Lies My Guru Told Me

*A Memoir of Life
in Silo's Humanist Movement*

Lies My Guru Told Me

*A Memoir of Life
in Silo's Humanist Movement*

Rex Voluntas

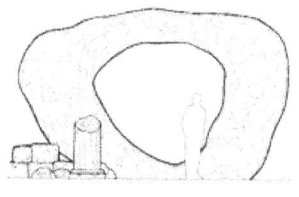

GUARDIAN OF
FOREVER PUBLISHING

Text © 2013 by 7609159 Canada Inc.

All rights reserved. No part of this publication may be reproduced, stored in a retrieval system or transmitted, in any form or by any means, digital, mechanical, photocopying, recording or otherwise, without the prior consent of the publisher.

Guardian of Forever Publishing

Cover design by Viviane Katz
Editor: Allister Thompson
Associate editing: Traductions alchimistes
Translation from French: Traductions alchimistes
Spanish editing: Pierre LaRocque

FRONT COVER ILLUSTRATION: Pro-Siloist graffiti on outdoor wall in Chile. The outstretched hands with three-finger salute are a typical Siloist greeting on first meeting. The man and woman represent "The Ideal Couple" in Siloist doctrine and New Age tapes, contributing to the Movement's feelings of distorted unreality and childlike naiveté.

Print ISBN 978-0-9918275-0-3
Kindle Ebook ISBN 978-0-9918275-1-0

Printed in the United States of America

17 16 15 14 13   5 4 3 2 1

Legal deposit, Library and Archives Canada, 2013

Library and Archives Canada Cataloguing in Publication

Voluntas, Rex
    Lies my guru told me : a memoir of life in Silo's humanist movement / Rex Voluntas.

Includes bibliographical references, discography, and videography.
Issued also in electronic format.
ISBN 978-0-9918275-0-3

    1. Silo, 1938- --Cult. 2. Cults--Canada. 3. Cults--Psychological aspects. 4. Humanism. 5. Voluntas, Rex. 6. Ex-cultists--Canada--Biography. 7. Humanists--Canada--Biography. I. Title.

BL2747.6.V64 2013   299'.93   C2013-900071-2

CONTENTS

Author's Introduction		1
I	The Mind of Enrico Barrier	3
II	Enrico's Control of Sex	28
III	A Spiritual Journey	40
IV	Prelude to the Abyss	55
V	A Friday in May	68
VI	The Sun, the Moon and the Truth	100
VII	Notes from Cuba	118
VIII	The Spider and her Prey	127
IX	The Sisterhood and her War Against Men	144
X	Marie-Claude Avenges Herself on the Male Species	161
XI	Martyr to the Cause	178
Epilogue		199
Dedication and Acknowledgements		207
Bibliography		209
Discography and Videography		211

AUTHOR'S INTRODUCTION

THE LAST THING I wanted to do when writing this book was create a doctrinal study of Siloism, for the ideology of such groups is nothing more than filler. And so I have avoided doing so. Instead, this is the first book in English critical of Siloists or Siloism. The book is written in the spirit of the Hebrew doctrine of *tikkun olam*, which means the world is broken and must be repaired through social action and social justice. I have focused on the experience of the protagonist, an Everyman character whose challenge was foretold by the ancient prophet who cautioned, "Waste not your time in idle chatter with fools or women." He is sandwiched between two antagonists, one a fool and the other a woman. Sometimes people ask me what it was like to suffer such a fool or if I can strain to remember what she looked like, her melodic voice or how such an otherwise average woman could do such harm. Thus, I have found it best to write my memoirs now so I may not have to remember so well when I am older.

To dispense with the legal formalities, *Lies My Guru Told Me* is based on a true story and the events described comprise the ninety-nine percent of the story that was left out of a legal proceeding that went through the court system in the Canadian jurisdiction of Quebec. Names of real people have been changed, with the exception of Silo and his Movement, which are unchanged.

Lies My Guru Told Me is not a story for children and I recommend taking a break between chapters. I have never been a great fan of the *Star Wars* franchise, and "The Force" that is discussed herein has absolutely nothing to do with the Force in *Star Wars*; the two are not related. Although I am a great fan of *Star Trek*, this book is not

Introduction

about *Star Trek* per se, though it is mentioned a few times. In terms of style, the book is written in Canadian English and Canadian spellings are favoured throughout with translations from French or Spanish. Every effort has been made to present the original quotes as they first appeared in their original language. For this reason, some French text appears without French accents, since the original appeared that way; they are not marked [sic] as errors would be. « French chevrons are used to quote French text ».

I decided to write in the third person limited omniscient since I thought it would be easier to tell the story and easier for the reader as well. I chose my pseudonym from the Latin used in a Siloist Guided Experience (book on tape with New Age music and sound effects) titled *The Saving Action* which describes a nightmarish post-nuclear war landscape where water is contaminated, cities are destroyed and chaos is all around. Participants are asked to imagine themselves inside this Armageddon and decide what unselfish action they would take to save their fellow man. Lacking useful information, the radio has only one station that is reduced to repeating the same line in an authoritarian manner "Rex Voluntas! Rex Voluntas! Rex Voluntas!" [The King's will], i.e. your will is King, your personal ego is all that matters. *Lies My Guru Told Me* has three very different audiences. To pro-Siloists who may be shocked at the contents, I say, believe it or not, your will is King. To former Siloists, I say believe it. To the public who may be curious about the inner workings of such groups, I say read on, gentle reader.

—Rex Voluntas

I — THE MIND OF ENRICO BARRIER

"It may easily come to pass that a vain man may become proud and imagine himself pleasing to all when he is in reality a universal nuisance."
—Baruch Spinoza

MONTREAL in the summer of the Olympic Games was a place of optimistic energy, youthful enthusiasm and great anticipation for a city in its heyday. Fresh from her fruit-picking sojourn in British Columbia's Okanagan Valley, eighteen-year-old Marie-Claude Desrochers enjoyed her share of it, taking in the sun, visiting friends and seeing the Olympic Park, then climbing on the back of her boyfriend's motorcycle for the long trip home to the suburbs. She held his waist as he navigated the route north to Laval and across the bridge spanning the Back River, then back to his parents' home. After parking the motorcycle in the open garage, they dismounted. They flirtatiously hugged and kissed a bit, then he wanted more. He guided her hand onto his crotch as he grabbed at her breasts. She went along, but only so far, until her sense of decorum could not withstand his hands. He forced her down on her knees, liberated his penis from his blue jeans and ordered her to perform oral sex on him. Even though his parents were away on vacation, anybody could see from the street with the garage door still open and enough sunlight remaining. They were practically outdoors and Marie-Claude (M-C) was completely humiliated. He was rough with her, placing his hands on her shoulders, pressing down and keeping her in that position for the duration of the assault. The worst part of it for M-C was his hands on her shoulders, but she felt she had no choice. She swallowed her pride, gave him what he wanted and kept the trauma to herself.

* * *

Unbeknown to M-C, just six kilometres to the west, nine-year-old Adam was also enduring an abusive childhood on the same island where his parents had raised him half-observant in the traditions of Ashkenazic Jewry. Indeed, Jewish emigration to Canada had become so popular that Yiddish was the third language of Montreal by the mid-twentieth century, behind French and English. Lithuanian Jews particularly, including Adam's maternal great-grandparents, so favoured Montreal that it became known as the "Vilna of North America." His paternal grandparents had settled in Winnipeg's hard-scrabble North End, where his grandfather was a Hebrew teacher, his grandmother a piano teacher. Adam would not meet M-C for another ten years.

Enrico Barrier, nearly a decade M-C's senior, had immigrated to Canada from Chile the previous year and settled in Toronto. Fresh off the plane, his wife seemed eager to divorce him and did so at the earliest opportunity by availing herself of Canada's liberal divorce laws and keeping custody of their three children in the process. Enrico worked in engineering jobs in Toronto for several years before abandoning his family, thereby forsaking his visiting rights to live in Montreal and organize his own team in Silo's Humanist Movement, where he later met M-C.

Enrico had lived in Canada for fifteen years the day Adam became his new roommate in Enrico's Frère-André Street apartment. Named in memory of Brother André Bessette, a Catholic lay spiritual leader, miracle worker and folk hero of French Canada, the street was short — no more than 150 metres — and featured a half-dozen interconnected asymmetrical apartment buildings of English Arts and Crafts design. Frère-André Street was gated at its western limit, after which it ran directly into the extensive grounds of the towering St. Joseph's Oratory, the largest Christian shrine to St. Joseph in the world, the construction of which was due in large part to donations made in the name of Brother André's works. Inside the shrine, Brother André's heart was preserved in a reliquary, which Adam had seen with his French immersion class on a school trip. Like the cross atop Mount Royal, the French architecture of the old port, the St. Lawrence River or the Montreal Canadiens hockey club, St. Joseph's Oratory had become a symbol of central pride accessible to all Montrealers, religion or language not being a barrier in this multiethnic, multilingual urban mosaic. In summertime, Enrico's visitors could hear angels singing and believed they had died and gone to heaven. It was in fact the Mount Royal Chorus whose angelic voices wafted from their practice chambers in the Oratory through the summer air and into any open window. At nightfall, the shrine's copper-greened exterior illuminated the neighbourhood skyline with a bright orange light, though it could be white or purple other nights. Adam wondered if there was a liturgical meaning to it. Tucked away, isolated and sheltered from the bustle of this city of over three million people by tall pine trees, Adam saw the second-storey apartment nestled under the northern flank of Westmount as an ideally quiet place to read, study, contemplate and pursue his college studies.

Frère-André Street was at the crossroads of four very different paths. The cross street Côte-des-Neiges Road was a major north-south artery built on a slope between two of Mount Royal's three peaks. Following it south past the gates to opulent Westmount on the right and the Trafalgar Stairs up to the mountain's summit on the left, one would reach Downtown Montreal and spectacular Sherbrooke Street. Following it laboriously north up the steep incline from Sherbrooke, the first cross street past Frère-André was Queen Mary Road. What followed was the highly multicultural Côte-des-Neiges neighbourhood: Africanized and Islamicized, with the University of Montreal on the right and the Jewish General Hospital on the left. It was bracketed by Caribbean spice shops; Vietnamese fare; Maghrebian coffee shops; music, book or print shops; and city parks all the way to the well-to-do and adroit Town of Mount Royal at the terminal. At that point, Mount Royal itself would be behind one's back. Queen Mary Road led to the right, east up another slope to the École Polytechnique, where Enrico studied bio-medical engineering. To the west were the residential neighbourhoods that comprised the cultural heart of the Jewish community, including the Saidye Bronfman Centre, the Jewish Public Library, the Young Men's Hebrew Association, kosher bakeries, Hebrew bookstores and several synagogues — all of the above Judaica were more English than French-speaking.

Adam had set up his bed, but most of his boxes were still packed. Exhausted, he went into the living room to relax after an arduous day. Adam was minding his own business when Enrico arrived after the movers had left and within minutes started an unsolicited monologue on the subject of women and sex. He would not let Adam talk while he recounted, in the most disgusting terms, everything about how he talked to and picked up women, how Adam should talk to and pick up women, conditions under which women would tell Adam "Fuck you!" (not that he had asked), how Enrico had sex with women, how Adam should have sex with women, Enrico's sexual adventures and prowess with women, sex toys women use in private when they don't have men, how women touch themselves in private, how Enrico touched women, how women touched Enrico, a detailed description of his girlfriend Lola's naked body, how Enrico touched his girlfriend Lola, how Lola touched Enrico, how Lola touched Enrico's genitals, how Enrico touched Lola's vulva and how Adam should touch women, the emotional involvement of a woman towards a man, how sexual relationships can be used for spiritual growth, nonverbal sexual communication between women and women, nonverbal sexual communication between Lola and women from other countries, nonverbal sexual communication between women and men, and how a person's sex will modify the sequence of his own thoughts.

Enrico continued to vex Adam, taking a prurient interest in his mother. "All the time while you were growing up, your mother had to get up early in the morning and cook breakfast for you and your father..." Adam tried to object that they did not have traditional family breakfasts every morning, but Enrico kept right on going over his objections "No! But what do you know? You don't know! And she had to work in that store all day and at night..." Adam tried to object that his mother did not work in the store when he was a little kid; the store was a recent development in their family history. Enrico cut Adam off, and Adam was never able to get the words out. "She had to cook supper for your father and do the dishes and do the laundry and then after you kids went to bed, then your mother had to open her legs for him..." Enrico said, probing further. Raising a finger, Adam tried to object, but Enrico yelled "NOOOOOOOOOOOO! BUT YOU WEREN'T THERE, Adam! You don't know what went on between them. You don't know what your parents had, so who are you to talk?"

He took a long time berating Adam, while puffing on his briar pipe in the authoritarian manner of Joseph Stalin. Adam was completely humiliated; he could not say a word and had not even asked any questions to deserve such a harangue. From the time he first walked in the door, Enrico hadn't wasted any time establishing their domestic relationship in terms of an extension of his own authoritarian dominance, machismo and masculine hegemony. Enrico disassembled and cleaned his pipe, which mesmerized Adam, who drifted into daydreams and began thinking about his situation; he felt trapped and started to wonder if it were not a terrible mistake on his part to move in with Enrico. It would have been very difficult to end their arrangement, given that he had no place to go, had cancelled his previous lease, had sent the movers away and had no job or money to find a more expensive apartment on his own. Enrico had put Adam on the spot because he had to decide immediately, under duress and coercion, if he would pack his boxes and leave or stay and be subjected to Enrico's abuse. Adam watched the pipe smoke drift away, and his freedom went with it. Of course, Adam could not really leave the apartment, and they both knew that.

It was especially confusing for Adam to be confronted with the prospect of leaving the apartment since he had left the Movement just a few months earlier for the same reason. Now that Enrico was abusive again, did it mean that Enrico had somehow re-admitted him to the Movement, or would he be expected to rejoin the Movement while living there? For Adam to admit he needed to leave the apartment, he would first have to understand he had never left the Movement.

Only by understanding and admitting that he was still in the organic structure of the Movement could Adam then leave the physical structure of the apartment, Enrico's Movement headquarters. In other words, Enrico created of Adam's mind a prison, within the prison of the apartment, within the prison of the Movement. To stay was as equally ridiculous a choice as deciding to leave, but economically and practically, he had no choice. The only real choice he could make was to overturn his own previous choice of moving into that apartment; such a decision would be against his own best interests. It would be as much a mistake for Adam to leave the apartment as it was to stay. Thus, he felt uncomfortable and thwarted throughout the entire duration of his stay. Enrico had wrested psychological, verbal and emotional control over Adam and sustained this for the ensuing two years.

    The building had twelve apartment units over three floors, sharing a common roof and basement laundry. The complex was E-shaped, with the three prongs pointing to Frère-André; the middle prong was a courtyard. Enrico's apartment was in the middle floor with the back walls closer to Queen Mary Road. There was no backyard separating the two streets, only a thin lane. From the front door, the high archway to the living room was at the first right, the hall closet at left. The ceilings were stuccoed, the floors creaky and the cornices and mouldings original to the 1930s construction. The living room walls were lined with stacks of scientific papers, some yellowed or brittle, which Enrico had read or not yet but intended to read some day. The room featured a doublewide window to the right that opened sideways on the courtyard and a working fireplace on the far wall that hosted Enrico's pipe paraphernalia on the mantle. Between the window and fireplace, Enrico's modern television proffered a range of colours: black, off black, blue, grey, light black, dark blue, blackish blue, greyish blue, blueish black, off blue distorted static and white. Enrico's bookshelf included a catalogue of weird books, many of which he had stolen from the library of the Universidad Católica de Valparaíso. The tiny kitchen was at the end of the front hall and had a puny window, while the two bedrooms branched off to the right of the kitchen door. Adam's bedroom was the first door to the left while Enrico's was the last door with the bathroom on the right. A closet in Enrico's bedroom concealed books that were too unusual to be displayed in the living room.

Throughout the summer, Enrico cornered Adam with impromptu sermons and inflicted upon him spontaneous meetings of the Movement, introductory meetings of the Movement, introductory seminars, doctrinal seminars and long, rambling, didactic harangues of the Movement. Such spontaneous events could begin at any time, without warning and run on for hours well after midnight, until Adam could no longer think straight and was swimming in Enrico's words. When visitors came from the Movement, Enrico conducted a spontaneous meeting. At any moment, Enrico re-enacted any meeting of the Movement, which he judged Adam had missed whether Adam was using the kitchen, sitting in the living room or resting in his bedroom. After his weekly meetings, Enrico got maniacally hyper and updated Adam on the themes and topics that were discussed by putting him through an exhaustive discourse and unsolicited re-enactment. When people arrived two hours before the meeting started, Enrico conducted a two-hour spontaneous pre-meeting, followed by the regular weekly meeting. If Adam made a single move, utterance or decision that departed from the thought of the Movement and the themes of the most recent meeting, Enrico reminded him of it in no friendly way! Enrico analyzed Adam's every single word, movement, comment and gesture in terms of its relevance to the project of the Movement, twenty-four hours a day, every day, incessantly.

Enrico's weekly meetings took much more than the forty-five minutes advertised; they went on for hours and hours, into the morning. The meetings were preceded by the pre-meeting and followed by the post meeting. After the post-meeting came the after-post meeting; after that, several members of the team would stay to wind down, light the fireplace, chat and play Enrico's LP albums. Enrico would again bring up the themes of the Movement to reconstitute the evening, which by that time had become night. After everybody finally left, Enrico tried to engage Adam in more Movement-related conversation by asking him "So, how did you like the meeting?" Adam was no longer in the Movement, so he shrugged off the question. "So, how did you like the meeting?" Enrico repeated the same question endlessly until Adam answered. In so doing, Enrico steam-rolled directly over Adam's obvious fatigue and tried to break Adam's will by exhausting him even further and depriving him of his sleep, his domestic comfort, his privacy and his peace of mind.

Enrico was the first Chilean Adam had ever met. When Enrico spoke about the project of the Humanist Movement, he often highlighted the situation of political violence in Chile, the kidnapping, torture and murder of political dissidents in Chile and the subsequent flight or exile of survivors to countries like Canada. Adam got the mistaken impression that Enrico had been involved in these situations and sympathized with him. Enrico often spoke about "Humanizing the Earth" as the worthwhile project of the Humanists and said he wanted to build a "Universal Human Nation." Despite this call for a world without borders or prejudice, all of Enrico's examples and instruction were based on stories from Chile or the situation there. Enrico had visitors from Humanist groups in South America who came to Montreal. They all spoke the same way Enrico did; Adam felt like everybody in the Movement was either a modern-era Simón Bolívar or shared a joint sympathy for the Latin American situation linked through a form of Liberation Theology. Increasingly, Adam felt like the Movement was on a mission to make North Americans feel guilty for all the suffering and violence that had happened in South America. Adam observed how, despite the Movement's plea for a Universal Human Nation, it was rather a Monolithic Hispanic Nation, a group not at all reflective of the Earth's diverse peoples, but more concerned with discussing revolution over coffee and cigarettes.

In Chile, Carmen was preparing for a day of protest against military dictator Augusto Pinochet. Her small group was intercepted by the military, which severely beat the young people, then poured petrol on them and set fire to them. Carmen was the only survivor. She was flown to Montreal to receive medical care and skin grafts (not easily available in Chile). Naturally, she had no money, no friends in Montreal and much personal anguish. When Adam saw the report on the local news, he thought it encouraging that the smallish Chilean community in Montreal was rallying to do what it could to help Carmen with personal and moral support, visits to the hospital, gifts of food and cash. Adam thought it a golden opportunity for Enrico and his team to get involved with a concrete application of the highly abstract ideas he espoused in the meetings between admonishments of Pinochet and cries for more humanity.

"No. Why should we?" was Enrico's reply.

Enrico overloaded Adam with information to loosen control over his faculties. Nearly every day, Enrico recounted with glee how he identified with the Conquistadors, who had conquered Chile by humiliating and destroying the native Chilean peoples and cultures. Enrico described the detailed and carefully engineered psychological and spiritual rape involving architecture, among other techniques, to destroy the native peoples and establish the hegemony of the Conquistadors. On the occasions where Adam tried to actively resist Enrico's long didactic monologues, his spontaneous meetings, interrogation and harassment, Enrico turned it into an opportunity for his peculiar sexual behaviour. "Oh! Give it to me! That's it! Give it to me! Let me have it! Give it to me, Adam! Give it to me! That's it! That's it! Give it to me!" Enrico said, pounding and stroking his chest. While looking at Adam sensually and calling out, Enrico reached down to caress his own genitals through his jeans.

From Adam's earliest days in the Frère-André apartment, Enrico acted out sexual dramas on the living room floor. You could call these dramas "air penis" for their similarity to "air guitar." Nearly every day, Enrico waited until Adam was seated in the living room, minding his own business. Enrico squatted on the living room floor and proceeded to insert an imaginary penis into his rectum, or his imaginary vagina. Enrico feigned full penetration, coitus, sexual rapture and passion up to and including orgasm, while providing complete sound effects and calling out "Thrusting and releasing, thrusting and releasing." The air penis became a regular activity for Enrico, who rode it while reading the newspaper, or computing his math formulae, or chatting with Adam. Sometimes Enrico would stop briefly, declare "It slipped out…" and then reinsert the air penis into the orifice from whence it came. These dramas could have been between two men, or two women or a straight couple, Enrico did not say if he was imitating himself, or if he included Adam in the drama, or if there were a third person. The woman whose voice Enrico imitated, however, had a Jewish accent when calling out "Oh my God! Oh my God!"

Enrico impersonated Adam's mother having sex, right to his face. The air penis was Enrico's way of saying he wanted to hurt Adam sexually, but Enrico was limited by the fact that he was not openly gay. If only Enrico had some way to assault Adam in a direct sexual way, in addition to what he was already doing to him in the apartment—in this way, the air penis was a kind of forewarning of things to come. Enrico rode the air penis without removing the pipe from his mouth, bobbing his torso up and down on it, while looking Adam straight in the eye.

Enrico explained in detail how he could tell from his bio-medical lab exactly which muscles were weak in a person's back and how many years they could go without developing back problems. He claimed he could also deduce which people had more psychological, sexual and emotional stress in their lives as a result of muscular pain. Enrico then linked that stress to the project of the Movement and pointed out how bio-medical engineering was relevant to his Siloist work. He showed Adam passages from Movement books and asked Adam if he knew the difference between an engineer, a technician and a technologist.

"Um, I don't care?" Adam replied, sensing a long explanation. Enrico was furious, unable to accept Adam's reason that he had no aptitude for engineering, technical work or mathematics. Enrico then observed that Adam would make a good test subject in his lab and made a move to grab at Adam's sides. Adam swerved out of the way and narrowly escaped Enrico's clutching hands. He retreated to his bedroom with Enrico in pursuit, frustrated that he could not use Adam for his experiments on stress, sexuality and pain. At least for the moment.

Enrico's meetings were pretty weird. The greatest care was taken to welcome every brand of weirdo and make them feel at home. "We're from the future," Enrico told them when they sat down. "The Movement doesn't exist. Nobody out there knows about the Movement and they won't believe anything you tell them." They left the place bewildered, asking themselves "What? What? What?"

One week, Enrico told the story of a Chilean woman in Toronto who had a light bulb that had never burned out for twenty years and a car that ran on a single gallon of gasoline, never needing a refill. "Yeah, it's called planned obsolescence," Adam quipped from the sofa. Enrico incredulously demanded to know who told Adam that.

"In first year economics or political science they tell you that. Companies can make their products far more efficient, but they don't so that people will buy their products more often. The companies know in advance when certain models will break down and when it's time to introduce new products to the market."

Enrico looked at Adam as if he had betrayed a family secret and insisted such things happened only to his Chilean friend in Toronto! Another time Enrico told about how the Movement was open to human diversity and used his friend's background as an example. Enrico said his absent friend had Chinese parents, was born in Jamaica and spoke with a Jamaican accent. Adam joined in with an example of a pastry chef he knew who was of Vietnamese heritage, born and raised in Madagascar and his first language is French. Enrico was again incredulous and demeaned Adam for telling such an irrelevant story during a meeting of the Movement!

For the Summer Solstice, Enrico pressured Adam without subtlety to rejoin. Adam said he was not interested. Over Adam's objections, Enrico reprised Silo's own words: "I know my way in this human landscape, but what will happen if we pass each other going in opposite directions?" He had anticipated Adam's response and reinterpreted his refusal through the filter of his Movement. He then started reading to Adam verbatim Silo's story of "The Rider and His Shadow":

> I renounce every faction that proclaims an ideal higher than life and every cause that, to impose itself, generates suffering. So before you accuse me of not being part of any faction, examine your own hands — you may find on them the blood of complicity. If you believe it valiant to commit yourself to those factions,

what will you say of one whom all the murderous bands accuse of being uncommitted? I want a cause worthy of the human landscape: a cause committed to surpassing pain and suffering.

Adam objected that he was not in the Movement and did not want to be subjected to this! Enrico stepped up his coercion by pressuring Adam to contribute to the financial campaign, even though Adam refused. If Adam had paid, he would be automatically considered a bona fide Movement member. Enrico absolutely would not let Adam go until he paid and told Adam to prepare a cheque payable to Marie-Claude Desrochers. Adam wrote on the subject line of the check "Movement duress." Enrico laughed at him. A few days later, Enrico pressured Adam to become the Support in the team. "Oh, Adam. You're more in theme with the Movement than many people who just say they are but aren't really," Enrico said, attempting to caress Adam's ego.

For years, Enrico had always asked "What are you compensating?" and told Adam to "Be honest with yourself!" for each answer Adam gave, until Adam gave the one he thought Enrico wanted to hear. Enrico also told Adam he had "resistances" and that Adam's words and actions were merely "compensations" to some resistance lodged deep in his psyche. Adam was baffled and did not understand him.

Enrico stepped up the questioning in the summer, telling Adam more specifically that his words and actions were given to prevent him from re-joining the Movement. Adam never did or said anything without Enrico saying it was either a resistance or compensation. Enrico tried many times to control Adam's dreams. He told stories about caverns and underground lockers in dreams and that Adam should unlock each locker to explore the cavern inside. He also told stories about his own dreams, particularly one in which he was a passenger in a hydroplane. The pilot suggested it was time to land on the water, but Enrico was nervous. Waking, he told Adam his reluctance to land on the water in the dream was a resistance to doing something important in his conscious life and that his job now was to reflect on what that thing was, identify it and then overcome the resistance. Enrico told Adam he had to do the same thing, meaning Adam had to overcome his resistance to joining the Movement.

One June afternoon, Adam was walking home from the Côte-des-Neiges Station of the "Metro," Montrealers' name for their subway system that had gained a favourable international reputation as an underground city. The Metro was one of Mayor Jean Drapeau's crowning achievements, along with the Summer Olympics, the Place des Arts Concert Hall and the World's Fair and Universal Exposition hosted in Montreal during that summer Montrealers have forever since affectionately known as "Expo67."

Some people, about three or four youths, passed Adam in the opposite direction. They all recognized him and called out to him. Adam didn't know who they were, but they seemed harmless, so he asked them how they knew him. They said they were all from Kitchener, Ontario, and knew Adam from the Movement. Adam was no longer in the Movement and as such, not particularly pleased to see them. Arriving home, he found that his entire apartment was contaminated with these Movement visitors from Kitchener! They were sitting in the living room, and others were crowded into the kitchen eating Adam's food. They hung out in Adam's bedroom, they were using the bathroom, their lit cigarettes rested on Adam's wooden bookshelf; he was like a prisoner in his own home. They implored him to sit with them. Adam sat on the sofa and after a few minutes of exposure to this group began to feel shock. He trembled nervously and felt panicky. His entire life was being taken over by Enrico and his Movement.

By contrast, when Adam had visitors, Enrico attempted to hypnotize them using artwork hung on the living room walls, including works by Rafael Edwards and da Vinci's Vitruvian Man, and conducted a spontaneous introductory meeting using Siloist themes. Enrico would not permit Adam to receive telephone calls from the outside world. He insulted the callers or hung up on them. He also deliberately erased messages Adam's aunt had left for him, then declared, "This is not a talent agency." He forbade Adam from talking to one of his own cousins, and on another occasion he enquired about the political career of Adam's other cousin and the extent of his power in Montreal.

If somebody called for Enrico, however, he expected Adam to

observe only the highest standards of telephone courtesy. Once, Adam answered a call from a young woman who claimed to be Enrico's daughter. Adam took the message and told Enrico when he returned that his daughter had called. Enrico flew off the handle and started screaming that he had two daughters, and unless Adam told him which daughter had called, he would have no way of knowing! Adam did not know Enrico had two daughters. He told Enrico so and added that Enrico should welcome any chance to talk to his daughters, and furthermore, Adam was not responsible for Enrico's failings as a father. It turned out Enrico's daughters both lived in the same Toronto house.

Enrico, who seldom saw his son Insolencio in Toronto, objected when Adam ate ice cream or kept a teddy bear on his bed or hung *Star Trek* posters on his bedroom wall, asserting that all three were immature. Enrico's intrusions and attitude problems got to be so bad that Adam bought a separate telephone number just for his bedroom, to which Enrico reacted with "You fucking asshole!"

Adam had developed the habit of recording his journal into his tape recorder, outside the apartment. One afternoon in August, it was a nice day so he went up on the gabled roof with his machine. Amidst the stone chimneys, he recorded his journal entry, which included all his most personal and private thoughts. A few days later, he sat down to transcribe his journal from the tape into a computer file. He set the tape to the beginning and began listening with the headphones. Where he expected to hear the beginning of his own voice, he heard in its place: "Adam, have a good talk ... think of me ... bye." He couldn't understand where that voice was coming from, so he played it again. It was Enrico! Knowing Adam was going upstairs to record his journal, Enrico had taken the tape recorder and recorded his own message on it, changing the sequence of recordings, just as he had described the sequence of shifting sexual thoughts on moving day. A journal is a very personal document; although Adam thought he knew its contents and the order in which the recordings were made, he was wrong. Only Enrico knew what he had done, until Adam discovered the tampering.

From his earliest days at Frère-André, Enrico physically intimidated Adam and subjected him to constant ridicule, harassment and pressure. Enrico tried slapping Adam's face repeatedly every second day, coming within one millimetre of his face each time while providing sound effects: "Kish! Kish! Kish! Kish! Get the fuck out of my way, you bitch!" He also subjected Adam to daily cries of "Fuck you!" "Who the fuck are you?" and "Get the fuck out of my way, you bitch!" He alternated these insults with criticism that Adam did not laugh enough accompanied by sudden commands of "Laugh! Laugh!" screamed in his face. Enrico alternated that with "Jew! Jew! You greasy Jew!" At other times, Enrico would claim to be Jewish. But for anything Adam wanted to say, Enrico gave him, "Excuse me, you must have mistaken me for someone who gives a shit!" Enrico told long, tiresome stories about unfunny Holocaust jokes he had shared in the past with his peer, Yorgo. Enrico controlled Adam's comings and goings any time Adam ventured out of the apartment. But if Adam inquired about Enrico's movements, he gave him a dirty look. "Fuck you, Adam!" If Adam dared ask why, Enrico would make it look like he was the offended party, giving his ultra-insincere "Movement apology" in a sugary, cajoling voice, showing he was clearly not sorry. "Oh sorry! Gee, I'm so sorry, Adam, that I hurt your feelings."

Enrico enjoyed placing his body in the doorway of the kitchen once Adam was inside, preventing him from getting out. Once Adam was trapped, Enrico exposed him to his spontaneous meetings, placing resistances upon Adam, interrogation, sexual humiliations and whatever he pleased. Enrico would often hide in the house and suddenly scare Adam. He often locked the front door to keep Adam from getting in, then unlocked it while telling him to turn the key in the door. Once Adam had locked himself out at Enrico's insistence, Enrico anticipated the next move each time and did the opposite so that Adam continuously locked the door from the outside while Enrico opened it from the inside. Enrico often rang the doorbell from downstairs and arrived upstairs and let himself in before Adam could answer, often swinging the door open in his face. He said that Adam was the one having "locked doors and resistance" and that Enrico's door was always open, his metaphor to enter the Movement.

Earlier that summer, Adam was cleaning his bedroom. He tore

up some old papers then discarded them. "There! There you are in your own house. Why should you tear up papers like that? Who are you afraid of?" Enrico demanded.

"I dunno, Enrico, you know … it's the ghosts..." Adam said. Enrico scurried away and returned with his copy of *A Midsummer Night's Dream*, from which he read aloud these lines:

> If we shadows have offended,
> Think but this, and all is mended,
> That you have but slumber'd here
> While these visions did appear.
> And this weak and idle theme,
> No more yielding but a dream,
> Gentles, do not reprehend:
> If you pardon, we will mend.
> And, as I am an honest puck,
> If we have unearned luck
> Now to 'scape the serpent's tongue,
> We will make amends ere long;
> Else the Puck a liar call.
> So, goodnight unto you all.

Adam's reaction was incredulous despair. *Why do I have to live with this weird guy who has an answer to everything, already prepared? And why is he always lurking around the corner, waiting to answer and tell me things, anyway? It's as though his whole life is built around changing me!*

Enrico often told "Silo stories," which invariably involved non-Siloists being humiliated, cheated or yelled at by Silo. Even when Enrico knew Silo personally in South America, the stories that resulted were still humiliating for Enrico, who was left in a state more profoundly insignificant than non-existence. Silo had once proclaimed, "Only ten percent of our people truly understand what we're trying to accomplish." Many years earlier, Silo had conducted a training camp in the Andes which Enrico and Yorgo had attended under the code names Juno and Pecto. Included in the exercises was one where Silo instructed them to run from the top of a tall hill to the bottom while counting silently by threes. Furthermore, they were to veer from left to right and change directions around rocks while loudly calling out "¡Madre!" [Mother] at intervals of nine and alternately "¡Padre!" [Father], and not lose step or count or muddle speech all the way down to the bottom.

Neither Enrico nor Adam had ever seen Disney's *Fantasia* the day Enrico told Adam Silo's "Story of the Apprentice." There was a young man who worked as an apprentice to a wizard. One day, the wizard said he was leaving the workshop to run errands. It was the apprentice's job to clean up the workshop with a broom. The apprentice swept the workshop while the wizard was gone, but he found the work slow. He saw the wizard's book of magic incantations on the bookshelf and wondered if he could find one to help him clean up the workshop. The apprentice looked in the book and found an incantation that would cause the broom to multiply itself into two brooms and clean the workshop on their own. The apprentice thought this would be an excellent way to avoid doing his own work. He read the incantation aloud and invoked the magic powers. He bid the broom to divide in two and clean the workshop. The broom split in two and both brooms went about cleaning the workshop without any effort from the apprentice. The apprentice rejoiced at his skill in using the wizard's own magic spells in his absence. At the same time, the two brooms split in two and made four brooms; these divided in two each and left eight brooms. The apprentice bid the brooms to stop, but they did not. They split in two and made sixteen brooms, each cleaning the workshop. Soon, there were thirty-two brooms. The apprentice became frantic and panicky. He grasped at the book and looked for a way to reverse the magical effect. It did not work, instead leaving sixty-four brooms. There were 128 brooms cleaning the workshop when the wizard returned home and found the apprentice in tears. The apprentice explained what happened. The wizard raised his finger and said, "Now you know what happens when you play with powers you don't understand!"

Adam was terrified when Enrico told him this story. Was this

The Mind of Enrico Barrier

Enrico's weirdo way of saying it was time to clean the apartment? It was yet another attempt to control Adam's mind by inserting the thought that Enrico, "the wizard," knew exactly what Adam, "the apprentice," was doing in his absence, that Adam was up to no good and that Enrico was in control of Adam. Adam had no idea what he had done wrong, but he felt very self-conscious and uncomfortable. When Enrico came home daily, he would purport that he knew what Adam was doing while he was gone, that his activities were dishonest and that he was going to interrogate Adam to find some hidden truth and hold it against him. Even when Adam thought he was alone in the apartment, Enrico didn't want him to make the mistake of thinking that he wasn't watching him.

Enrico cultivated his narcissism to supplant Adam's personality. Quite different from his offensive remarks about Adam's own family, he told stories about himself much like the enchanted birth stories told by followers of the Buddha. Enrico claimed that as a child in Chile, he was awoken every morning by his uncle, who had fashioned a local fruit into a kind of flute. Enrico was serenaded at his bedroom door by his uncle, who played gentle music to wake him gradually, because Enrico was such a special child. Enrico boasted a childhood enriched by a Jesuit education in private British schools in Chile, where they sang "God Save the Queen" every morning, in English. Adam thought the combinations extremely unusual. Enrico purported to have been the class clown and the only student capable of flustering the Jesuit fathers, who expelled him from the classroom daily. After claiming to be an atheist, he went fishing for compliments, asserting he had memorized vast sections of the catechism and could recite it from memory. Adam told him he was a good Catholic, at which Enrico became insulted.

In the kitchen, Enrico repeatedly tried to convince Adam that he was jealous of his cooking and that Adam longed to taste his food. Adam told him he was not jealous, had no cravings for Enrico's food and did not share his tastes. Enrico said that Adam secretly wished to share his food, and Enrico refused to share. Sitting at the kitchen table to eat his meals, Enrico again taunted Adam that his food was so delicious, Adam was so jealous and envious of him and could only long to have what Enrico had. He covered his plate with both arms and did so every time Adam passed by or looked his way while he was eating. He aggressively called out that Adam was not allowed to take his food. In contrast, when Adam cooked and ate his own food, Enrico insulted him by saying he was "pigging out." Enrico also bragged about the honey given to him by a local bee farmer. He said the honey was of a superior quality, and the farmer giving some to Enrico was a reflection of Enrico's superior qualities as a human being. As with many other objects, the good quality of the honey was a sign of Enrico's excellence and reflected well on his good taste. The honey sat untouched for months or years.

Enrico tried to make Adam jealous of his computer and peripheral equipment. He did this by accusing him repeatedly: "You go through my computer when I'm not here, don't you?" "You turn on my computer, you read my letters, you try to get into the files that are locked…" Adam denied it and asked if there was a problem that would cause him to believe this. Enrico pretended not to understand. "You go into my room when I'm not here and you play with my computer, don't you? You open my drawers, you look at my things." Adam stated that he had his own computer and didn't need Enrico's. He also asked Enrico if his papers had been disturbed. Enrico refused to answer but made a point of asserting he had the best computer equipment known to mankind and that his printer was by far superior to Adam's. Enrico had an IBM-DOS compatible clone of a 386 machine, a monochrome greyscale monitor emulating 256 shades of grey, and a dot matrix printer.

During a discussion of poetry, Adam mentioned his admiration of William Blake's oeuvre, particularly "The Little Black Boy" and "The Chimney Sweep." Enrico said those poems were irrelevant to "The Human Being," and only Blake's poem "The Smile" was connected to the themes of the Movement. Another time, Adam was playing taped music in his bedroom with the door open, and Enrico was in his bedroom. Enrico asked him what it was. Adam said it was Vivaldi. "Oh, fuck! I know it's Vivaldi, fuck! What opus number is it?" Enrico blustered to reinforce that his own background and knowledge were so prestigious that he could recognize the composer of any classical piece or instil jealousy in anyone.

Enrico made a point of making Adam feel insignificant about his own tastes in music, literature, cooking, art and every other subject, each time filtering out his own personality and replacing it with Enrico's. When Enrico spoke about philosophy, literature, the arts, social sciences, science, classical music, computers or any part of human knowledge or activity, he always spoke as if he had been on site when the work of art or scientific feat was created. Furthermore, he knew the persons involved intimately, and their work was done in the spirit of Silo's Humanist Movement, which reflected well on Enrico personally. Specifically, Enrico named Baruch Spinoza, Leonardo da Vinci, George Gurdjieff and Martin Heidegger in addition to the authors of books such as *The Tibetan Book of the Dead*, *Starmaker*, and *Gödel, Escher, Bach: An Eternal Golden Braid* and attempted to enlist them all as consenting forerunners of Silo. According to Enrico, they were all Siloists.

The previous year, Adam had been struck by a car while crossing the street and was nearly killed. He was in a coma with trauma for nine hours and was hospitalized for nearly three weeks but remembered nothing at all about the accident itself. He suffered a fractured skull, encephalitis, hematoma beneath the skull, compressed vertebrae and loss of smell (anosmia) and taste. In addition to being told by his doctor that the accident had taken a few years off his life, Adam had to get used to the idea of never enjoying another meal, flower or fragrance for the rest of his life. The doubt of not knowing what after-effects could linger if his injuries completely healed compounded an already difficult road to recovery.

Adam had several visits in hospital from his peer and good friend, Raymond, who on one occasion brought Enrico with him. Without saying a word of comfort, Enrico asked, "What colour is the pain?" He led Adam through an unwanted pseudo-Buddhist mumbo-jumbo exercise in which Adam had to imagine the pain diminishing in colour from black and purple to orange and white. A bedridden and listless Adam had to suffer through Enrico's selfish need to be glorified in public. In fact, Adam was heavily medicated at the time and did not feel pain. As a result of the accident, his physical strength was diminished and he was left with chronic headaches, vertigo, nausea, language problems, short-term memory loss, a loss of purpose, and loss of meaning and direction in daily life.

Enrico exploited the trauma of Adam's accident as another opportunity to impose the Movement's ideology. He did everything he could to provoke headaches in Adam and force him to relive the psychological trauma of the accident and the pain of his head injuries. Enrico made sudden and frequent banging noises in the kitchen with knives, pots and pans, salt shakers or other equipment whenever Adam was nearby. Adam got headaches and went to lie down on his bed, often taking a Tylenol first. Typically, Enrico responded immediately. He went to see Adam in his bedroom and started to lecture him about the importance of working with images, the tendency of thoughts to produce and attract actions and the correct position to take towards life.

On one such occasion, Enrico smacked Adam in the head with his open fist four or five times consecutively to prove that his headaches were just an illusion, which Enrico could cure with Movement techniques. Adam started to feel the onset of a headache and went to his bedroom. Enrico followed him there and lectured him at length about how the headaches were an illusion he used to develop an emotional bond with and chemical dependence on Aspirin. He said Adam exhibited classic symptoms of chemical dependence and that the pain only disappeared at first when Adam took Aspirin, but after that the pain would stay away only if Adam took Aspirin and would come back if Adam failed to take it. Adam told Enrico he was wrong, but Enrico would not leave him alone and continued to talk about case studies that had been done during the Korean War on soldiers who were prescribed morphine for their injuries. Adam said he was not interested in hearing these stories and already knew this information from *M*A*S*H*.

Enrico asked, "What is *M*A*S*H*?" and Adam told him about the television show set in the Korean War. Enrico objected that the doctors in that show were not real doctors, Adam reminded Enrico that he was not a real doctor either! Enrico replied "Yes, I am."

Incensed, Adam asked Enrico to repeat himself then told Enrico that he was not a doctor. Enrico explained that as a requirement for his degree in biomedical engineering, he had to take the same courses in the same classrooms as students at the Faculty of Medicine. He said he had the same knowledge as them and that made him a doctor. Adam told him that while he might think he was a doctor, he was not Adam's doctor, that there are medical ethics and such a thing called informed consent which allows a patient to consent to treatment and to choose their own doctor.

Enrico began laughing hysterically while jumping in the air and slapping his knee, then repeated his boast. Adam told him that his own real doctor had prescribed Tylenol, not Aspirin and said Adam could take it any time he had pain! Adam got a severe headache from Enrico's assault, naturally, and had to lie down for the rest of the day.

Enrico exploited Adam's precarious health to further weaken his resistance. He conducted daily rally and pep-sessions aimed at working Adam into a frenzy. Enrico did this to influence the emotional form he wanted Adam to take, but also his mood and attitude, the direction of his actions, his level of communication, the position of his body and especially of his head and breathing. If Adam felt happy, Enrico would appropriate the happiness for himself then subject Adam to a complete psychoanalysis and commentary on his life, past, present and future, with special focus on resolving his road accident. Enrico built his harangues around overly deep and heavy themes that could last hours, such as his own popular interrogative "What is time other than the biological processes of your own body?" He was preoccupied with Adam's mortality and persistently badgered Adam about the imminence of his death and the meaning of his life, linking those themes to the significance of every move, decision and action Adam made. He then linked that to the project of the Movement and provided unsolicited and exhaustive psychoanalysis and commentary. Later in the year, Enrico offered Adam immortality. "So what if you die? Big deal!" he said frequently, adding that he had a special gift for Adam. He quoted from a passage by Silo, which became part of the daily pep sessions.

> I declare to you my unshakable faith and my certainty
> from experience that death does not hold back the

future. That death, on the contrary, modifies the provisional state of our existence to launch us blissfully toward immortal transcendence.

Enrico exploited Adam's anosmia handicap to loosen Adam's control over his senses. One Saturday in June, they went up on the roof of their building, ostensibly just to be outside and take the air. Instead, Adam discovered Enrico was doing his weird pseudo-Buddhist doctor act.

"Did you hear the colour of that bird flying by?" Enrico asked.

"Yeah," Adam responded without hesitation. He noticed that Enrico had chosen to express himself using synesthesia, rather than natural language. Adam thought it was a little unusual given that synesthesia was a trope used in poetry. Nonetheless, Adam was familiar with this practice of expressing one sense in terms of another, as in Swenson's "...the seven fragrances of the rainbow," Lorca's "...green wind..." or Milton's "...blind mouths..." so he expressed no surprise. At the time, Adam was aware of the significance of synesthesia in literature and poetry only, not medicine. When Adam did not ask for an explanation, Enrico asked Adam repeatedly if he had understood his question and if he wanted Enrico to explain it. Adam declined. Enrico seemed very frustrated in his failed efforts to alter Adam's senses and perception of reality. At least for the moment.

Enrico exploited Adam's weakened condition to control his thoughts and language. He interrupted whenever Adam tried to speak by making loud noises or creating long, rambling stories and pointed sermons. Due to his problems with short-term memory loss, Adam would lose his train of thought. When it did return, his ideas were gone and he had forgotten what he wanted to say. Enrico's words, however, were omnipresent and took over from Adam's own thoughts. While his thoughts had been muddy, unclear and increasingly inaccessible since moving in, Enrico's thoughts were extremely detailed, complex and highly organized super-structures. He boasted he could "disarticulate" Adam at any time and often did. To better understand Enrico, his mumbling and his thick Spanish accent, Adam asked for explanations and Enrico obliged, further restricting Adam's own ability to speak and think for himself. Enrico waited and watched his every move. Each time Adam tried to think, Enrico instantly started talking to prevent him from thinking. Each time Enrico pushed Adam off his train of thought, he forgot what he was thinking and was only aware of Enrico's words and thoughts. Even when Adam tried to talk, he could not express himself clearly because his speech had become slurred since the accident and he could not form words easily. Progressively, he could neither think nor speak for himself as Enrico filtered out his thoughts and personality, replacing them with Enrico's thoughts, his personality.

Enrico used coded words that were in fact Movement vocabulary. Each word was charged with meaning and was accompanied by a detailed explanation that represented hundreds, sometimes thousands of words that took hours to explain. Since Adam's own thoughts were unclear, Enrico's method of speaking with meaning-enhanced words, each representing a world of significance, replaced his own system of thought. For example, "reversibility," meaning "the ability and practice of the conscience to reflect on itself," was Enrico's introduction of Movement vocabulary into Adam's brain. It came to replace, however, many previous definitions from idiomatic Canadian English and associated actions, each with their own feelings and connotations. Enrico would start by telling Adam that the conscience cannot conceive of its own death. He would then follow up with long, detailed explanations of how conscience is self-reflective and give instructions on how to develop a sense of observing oneself through one's own brain. Starting the next night, Adam had nightmares in which he removed his own head with his bare hands and used it, detached and bloodied, to look at his own body, asleep on his bed.

One summer evening, Enrico was driving home with Adam in the passenger seat. He insisted on starting an involved discussion about a controversial topic, and Adam tried interjecting. As they drove west through downtown, Enrico gave his point of view. He navigated the complex system of streets through Pine, Cedar and Doctor Penfield Avenues and past Pierre Trudeau's house in Montreal's Golden Square

Mile. Once the wealthiest borough in Canada, the Square Mile was home to the captains of industry who would, from this vantage point, watch their ships arriving in the Old Port. Perched in their mansions on the south side of the mountain, they spied with binoculars on their longshoremen who toiled like ants four kilometres downhill. Not unlike Don Quixote's beleaguered horse Rocinante, Enrico's red Honda Civic rusted car, an unwilling veteran of fifteen winters, plodded past the cemetery to Côte-des-Neiges Road and on up to Frère-André as Adam took a position contrary to Enrico's and pointed out the fallacy.

Enrico retraced the entire flow of the conversation, matching the streets and buildings they had passed. The asphalt became a transcript and Rocinante's rubber hoofs witnesses to their conversation. Relying on the transcript, Enrico said what street they were on at which time, which building they had passed when he said the next phrase, which street he had turned onto when Adam spoke and which street they turned away from when he answered. He went on to say that each progressive traffic move had followed in the sequence he described and matched each verbal phrase uttered just as fixedly as the city's layout and the streets in their beds. Sudden verbal turns were not permitted, since no right turn was possible at that corner. A twist in Adam's reasoning was disallowed, since the road sign said no U-turns. For these reasons, Enrico refused Adam the right to connect his own thoughts, given that their corresponding streets did not connect, but were as physically separate as his own disconnected thoughts. Enrico won the argument and destabilized Adam further. Adam's feelings of vertigo and nausea, sporadic since his road accident, began to return. He sat silent, stewing, brooding and very confused about his sense of direction.

II — ENRICO'S CONTROL OF SEX

> "A man who has been the indisputable favourite of his mother keeps for life the feeling of a conqueror."
> —Sigmund Freud

ENRICO BOASTED many unsolicited sexual stories to Adam. Included in these were his sexual assault of a young drifter in Toronto; the seduction of his mother's friend in Chile when his mother Consuela lay dying in hospital; his deflowering of young girls in Chile; his sexual harassment of women at his job and at engineering conferences. Enrico related with pride how his brother Miguel — a rival for his mother's affection — had died under mysterious circumstances before the age of ten. Consuela had died suddenly when Enrico was only thirteen. He recounted that he suffered a grief so profound and a shock so severe that he had to be sedated by the doctors on duty that evening. Since then, Enrico had always missed his mother terribly and saw her in other women, especially those who were the mothers of young men in his team.

    Enrico's moods often led him back to thoughts of Consuela when he was feeling melancholic or homesick for Valparaíso. On these occasions, he would make a special kind of soup or dish she made during his childhood. Enrico's father, David, was also an engineer, a specialist in turbines and turbine technology. Enrico recalled with fondness how his father took him to art shows in Santiago, yet Enrico felt no regret when he allowed his efforts in the Movement to poison his relationship with his father. Enrico never healed the rift with David, who died the following year, estranged from his only son, thousands of kilometres and two continents distant.

Enrico frequently told unsolicited stories about his sex life with Lola, a cold, frugal economist and political scientist from Nova Scotia. He boasted that he knew every inch of Lola's body and included details about the specific sexual positions he had tried with her. Once, Enrico told Adam about an incident when Lola lived in the apartment with him, before Adam. Lola and Enrico were about to have sex and were in Enrico's bedroom when they noticed a man on the roof of the building opposite them, on Queen Mary Road. They took a look at what he was doing. According to Enrico only (not Lola), the man had gone up on the roof with binoculars when he saw Enrico and Lola undressing and was planning to watch them have sex. Enrico said he drew the blinds and considered it an intrusive and shocking incident. In telling Adam this story, Enrico turned Adam into a voyeur and, by reversing the point of view, planted the suggestion in his mind that somebody was watching him.

In the same vein, Enrico made Adam listen to the sound of the woman in the next building allegedly having sex. During the daytime, Enrico said, "Hear that?" Adam couldn't hear a thing and told Enrico so. Enrico insisted that he'd heard something. Adam asked him what he heard. Enrico said it was the woman in the adjacent building on Frère-André Street having sex. Leaning out their front window, Enrico claimed that he could hear the faint sounds of her lovemaking emanating from her apartment, through her closed windows. He urged Adam to listen again, this time being completely silent for several moments. Leaning out the window himself, Adam listened and listened. The street was, by nature, very quiet. The busy Côte-des-Neiges Road, however, was only a few meters away, and Queen Mary Road directly behind them. Adam heard some sounds that might be traffic-related, but nothing sexual. Just then Enrico called out, "Hear that?"

Adam listened very carefully but could not hear anything. "No, really; I don't hear it, sorry." But Enrico claimed that he could hear someone having sex at a distance outside his own building, with the windows shut. If the tables of espionage were turned on him, Enrico claimed he could detect someone spying on him from another elevation atop another building. In both cases, Enrico saw, heard and knew everything. The cumulative effect of Enrico's stories was to let Adam know that he was being watched, observed, listened to and somehow recorded.

Enrico tried to make Adam believe everybody in the building was watching him and reported back to Enrico: Hazel from across the hall, the people downstairs and especially Brianna, whom he called "the lady upstairs." Enrico tried to edit and control Adam's speech on the grounds that the lady upstairs could hear him through the ventilation shaft in the bathroom and, disapproving of Adam, would report her displeasure to Enrico. He also told Adam that he controlled Brianna sexually.

"Oh fuck, I don't understand this Brianna, man. I mean, usually by this time with a woman, I would have had her in bed already!" Enrico said. One day, Enrico invited Brianna to his bedroom ostensibly to show her his engineering project and closed the door behind them. Within five minutes, the door was flung open and Brianna ran screaming from his bedroom.

Later in the autumn, Enrico said that he had accompanied Brianna to the hospital and had driven her home after her treatment. Enrico undressed her in her apartment and laid her down on her bed. While she slept, Enrico boastfully claimed to have inserted his finger in Brianna's anus, then sniffed his finger and frowned. *So don't put your finger there!* Adam thought. Thus, with Brianna under Enrico's sexual control, Enrico said that Adam was under Brianna's aural control and that Brianna reported back to Enrico about his doings while Enrico was gone. Brianna's next-door neighbour, Lindsay, lived in another apartment upstairs when Adam first moved in. Enrico said that he had gone onto the roof when Lindsay was sunbathing and surprised her. He made inappropriate sexual remarks to Lindsay in an effort to seduce her.

Enrico invited Adam to take the sun on the roof with his guest and peer, Fan, a Team Delegate Adam had known in the Movement. Enrico told the story of his gay roommate in Toronto. He always had the sensation of being watched by the roommate. The roommate practised anal masturbation with a butt-plug he had purchased in a sex store. Enrico preferred to leave his door open while sleeping but sometimes awoke to the sensation that the gay roommate was standing in darkness in the doorway, watching him. Fan looked at Adam disapprovingly and blurted, "That's terrible." The previous year at a Movement event in Montreal, Adam saw Enrico down on one knee, holding that position for several minutes, gazing at a closed door, with a broad Cheshire-cat smile. Eventually, the door opened and Fan emerged: she had been in the women's bathroom! Enrico held the position and the grin and asked Fan if she had noticed him. Fan said no and asked Enrico what he meant. Enrico went to the trouble of explaining to her that he had been watching her in the bathroom all the while she was inside, and that given his eyes were level with her body, he could see everything she was doing in private through the closed door.

Enrico enjoyed bursting into the bathroom when he knew Adam was bathing, catching him while still in the bath. Adam pointed out that he was using the bath, that he was naked and that he would like Enrico to leave out of respect for his privacy. Enrico refused to leave, but approached even closer and stood over him, looking at his privates, giggling, making sexual comments and sexual jokes. Alternatively, when Adam was standing in the shower, Enrico would burst in when he knew Adam was standing with the curtain open, according to cues from the plumbing sounds. Adam again pointed out that he was using the shower, that he was naked and that he would like Enrico to leave out of respect for his privacy. Enrico refused to leave but approached closer and, standing right next to the shower, stared at Adam up and down, sized him up and made muffled sexual sounds with sexual gestures. Adam was in a vulnerable situation owing to his position and limited mobility in the shower.

For his part, Enrico insisted on leaving the bathroom door open even when he sat on the toilet and accused Adam of watching him. Adam had full use of a hallway closet, as his own bedroom had none; he hung up his clothing and Enrico protested "Don't look at me!" from his seat on the toilet barely three metres away.

"Nobody's looking at you, Enrico. If you don't have manners that's your problem."

Another time in the living room, Adam asked, "Enrico, do you have a mirror I could borrow?"

"Why? Because you want to play with your asshole?" Enrico responded.

"At least my asshole knows its place," Adam said as he walked away, "and doesn't try to take over my entire personality."

"Fuck you, Jack!" Enrico yelled after him.

"Fuck you, Jasper," Adam countered nonchalantly, having read it in a Kurt Vonnegut novel.

"Eh! You call me 'Yasper'! My name is not 'Yasper'!" Enrico objected.

"My name is not 'Jack'," Adam reminded Enrico, leaving him perplexed.

* * *

In public settings in restaurants, cinemas, or Movement gatherings, Enrico often tried to make Adam believe that waitresses, cashiers or other women were interested in Adam sexually. Enrico urged Adam to approach the women and make sexual advances to them; Adam always refused. Afterward, Enrico told him that Adam had offended a woman and she had complained about Adam to Enrico, as though she saw Adam under Enrico's control. Adam asked him to give names and details to explain what he was talking about. Enrico always refused such requests but told Adam he would have to remember this incident for when "somebody" offended Adam in the future.

Enrico stayed omniscient in Adam's affairs with women, often showing more interest in the women than Adam had himself! There was the case of Jill, a Native Canadian girl Adam knew from university. Enrico asked Adam for regular updates about her and kept asking for updates long after Adam had stopped seeing her. He also asked for updates about Karen, an American girl Adam had not seen since her visit four years earlier! After showing that he was more interested in Karen than Adam was, Enrico tried to change the facts surrounding her visit, claiming Karen and Adam had irritated Lola by dropping in on short notice. Similarly, Enrico told a detailed account of the time Adam ran away from home as a child. In fact, Adam had never run away from home as a child, nor did he ever tell Enrico any story resembling that.

Andrea was a Protestant single mother from Ontario and Adam's study partner at school. Enrico took an exceptionally deep interest, to the point of spying on Andrea and Adam when Andrea visited. Adam felt like Enrico was always around the corner, listening to every word and sound. One evening, Andrea kissed Adam in the hallway when Enrico was in his bedroom. After Andrea left, Enrico appeared suddenly and said, "Hey, hey, hey! Andrea!" Adam asked him what he was talking about. Enrico repeated the same thing and Adam asked him what it meant. Enrico repeated it again.

Adam said, "Hey, hey, hey Andrea, what?"

"Yeah! You guys kissed!" Enrico beamed.

Adam asked Enrico how he could know Andrea kissed him if he was in his bedroom, working hard on his Masters thesis in bio-medical engineering. "I heard the smack." Enrico said, smiling.

How can someone hear the smack of kissing lips from another room unless he is *listening* for the smack?

Alison was a young woman from Trinidad and Tobago whom Adam met at school. They had an evening out and Adam returned home on his own only to find his peer Gus there with Enrico, who had already informed Gus that Adam had a "date" with Alison. Adam called Raymond on the phone, and Raymond told Adam he already knew about his "date". He speculated that the entire council knew about it, even Silo in Argentina. In fact, Alison's agreement with Adam was that their evening out was not a date.

Adam met by chance in the Montreal Metro a young Caribbean single mother, Kelly. They talked a little bit and exchanged phone numbers. Adam never considered Kelly to be a serious interest. He seldom called her and did not provide his new phone number. By the following summer, Kelly was calling Adam almost every month at his old number and Enrico intercepted the calls. He told Adam, while they were at a barbecue at the home of Gus and his wife Lethe, that Kelly had called. It was clear that Enrico was interested in taking

Enrico's Control of Sex

Kelly for himself, never having met her. Apathetic, Adam thought it was a perfectly stupid idea, but in any case, he had no interest in Kelly himself. Enrico and Gus accused Adam to his face of possessiveness and of harbouring suspicion toward Enrico's intentions.

Gus and Lethe had been joined in civil union in an informal ceremony conducted by the Community for the Equilibrium and Development of the Human Being, one of the Movement's front groups, and were thus not legally married. Lethe was also a member of Enrico's team, and Gus often appeared fearful that someone would tamper with her sexually. A Friar Tuck character, jocular, rotund and extroverted, Gus had left Chile for Canada twelve years earlier. Porcine and florid, Lethe was red-haired and scatter-brained, from a local French Canadian family. They had one child together. Gus confided in Adam that at least ninety percent of women were sexier than Lethe, and if it weren't for the lure of cheating, he would never stay married. Gus routinely made wild promises to Enrico about building large teams full of "fifty-two members" but got sidetracked with frequent careless fender benders and seldom recruited anyone other than his circle of varied bums, young punks or unemployed Hispanic refugees. He indulged in recreational snacking after hearty breakfasts and lunches when the afternoon doldrums pushed him to visit fried chicken restaurants between meals while Lethe prepared their evening supper.

At midnight, Gus could go out for a plate of "spaghetti Caruso" with several slices of fatty smoked meat layered on top. Enrico often insulted Gus in the team meetings, calling him fat, lazy or stupid and Lethe *la Gorda* [the fat woman]. People rarely mistook Lethe for Marie Curie or Albert Einstein. Following a group discussion of the Armageddon in *The Saving Action*, Lethe exclaimed "That was fun!" and that it would be great for children because it had colours and animals in it. She was referring to the Four Horsemen of the Apocalypse: white, red, black and pale that could symbolize conquest, war, famine and death. Similarly, she identified Raymond's book on heraldry as children's literature because it included colourful pictures of dragons, lions and unicorns.

As time went on, Raymond noticed Enrico's behaviour was

nearly always inappropriate or offensive and his words tinged with innuendoes. Enrico fostered resentment and discomfort among the team members. As the months turned into years, different stories came to Adam's ears about how Enrico's behaviour and speech were imbued with sexual overtones and scatological imagery. Raymond especially told of how he and Gus had been insulted and abused by Enrico, who had alienated and repulsed many young females with crude comments and vulgar demonstrations, causing them to flee the team and shun Raymond, who had invited the women to the meetings.

The limits of Adam's patience about the sanctity of his privacy and mental space had been completely breached by Enrico only eleven days after Adam moved in. They were in the kitchen and Enrico asked, "Where are you going?" Adam said he was going to visit his mother in Laval. Enrico pinned Adam against the wall while his feet were caught under the low bench. Enrico gyrated his hips wildly and stroked his chest erotically with circular hand movements and, clearly jealous of Adam's mother, called out "Oh, love me! Love me!" over and over again. Adam recorded the incident in his journal, noting Enrico's Oedipus complex was in high form.

That summer, Raymond went with his mother to France. Enrico asked Adam what Raymond was going to do with "that lady" in France. Adam asked Enrico which lady he meant. Enrico referred to Raymond's mother once again as "that lady." Adam explained that the lady was Raymond's mother, that Raymond didn't call her "that lady," he just called her Mom. Enrico asked Adam how Raymond could pick up girls in France with "that lady" dragging along.

Enrico had an expansive Oedipus complex so large and complicated it extended beyond his own mother to the mothers of any young men he met. Later that summer, Raymond had broken up with a girlfriend. "Yeah! If you had a baby for every time you got screwed, you'd be a daddy many times over already!" Enrico said. Enrico was frequently abusive and disrespectful toward Raymond, who sometimes complained to Adam about him. By autumn, in front of Raymond's entire team, Enrico said, "Look at Raymond, he's a bum. Get laid already! Why don't you get laid already! Get it over with!" Raymond told Adam privately that Enrico used humiliation techniques like a torturer against him, creating a deep wound, then cauterizing it very quickly.

In November, Enrico convened a special Inquisitional Tribunal against Raymond, who referred to the Tribunal as "The Spanish Inquisition," and aptly so. Based on trumped up charges of sexual harassment and with no written policies, Enrico served as both judge and prosecutor in the spirit of Tomás de Torquemada, while Raymond was left to defend himself alone, without the benefit of a lawyer, counsellor or social worker. The Tribunal was held in Enrico's apartment, while Adam stayed in his bedroom. Enrico allowed several female witnesses, including Lethe, to attack Raymond at the same time, while Enrico joined in. By the end of the Inquisition, Raymond was left deeply wounded, emotionally exhausted, in tears, exasperated, frustrated, angry and inconsolably despondent. In the days that followed, Enrico relentlessly continued his attack on Raymond, raising painful memories of Raymond's childhood, especially his grandmother, possibly the ultimate Oedipal fantasy for Enrico. He elaborated an insulting scenario in which he asked Raymond what he would say to his grandmother if he could reach her in heaven by cell phone. Raymond said he would hang up.

Lisette came to Enrico's team the same summer after a few years in Vancouver, where she had fallen in with the wrong crowd of seekers, mystics and granolas who sometimes took advantage of her. She was an extremely weak and vulnerable woman of thirty with few friends or career prospects. She was more deeply exploited by Enrico than any other woman Adam had known. She was unemployed, partially illiterate, and often hungry and given to picking objects from dumpsters. Enrico started having sex with Lisette soon after he hypnotized her and integrated her into his team. Enrico told Adam that he just wanted to use her for sex, that he knew she was vulnerable and idolized him and that they had sex without protection at Lisette's risk. He also explicitly told Adam not to tell anyone what he was doing to Lisette. Adam was a witness as Enrico psychoanalyzed and reduced her to a childish state; he also saw how Enrico treated her like a rag doll, throwing her into the air and catching her while shouting "¡Mujer! Mujer!" [Woman! Woman!], slapping his knee repeatedly. Adam also watched as Enrico berated and screamed at her while he turned her into his patient, his maid, his math pupil and after Adam got his own telephone line, his secretary and receptionist. All the while, Enrico severely criticized her for not being perfect.

Overwhelmed and mismatched, Lisette quickly became emotionally dependent on Enrico not just for sex, but for everything ranging from the dispensing of meaning, to food, to companionship. She came to see Enrico hours or even a full day before the weekly meeting and slept over afterward. In effect, she became Enrico's live-in whore whom he kept for his own convenience, just to have somebody to victimize when he felt exalted after the meetings. In addition to having very poor self-esteem, an irritatingly nervous laugh and facial tics, Lisette was so undernourished that she went into shock when Enrico fed her, trembling convulsively as she consumed melted cheese on bread, or whatever scraps Enrico saw fit to throw her way. She became the Support in Enrico's team, deriving meaning from working directly for him. After a while, she was so dependent on Enrico that she could not even speak to anybody else or to be told anything meaningful; all meaning had to come from Enrico. After several months of ritual sexual exploitation, Enrico decided to dump Lisette. She did not take it well. She called Enrico nearly every day, pleading with him to take her back. He refused but kept her on the team to better manipulate her awhile longer. Sadly for Lisette, so much of her personal identity was already tied up in the Movement; she could not leave. She stayed in the team after being Enrico's unwitting sexual appliance and became jealous of every woman whom Enrico subsequently hypnotized then sexually assaulted after the meeting.

In June, Enrico's beloved Lola broke up with him by phone from Ottawa, but he kept the news from Adam. Soon after, he spoke of something he called "the problem of sex and death." He gave detailed accounts of how "the problem of sex and death" was so important to him and what it involved. Adam did not understand a word he said. He asked Enrico if it was something like when Jim Morrison of the Doors sang "I touched her thigh and death smiled…?" Enrico said sort of, but not really. Adam lost interest in guessing.

Enrico's Control of Sex

Enrico asked Adam every week thereafter when Adam would get a "new girlfriend" and urged him repeatedly to do so during the ensuing year, including repeated discussions of "the problem of sex and death." After being dumped by Lola, Enrico went on a rampage, during which time he hypnotized and assaulted every woman he was able to. He used each of his new conquests, typically from the Movement, to foster a kind of competitive game with Adam, in which Enrico lorded his sexual power over Adam and dared him to match. Adam wanted no part of his game.

Enrico's team contacted Manon, a New Age vegetarian waif, after she went through severe depression and suicide attempts the previous year. Manon was completely ignorant of the Movement and felt an enormously disturbing pressure to join upon being first contacted. In a rapid sequence of events, she became infatuated by Enrico, joined the Movement in Enrico's team, became Enrico's sexual victim, became disenchanted by Enrico, left the Movement and broke up with Enrico. With Manon, it was the same pattern as with Enrico's other sexual casualties. She arrived in advance of the meeting, participated in the meeting and was shown off to the team as Enrico's plaything. Manon stayed after the meeting and slept in Enrico's bed, occupying a prestige position in the eyes of Lisette, with whom she clashed. Manon did not speak English very well and Spanish not at all. Enrico did not speak French any better than the prototypical Spanish cow and looked down on French Canadians as deformed clowns beset with genetic diseases. It is not clear how or why Manon communicated with Enrico, although Manon was slightly better at handling herself in situations than was Lisette. Thus, Manon made supper for Enrico, who knew full well that Manon was a vegetarian when he said to her face, "This stuff is shit!" insulting her bland whole wheat pasta with sesame seed sauce. He was similarly abusive and disrespectful to her in all other aspects of their relationship.

Manon's relationship with Enrico broke off by November, and she left the Movement at the same time, her usefulness having been bound solely to Enrico's sexuality. Manon visited Frère-André while Enrico was attending an engineer's conference in Florida. Adam told her Enrico was not available, and she proceeded to tell Adam how much she hated Enrico and how he had done so much harm to her. She had suffered greatly and had been lied to by him. Manon farted all over Enrico's bedroom then told Adam she would like to defecate on Enrico's bed — right then and there — to show Enrico what she really thought of him. She squatted on the floor and continued farting abundantly. Adam told Manon that while he sympathized with her situation from personal experience, he discouraged her from defecating in Enrico's bedroom. Instead, Manon wrote a vicious letter to Enrico, left it for him on his bed, and nobody ever heard from her again.

III — A SPIRITUAL JOURNEY

"Maybe we weren't meant for paradise...
Maybe we can't stroll to the music of the lute.
We must march to the sound of drums."
— James T. Kirk

ONE DAY that summer, Enrico came home with his peer Pigpen, a Team Delegate in the Movement who himself was not too normal. Pigpen was from solid German Canadian stock and had been raised with good values in the Mennonite townships of Southern Ontario, yet he spurned his family and religious community so he could join the Movement. Pigpen now had no values, no scruples and as little soap, for he always appeared frog-faced and unkempt, wearing shabby or torn clothing, unwashed and unshaven. Pigpen thought nothing of asking pushy, manipulative, prying, nosy personal questions. He also had a talent for making you feel like a first-rate hypocrite when your day had been going well before he opened his uncouth mouth. The experience of talking to Pigpen was comparable to that of talking to a homeless alcoholic. To stir the pot, Pigpen married a woman who hated Latinos, which produced bizarre contradictions and made their lives difficult in the Movement.

Enrico decided to show off for Pigpen. First, he assumed an intimidating posture and placed his body in Adam's path. Then he barked at Adam: "What do you do when I'm not here? What have you been doing? Were you playing with yourself!?" Then he turned to Pigpen and said: "This guy likes to play with himself when I'm not here." (Pigpen nodded.) "Yeah; this guy's an asshole!"

Then Enrico defied Adam, in front of Pigpen, from getting into Enrico's computer or through the password. He claimed that even if Adam thought he could get through the password, Enrico, in his genius, had devised a program to counteract any program that Adam would have made to break through passwords. Enrico progressively blended his psychological coercion with sexual abuse, eventually making them indistinguishable. After having falsely accused Adam of breaching his personal space and privacy, Enrico installed a piece of hardware on Adam's computer without telling him. In order to do this, he entered Adam's bedroom while he was gone, opened the computer's casing without Adam's knowledge or consent and altered the configuration of his computer hardware without his knowing. Through his intrusive behaviour, Enrico was telling Adam that he could get into his mental space any time he wanted, though the reverse would be impossible.

Also that July, Adam entertained Raymond, who explained the central values of the Movement: the human being as the central value, active non-violence, no discrimination, co-operativism, options, not monopoly. Enrico eavesdropped while Adam spoke the end of a sentence to Raymond: "…it's really easy."

Adam closed the door after Raymond and proceeded to his bedroom, because he had a headache. "Is it easy, Yellow?" Not allowing Adam to answer, Enrico called him back and again asked if Adam had heard what he said. "Is it easy, Yellow?"

Adam told Enrico that he had indeed heard him and that it was indeed yellow, not knowing or caring what "it" was. Enrico reminded Adam he had called him "Yellow" and asked where people called other people "Yellow." Exasperated, Adam ventured, "In the Wild West?"

Enrico held a finger up to Adam's face and exclaimed "In the Wild West!" He said he was calling Adam "Yellow" because Adam didn't have the guts to join the Movement — only to talk about it with people like Raymond. Enrico said that if Adam were a man, he wouldn't let Enrico call him "Yellow," but that in either case, Adam didn't have the guts to fight him any more than he had the guts to join the Movement.

A Spiritual Journey

Adam had more frequent personal discussions with Raymond throughout the summer. A polymath and polyglot, Raymond had been in Enrico's team for nearly seven years but had made little structural progress, having been an Admi in Enrico's team then an Orientor of his own team a few years earlier, rising temporarily to the position of Team Delegate, before losing his team. Adam rejoined the Movement voluntarily the second week of August as a member of Raymond's team, not Enrico's, after a team social outing to watch a moving pro-Siloist film titled *Hombre Mirando Al Sudeste* [Man Facing Southeast]. In capsule form, a patient turns up without papers at a psychiatric institution in Argentina. He says his name is Rantes and claims to be a visitor from another planet. Granted asylum, he keeps a shoebox under his bed full of newspaper clippings of violent acts, including massacres, wars, genocide, and murders, which he calls "the daily crimes." Rantes volunteers in the hospital's biology lab so he can study the human brain. He weighs one and takes notes in an unknown language. He asks questions about human nature, emotions and thought. Rantes slices a cadaver's brains and crumbles bits of it into a sink with running water. "There goes Einstein, there goes Bach," Rantes begins as brain matter washes down the drain. He continues, "Mr. Nobody, an assassin, a madman. What do you think, Doctor? Will this drain lead to heaven or hell?" The watchful psychiatrist has no answer.

Adam's membership in Raymond's team was both voluntary and satisfying, but Adam was not aware that Enrico took it as a triumph of his will over Adam's — a victory in his organized campaign of control. Adam wanted to work with Raymond because they had a common understanding; Adam did not have any understanding with Enrico and avoided his meetings — much to Enrico's chagrin. Adam mistakenly believed that by choosing Raymond's team over Enrico's, he could avoid Enrico's psychological coercion and sexual interference. Enrico had converted Adam to the Movement in seventy-four days.

In September, Adam became the Admi of Raymond's team and began working under the Admi of Enrico's team, Suzette, who had been contacted the same summer. Her numerous nervous tics, her irritating clown-like sycophantic laugh and sexual harassment of men all marked her presence in the team. Suzette confided in Adam that she had many sexually transmitted illnesses, including one for which the doctor told her she should use a condom during each sexual encounter for the rest of her life. She always tried to kiss the men in the team. She stood very close while talking and advanced steadily closer every few seconds until she was right in your face. To complicate matters, she hated her chin and was constantly picking at it until she drew blood. She seized the slightest excuse to kiss startled men all over the face, at which point they usually drew back. Sometimes, Suzette tried to hug and kiss Adam on the mouth, which he resisted with great urgency. In working with Suzette as his direct Admi supervisor beneath M-C, he came to understand Suzette's verbal marathons after practice. A native of the small town of Saint-Paul-d'Abbotsford south of Montreal, Suzette was otherwise frustrated with her life: she was thirty-five and still unmarried, without children, near bankruptcy, and had a creeping feeling that people found her obnoxious.

Suzette and Adam, in turn, both worked under the Central Administrator of the entire North American Council, Marie-Claude Desrochers. Based in Montreal, she was in a position of authority and power. In September, Adam began attending regular weekly meetings of Raymond's team, in a location away from Enrico. Suzette and Raymond taught Adam the ropes of the Admi sector and referred to M-C, with whom Adam sometimes had occasion to speak on the phone, to report monthly statistics, etc. Raymond also told him the importance of showing solidarity towards each member of the council and his administrative network. Raymond had spoken favourably about M-C, as had Suzette. Both Raymond and Suzette were instrumental in helping Adam learn his job, in seeing how he fit into the structure and in ensuring that all his Admi efforts were ultimately supervised by M-C. Increasingly, Adam saw M-C as a model to be followed and a paragon of efficiency.

In addition to being the Central Admi, M-C's level in the structure was a Team Delegate and member of the Council of Team Delegates. Team Delegates oriented teams of at least ten group delegates each. A General Delegate, Josh in turn oriented ten Team

Delegate Orientors, and also had under his purview the Team Delegate Support, Yorgo, and the Team Delegate Admi, M-C. Together, Josh, Yorgo and M-C formed the "triangle," a prestigious planning unit that co-ordinated orientation, administration and support for the entire council. Being Central Admi meant M-C was also Josh's executive secretary, Chief Information Officer and Chief Financial Officer as well the System Operator for the council's Bulletin Board System (BBS) and as such, wielded a lot of power. M-C was also a *vieja*, a Spanish word meaning "old-timer." The *viejos* [*viejo* for men, *vieja* for women] had been in the Movement for many years, in M-C's case, ten years. Over the years, the Movement had contacted thousands of people in Montreal, but M-C was one of only five *viejos* who rose to be Team Delegates in Montreal; the others were Enrico, Colleen, Fan and Renato.

The same basic structure was repeated for all teams and councils smaller and exponentially larger throughout the Movement. Above the General Delegate, a Co-ordinator oriented a team of ten General Delegates like Josh and his own peers, and by extension a thousand people around the world. Silo was a Co-ordinator, and the project of the Movement was to recruit "new people" to reproduce this same pyramid structure until every human being worked in a Siloist team. Above the Co-ordinator were the levels of Team Co-ordinator and General Co-ordinator, orienting the lives of ten thousand up to one hundred thousand people, though nobody had ever reached that level in the Movement while Silo remained satisfied with his olive vineyard and ever-growing bank account, both in Argentina. Much symbolism was attached to the sectors of the triangle and their functions. Some said the three functions of orientation, support and administration represented the past, present and future. Others pointed out it could represent the three cardinal virtues of a Siloist: peace, force and joy.

The son of a Holocaust survivor, Josh Zylberberg was born in the United States, where he had been a hippie and flower child. His first adult experience of Canada was backpacking when he was twenty-one; he emigrated permanently and studied History and Philosophy of Science, which led to a career in the media. Josh was an extremely charismatic and charming individual who bore a strong physical resemblance to the accomplished actor Eugene Levy. His voice had the hypnotic singsong quality of Bela Lugosi and his politics were akin to those of Noam Chomsky. Josh was given to utterances like "Psychophysics in the Soviet Union…" that had audiences enthralled. His sudden recovery from alleged lymphoma cancer transformed Josh into a messiah within the Movement. Notwithstanding, other less positive qualities left his detractors perplexed. For example, as a car owner, ardent meat-eater and polluter, Josh seemed hypocritical given the Movement's mission of improving the species and making the world a better place in which to live. Josh also adored the snob appeal of rubbing elbows with Silo and other Movement luminaries while he looked down on anybody who did not devote his or her life to Silo's cause. Gus, Raymond and in turn Adam had, on separate occasions, each been on the receiving end of Josh's penetrating glance when, with a deep drag of his cigarette which he did not exhale for up to an hour, he seemed to stare right through them and see deeply into their shortcomings with an askance look that said "What the fuck you doing with your life, man?" As a General Delegate, Josh was Silo's bagman in Toronto. He was an ambitious climber who could not be bothered to supervise the degraded antics and sex lives of his lowbrow acolytes.

On the last Sunday in October, Adam attended his first Admi seminar, conducted by M-C in her apartment on Waverly Street in Montreal. Every Admi in the council was invited and many came in from Ontario, in addition to those from Quebec. Adam represented Raymond's team and was eager to learn. Three autumns earlier, Adam had attended a council event when the Movement had a campaign about the environment and at which M-C was a prominent speaker. He observed her way of speaking and interacting with people. She was such an industrial-communistic woman, devoid of sentiment or warmth. Everything she did was for "The Cause." In her relations with others, Adam saw her to be a vicious, combative and confrontational person. In front of everyone, M-C discussed with Enrico his travel plans to Argentina. Enrico complained that the airline ticket she had found for him was too expensive. She yelled loudly back at him, and they engaged in an extended dispute. Adam was afraid of M-C.

A Spiritual Journey

She was a pugnacious person to be steered clear of, and he found no pleasure in talking to her. Adam heard rumours that she lived on Parthenais Street, in the shadow of the towering detention centre which harboured a prison; it seemed a perfect match for her personality: cold, austere, grey, inhuman. Now, after four years of knowing M-C, it was his first time in her home. It was difficult for him to find the apartment since he was not familiar with the Villeray neighbourhood. Her building was within a labyrinth of streets sandwiched between the garment sector to the north of the Metropolitan highway and the railway tracks to the west. A somewhat less attractive stretch of the Main to the east offered unfriendly shops for sewing machine repair or typewriter maintenance, among other dying arts.

The Admi seminar was very good, and Adam was thoroughly impressed with M-C's administrative talents. He watched her attentively while each Admi asked her questions and she fielded them all. It was the beginning of his admiration for her as an administrator, as his senior and a person with experience in the council, as a person to be listened to. Adam gained fulfilment, meaning and identity working for M-C as an administrator. When the meeting ended, he asked her if he could stay a few minutes to discuss certain problems relating to the smooth administration of his team. She became extremely uncomfortable when he asked this. After the other Admis left, she was visibly tense and asked him to explain his business quickly; Rania was coming, and Adam had to be hustled out of the house before Rania entered. He asked himself what the problem was. Was M-C so disgusted with him that she could not allow her daughter to be exposed to him for even a few minutes? So what if Rania and Adam should cross paths? It now seemed that M-C wanted a strict separation between the use of Waverly for Movement business and her personal life. She had allotted a certain amount of time for Movement business with the understanding that her personal time and space would not be infringed upon. Any activity that went beyond the purpose or the timing of the agreed Movement activity was unacceptable, even it was for the Movement. Adam had no choice but to accept her terms for the simple reason that it was her apartment. They discussed their

Movement business and Adam left quickly, ejected by an inhospitable and protective M-C. He was unwelcome in her home and there were no thoughts of friendship in his mind.

In the first week of December, M-C attended a meeting of Raymond's team, to evaluate Adam's work as an Admi. Adam listed her in his notes as "special guest star." She was harsh with him during the meeting, but when leaving she said, "You're doing a good job." It was a touching honour for him to get such a big compliment from M-C. Adam started to feel a sense of accomplishment working for her and began to reclaim some meaning in his life as a result of his Admi job, which he took very seriously and which became part of his identity.

In the second weekend of December, Adam attended his second Admi seminar with M-C. There were fewer people in attendance, all Admis from Enrico's council, but M-C continued to serve as a model for him. From start to finish, Adam entered and left with the understanding that the use of M-C's apartment was for Movement business only and that he was to be respectful of her time and space. He made no special requests for extra time at the end of the meeting, as he had done in October.

The Winter Solstice was the time of the "Seasonal" assembly, based on pagan traditions and held four times a year. Usually at this time, Enrico would attempt to address the issue of why so many people had left the team recently, instead of staying for more of his verbal abuse and sermonizing. He used the metaphor of the amoeba:

> "The team is like an organism, an organism like the amoeba. And all the amoeba does is it eats and it shits. This team eats and it shits. The new people the team takes in are like ... nutrition for the team; the team always needs to have new food, new nutrition. Then the organism digests the nourishment; that's where you people come in: the pillars of the team help the new people to integrate into the team. But they don't all stay because they haven't got the guts; so the team shits them out."

Enrico and M-C used words like "lumpen" when referring to people who had left the Movement. Adam asked Raymond what it meant. Raymond said it was derived from *lumpenproletariat* and was "an unofficial official vocabulary term of the Movement, drawn from Marxist ideology." It referred to losers. Enrico said the words spoken by lumpen and on occasion group delegates were "noise," since they disrupted the important business of the Movement. Enrico denigrated and chastised people outside the Movement, saying that people who never joined the Movement would never overcome the abyss and that the "lumpens" who left the Movement fell into the abyss soon after and would never leave it.

Raymond and Adam celebrated New Year's Day by boarding a flight to Toronto, with their final destination Santiago, Chile, for an international meeting of the Movement which Enrico did not attend. The Central Support Sector, Yorgo, was a cool guy, a superstar and sex symbol in the Movement, much to the chagrin of his faithful wife, who resembled a visitor in her own bed considering his dalliances. Born of mixed Spanish and Dutch heritage in Concepción, a city south of Santiago, Yorgo was there when Silo founded the Movement but fled to Canada to escape the repression and torture he allegedly suffered under Pinochet. Settled in Toronto, Yorgo became like a Canadian version of Don Juan — a charming and kind man with a good sense of humour, a man who uses his personality to exploit women for sex.

People like Yorgo gave the Movement its reputation for being an agency dedicated to helping Latin American émigrés find plentiful cigarettes, strong coffee and casual sex overseas. Yorgo was known to take an interest in the wellbeing of Siloists by marching into a room, thumping a man on the chest and asking "You doing well, man? Eating well, man? Sleeping well, man? Shitting well? Fucking well? I just have to take care of the vegetative-sexual."

Yorgo had a serious discussion with Adam during the flight about his sleeping and relaxation habits and his difficulties in working with the Force. Over Quito, Ecuador, Adam was inspired when Yorgo gave his vision for a bright future with the project of the Movement. "One day man, you're going to feel something you never felt before, and life will become an adventure for you, man!" Upon landing, Yorgo was on his home turf and he knew all the moves. With his sweater sleeves tied around his neck and sporting sunglasses, he mentored Adam (and Raymond) and was a welcome relief from Pigpen. There was exuberant talk of Viña del Mar and the Pacific Ocean. Raymond wanted to make a pilgrimage to Argentina. Gus salivated about the prospects for eating good Chilean food, especially shark fin soup, beef testicles and mountains of fresh local seafood at Santiago's Mercado Central.

Team Delegate Renato had arranged housing for some Canadian members in Chile. Adam shared a home with Renato, Raymond, Fan, Yorgo and Pigpen. Josh stayed with some "big cheeses" in the Movement while Team Delegate Ned and his wife Hex stayed in a hotel. Pigpen was on Adam's case from the first day in Chile, pestering him, harassing him and treating him like a fool. One day in Santiago, Adam was seated in the living room of the group house nearly 9,000 kilometres from Montreal when suddenly Pigpen turned directly to him and began a vociferous attack on *Star Trek*. Pigpen went on at great length deriding the show in very nasty terms and expanding his criticisms to Adam personally in a way that ridiculed him and his values, linking them to *Star Trek*. He lambasted Adam for watching and admiring the show and said that it had no place in the life of a Movement member.

Significantly, Adam could not recall any time where he had watched *Star Trek* with Pigpen or even discussed it with him. Neither did Adam raise the subject of the show that same trip. Yorgo and Fan joined with Pigpen in criticizing Adam. It was three against one, and Raymond could not help Adam. Pigpen was prepared with a particular *Star Trek* episode synopsis upon which to focus his efforts: "This Side of Paradise," seemingly his most hated. Adam was not impressed with Pigpen's summary of the episode, which he got wrong, saying that the crew of the *Enterprise* had constructed a paradise-like environment in which everybody engaged in endless pleasure with no responsibilities. Pigpen falsely claimed the crew had been "brainwashed." "That sounds like a cult to me!" he said, distancing the Movement from *Star Trek*.

Cult? Who said anything about a cult? Adam thought, astounded.

A Spiritual Journey

Was Pigpen trying to portray *Star Trek* as a cult? If so, how was this relevant to the Movement? Did Pigpen see the show as competition to the Movement? Pigpen motioned to Yorgo to have a turn at extinguishing Adam's values. Yorgo jumped into the fray and asked Adam to answer this question: "If you had a chance to watch a *Star Trek* episode you had never seen before or to meet a person you had never met before, but you could only do one, which one would you pick?" Adam felt like he was being forced to choose between *Star Trek* and the Movement — like Adam was being separated from his values, just as Adam was already physically separated from his home in Montreal.

"What a stupid question!" Adam exclaimed. The group awaited his answer.

Five autumns earlier, Adam had attended the ceremonial return of Josh, the council leader, from Montreal's Trudeau Airport, to Toronto where he worked as a producer, writer and researcher for a well-known nature program on Canadian television. Adam rode in the front seat while Enrico drove his car. Raymond and Gus were in the back seat. Raymond did his Dr. Strangelove imitations ("Yes, Dmitri. Yes, Dmitri. No, Dmitri. The change will do us some good, Dmitri. Yes, of course I care, Dmitri. And how is Mrs. Dmitri?") and made several funny jokes that Adam enjoyed, and Enrico was visibly jealous of their friendship. Raymond then started talking about *Star Trek*, his shared interests with Adam, who answered Raymond in turn.

"Do you think the Klingons are an inferior race?" Enrico asked Adam disrespectfully, interrupting Raymond.

"Inferior to whom?" Adam responded calmly, closing his left eye halfway. Enrico was flustered by this and repeated his question. Adam explained that there were many different races in the *Star Trek* universe and that one's point of view could vary quite a bit depending on which races were being compared, but that the imposition of the Organian Peace Treaty was crucial to understanding. Raymond was thoroughly impressed while Enrico was frustrated and visibly angry and repeated his theory in more detail, engaging in wild fantasy about the harmful effects of *Star Trek*. Adam had never heard such a theory before and thought it was particularly stupid.

"So how about you? Do you think the Klingons are an inferior race?" Adam asked Enrico.

"Who am I to blow against the wind?" Enrico answered cryptically. Enrico retreated from his position, unable to humiliate Adam about his personal values. At least, for the moment.

In Santiago, Adam explained to Yorgo, Pigpen and Fan how that was a trick question not worth an answer. They shouted at him that the person Adam had never met was waiting to meet him now, but would not wait for long. Adam had to make his decision right away. He felt trapped, like his values were being squeezed right out of him by Pigpen, who suddenly knew about his personal values without having shared any good moments with him before, who did not even know him. Adam wondered about this group of Pigpen, Yorgo and Fan; he noticed they were all Team Delegate peers of Enrico, who used Pigpen as a proxy. For Adam, this incident was a total humiliation, being chased across time and space to defend his values.

Adam had many meaningful experiences with people from around the world, got to serenade Silo with "Cumpleaños Feliz" on his birthday and felt he had finally had his most authentic experience of the Movement. In attendance at the Admi conference conducted by Silo's Admi Petruchia of Rome, Adam was the only Admi representing North America. He felt tremendous pride that he might take detailed notes for M-C to better inform her. Adam did not understand much of what was said in Spanish and Italian but he made new Admi friends from other councils and returned to Montreal with a sensation of having had a rewarding experience, Pigpen being the only exception. Highlights of Josh's council meeting revolved around nearly seven-foot-tall Alberta-born cowboy Ned, his British wife Hex and her sourpuss personality. While Josh was addressing the gathered, the bearded Ned could not resist taking a banana from a bowl of fruit and peeling it. Raymond reached for his camera, not wanting to pass up Ned-the-monkey and his long foldout legs eating a banana. The whole room's attention turned to Ned while Adam giggled. After his banana, Ned decided to get up and arbitrarily close the hotel room curtains in the middle of the January day, which in Chile is summer.

A Spiritual Journey

Hex interrupted Josh and in her best Monty Python voice called out: "Blast that Ned! Now look here! This is our last day in the sunshine! Tell him to OPEN THE FUCKING CURTAINS!" The council roared in laughter, and the monkey demurred.

In Chile, Adam also met and befriended a nice Swiss girl, who he saw every day and with whom he made love towards the end of the trip and missed his excursion to Viña del Mar. A disturbing pattern started to repeat itself, however, starting with their return flight from Arturo Benitez airport in Santiago. Yorgo bid the returning Canadians farewell, saying "See you on the astral plane." Pigpen asked Adam if he knew that the girl he had met in Chile would never write him back after he returned to Canada and she to Switzerland. "You know, she's not going to write you back. You know that, don't you? You should not get your hopes dashed. Learn to give and let go. Learn to give without expecting anything in return."

Adam said he didn't know; maybe she would write back, maybe she wouldn't. He planned to write her and knew that he would retain a good memory of her no matter what happened. Pigpen did not accept this answer and continued to stress that the girl would not write back, that Adam would never hear from her again and that he should erase her from his mind. In short order, Fan, Renato, Enrico and M-C all repeated the same line of reasoning. Adam was beginning to wonder what he gave off that people should address problems he never complained about or even knew he had. After landing in Toronto, Fan and Adam boarded the flight to Montreal and she asked him if he met anyone special in Chile. Adam told Fan about the girl and Fan made the same remarks that Pigpen had. Home in Montreal, Enrico asked if Adam had met anyone special in Chile. Adam told him about the girl. "You know, she's not going to write you back. You know that, don't you? Now you know you can have that special feeling with someone else." Adam shook his head back and forth, wondering what Enrico meant and with whom.

On the first Saturday in March, there was an event for Admis at Suzette's apartment in de Lille Street. Suzette was busy looking over the internal Movement *fiches*, i.e. membership files from the council.

Normally, she would have access only to her own team's fiches since she was the Admi. However, M-C, the Central Admi sympathised with Suzette's personal situation and her desire to find a mate. M-C breached confidentiality to make available fiches for every man in North America, since they contained information about hobbies, marital status, abilities, age, country of origin and other data that would help Suzette choose a man for her purposes.

There, M-C asked Adam about his trip to Chile and the rumour that he had met a girl there. Apparently, somebody had informed M-C that Adam was sexually active. Swerving between French and English, she peppered him with questions « Penses-tu qu'elle va t'écrire?» [You know she's not going to write you back.] "You know that, don't you? Adam, tu ne dois pas croire qu'elle va t'écrire; c'est un faux espoir. » [Adam, you musn't hope that she will write you. It's a false hope.] M-C said, invoking the Siloist doctrine of false hopes and thereby using her position of power to manipulate his sexual behaviour. M-C looked at Adam as if with real concern for an emotional basket case, a naive and vulnerable person who had to be told the cold, hard reality of life. Adam was mystified by this constant concern for him, at a time when he had no problems and did not feel any regret over the Swiss girl. Why was everybody in the Council of Team Delegates trying to manage his sex life? It was as though a note had been placed in his file. Adam objected to M-C's comments and told her so, at his own risk.

From Adam's early Siloist experiences, Enrico and other Movement members used the Force in their meetings. The Force was very hard for Adam to understand, and even harder to experience. Typically, he fretted and twitched and the others said he was too nervous to feel it. Enrico would arrange the group in a circle, turn down the lights then summon a force of energy from "the profound models" somewhere inside their bodies. Enrico shook violently and transmitted the Force to others. Adam did not understand what was going on and never felt the effect, even when he felt Enrico trembling next to him. Adam had sought explanations from Raymond and other Movement members, but was often rebuffed and the Force remained a mystery for years on end. Since the previous autumn, Raymond had guided his own sessions with the Force and showed more patience in explaining it to Adam. Raymond told Adam that he had indeed felt the Force many times on his own, but just did not recognise it as such. Raymond added that M-C had recommended after her December visit to their team that Adam should be made to work especially hard on the Force for the specific reason that he had problems with it. Gently, the Force started to rise in Adam. One evening late in March, Raymond and Adam attended a meeting of Enrico's team. The room was darkened at the end of the meeting for Enrico to summon the Force. Adam had been practising relaxation in Raymond's team and felt he was nearly ready to feel the Force.

The room was dark and silent. As they joined hands, Enrico conducted the Exercise of the Force. He described a solid luminous sphere appearing in front of their heads. Adam took the sphere inside his forehead and allowed it to enter his body. It descended down into his chest and began expanding and contracting. Silent and restful, without any nervous tics, he began to feel the Force as a strange euphoria surging inside him, at last. He felt it clearly for several seconds, without anguish or consternation for the first time ever. Could this be the feeling Yorgo had prophesied over Ecuador? Adam was able to control the Force in him and did not fear it. At that very moment, Raymond put his hand on Adam's knee and said, "Welcome." Raymond patted his knee a bit longer and repeated "Welcome to us." It was a momentous occasion. Adam had joined the spiritual plane of the Movement. He felt what they felt.

IV — PRELUDE TO THE ABYSS

"A woman, on the other hand... is in an entirely different position. If she wants to transgress expectations of her sex with masculine forms of aggression, she needs a kind of permission.
The process is psychological, one of gaining a sense of entitlement to act out forbidden ambitions."
— Patricia Pearson

IN THE WINTER after the Chile trip, Enrico said Adam's personal values were still "provisional values." He added that Raymond had long since passed this stage and had already absorbed all the Movement had to teach him. As a consequence, Raymond was losing interest in the Movement and would have to leave soon. Enrico also denigrated and ridiculed Raymond and told Adam that Raymond was more his peer than anyone else in the Movement's structure. Enrico pushed Adam to take Raymond's place and to start his own team, to become a Team Delegate. Later, in March, Adam learned that Raymond had been offered a contract to teach in Japan and would leave Canada later in the year, in July. It made Adam sad and fearful for their friendship and for being alone in the Movement, without Raymond's support.

* * *

Since Chile, it was a time of expanding horizons, new friends and experiences. Adam made friends with people he had known for years, but only slightly: Renato, Yorgo and M-C. Renato himself expressed perfectly the spirit of the times in his personal inscription on Adam's birthday card "*Un gran abrazo para mi nuevo amigo que ya comienza a ser un viejo amigo.*" [A big hug for my new friend who is starting to be an old friend.] Adam felt the same way about Renato, and also about Karim, Bassam, Tara, Yorgo and M-C. Adam loved them all in the same way, as comrades in the Movement. M-C attended his birthday party and signed his card after she was given the choicest spot (by Enrico), directly under the printed "Happy Birthday." M-C's inscription read "♥XXX M-C…" Where Adam came from, the heart symbol means "love" and the three Xs are symbolic kisses. Adam did not interpret these symbols for their literal or sexual meaning, as in "I love you and I want to give you three kisses." To him, it was merely a token show of love for his birthday and in keeping with the same spirit in which Adam loved his new friends in the council, like M-C.

On the first Friday in April, Enrico's entire team rented a van and drove to the council meeting in Kitchener, Ontario, a medium-sized city northwest of Toronto with a large German and Mennonite population, where the Movement had always done well. During the general council meetings, Josh spoke as they all listened. They did the experience of the Force; while some dozed, Enrico sat like a stone sculpture and M-C wept. Josh pointed out, "In some languages, like French or Spanish, 'meaning' and 'direction' are the same word." He urged them to ask themselves where they were going and to remember the twin significance of the question. Josh also discussed the "ludic" approach to life, using the glass bead game mentioned in Hermann Hesse's *Magister Ludi* as a paradigm example. Josh's remark and surrounding explanation had a very profound impact on Adam.

During a break in the council meeting Saturday, Adam was seated on a chair. M-C passed by his chair and knocked his coat off onto the floor. She picked it up and replaced it on the back of the chair. Then, grabbing the arms of the chair firmly on each side so Adam couldn't move, she leaned directly over him and looked down at him from on top. "Sorry. Don't hate me for that," she said. Only four days after using the [♥] symbol on his birthday card, M-C was accusing Adam of hating her.

Adam thought the word "hate" was rather strong for an incident that he was ready to see as a minor accident and a small inconvenience.

He had no other choice but to look up at M-C, towering over him. "Oh, I could never hate you," he tried to reassure her.

Turning his eyes down, he thought the incident was over.

"*Why not?*" M-C demanded in a deadpan voice.

Adam was incredulous that she would ask him "why not?" for a common courtesy on his part that was intended to leave her the benefit of the doubt. Was it not enough that he already said he wouldn't hate her? What would it take to make her go away? He looked up at her again; she was still grasping his chair firmly as ever, glaring down at him. When M-C used such a strong word as "hate," she left him little room to escape. The concept of "hate" was the exact opposite of what M-C had expressed to him on his birthday card, on which she used the word "love" just a few days earlier. Although Adam agreed with the sentiment of "love" in the sense of authentic camaraderie, he did not expect he would be tested on it so quickly!

"I could never hate you because … I love you." Adam said to counteract her "hate."

"Harrumph!" she grunted and seemed to make a mental observation, then walked away suddenly, without explanation.

Boy, what's her problem? Adam thought, shaking his head while wondering what just happened. It was true, Adam did not hate M-C, but how and why did he say he loved her when he never did before and never thought he would have? M-C had conditioned him to respond with love whenever she treated him to hatred. Adam did not understand any further, but somehow, she had tricked him to say "I love you" when Adam didn't mean it in any other way other than how he loved Renato or Yorgo. By exaggerating the emotional tone with the word "hate," M-C also elevated the minor incident with his jacket to a major offence. So when she said "Don't hate me for that" it was her way of gauging his reaction. During the weekend, Adam attended Admi meetings given by M-C. They got along well and his admiration for her excellent abilities as Central Admi grew stronger.

Home in Montreal and for several weeks after Kitchener, Enrico persistently remarked to Adam, "You need to have a stronger nervous system," and significantly, "You could be more aware of your surroundings. You know, somebody really likes you." Adam asked what he meant by that. Enrico declined to answer, saying Adam needed to have a stronger nervous system before he could hear the answers to his questions, that he was too weak to hear the answers now. However, Enrico said that there was a woman in the council who really liked Adam, and if he were more aware of his surroundings, he would pick up on it and turn it into an opportunity for sex. Adam thought about who it could be, but couldn't think of anyone in the council who seemed interested in him. He asked Enrico to tell him who it was. Enrico said he *could* do that, but that it would be more fun for him to watch Adam manage on his own; he made a link to developing a stronger nervous system. The only female Adam could think of was Christine, a plump woman from France who seemed to take an interest. Enrico said it wasn't Christine; he added that Christine was trouble and that Adam didn't want to get involved with her. Enrico specifically warned about her, but refused to warn about the dangerous plans of the woman he originally spoke of. Why did he prevent one danger yet leave another on the table? Enrico steadfastly refused Adam's repeated requests to say who it was.

At Frère-André, Adam enjoyed a bright and sunny afternoon in April after their return from Kitchener. He was lying on his bed with his bedroom door open, relaxing.

Enrico's phone rang and he answered it in his bedroom. Adam did not know who was on the other end but the conversation seemed to become confrontational. "There's nothing about it in the *Norms*," Enrico said and repeated it a second time, emphatically. *The* Norms *are like the Movement's constitution. Who's he talking to?* Adam asked himself.

That same evening at Frère-André, Enrico steered the conversation towards his favourite topic: sex. He was discussing how different women would approach a man to have sex with him, mentioning Colleen, among others. Enrico invoked M-C's name and got much more direct and personal than he had about the other women, speculating on how M-C, specifically, would approach a man for sex. "You know how M-C would do it? 'You! Get over here! Fuck this!'" At "fuck this," Enrico pointed straight at his crotch, burrowing his finger into his jeans, as he portrayed M-C's attitude like a cave woman who finds a mate by clubbing an unsuspecting caveman over the head with a thick truncheon. Adam thought it was a very unusual thing to say, but he didn't know what Enrico was talking about or what could motivate him to say such a disgusting thing. All he said was, "Uh ... I don't know..." Enrico put his pipe back in his mouth. Puffing and smirking, he looked Adam straight in the eye and watched him squirm.

In late April, Fan visited Frère-André. Adam assumed she was there to discuss Movement business with Enrico, but Adam was mistaken. Fan had broken up with Renato while in Chile and she had not had sex in about three months. Enrico entered his bedroom and closed the door behind him, with Fan lying face down on Enrico's bed. For the occasion, Fan wore a jeans-jacket and blue jeans just as Enrico did every day of the year. Fan and Enrico, both Team Delegates, spent the night together. After Fan left, Enrico told Adam the terms of their sexual contact was strictly casual; he was helping Fan out because she needed sex. They agreed there was to be no romance, no emotional attachment. Adam thought it unusual that Fan would not be completely repulsed by Enrico, given that he had spied on her in the women's bathroom in the past and used her to show his sexual control the previous summer. Apparently, Enrico controlled Fan also.

Enrico's team celebrated the Movement's anniversary one Saturday evening by having a little party at Frère-André. His entire team was in attendance when the doorbell rang. They opened the door and Adam was surprised to greet M-C. Suzette explained to him that since M-C did not really have a team of her own, she was a guest in Enrico's team and very welcome. Adam concurred. They had their party. At the end, they saw off their guests and Adam said goodbye to M-C. She hugged him and he hugged her back. She hugged him again and would not let go. *What's this all about?* Adam thought. He gave her one good squeeze more to signify the end of the hug, then released her. M-C was still hugging him and would not let go, wrapped around his midsection. At this point, Adam just stood there and let her hug him until she was finished, while everybody in his team watched. After having tricked him into saying "I love you" at a Movement meeting just one month earlier, M-C had tricked him into hugging her in front of Enrico's council. When she finally released him, Adam tried asking her if something was the matter, if she wanted to talk to him about something. M-C said nothing and left abruptly. With M-C out the door, Enrico said, "You have to strike when the iron is hot!"

"What iron?" Adam asked. He got the idea Enrico was making yet another meddlesome comment about women, as he had done on many occasions in the previous year. Adam told him he was being offensive and not to insult M-C. Enrico ventured no further comment.

One Sunday in May, Adam went to a meeting of the Movement called "Encounter Number Two," given by Mina (Colleen's Support) at her home in Verdun, a working-class neighbourhood in Montreal's southwest corner which Raymond referred to as "the heart of darkness." Adam scarcely knew Verdun, but the community preserved the story of the Irish passage to Canada and the suffering the Irish had endured with a large boulder that marked the spot where many had perished from typhus. Since their arrival 150 years earlier, the Irish Catholics in Quebec had the role of emissaries between English and French, since they mixed with the French at church and the English at school. It was through this utterly Canadian process that hockey had gone from being a sport for Anglo and Scots aristocratic gentlemen in the nineteenth century to a working-class sport for twentieth-century French Canadians.

When Adam got home, Enrico told him that M-C had called for him and wanted Adam to call her back. Since M-C was the Central Admi, she co-ordinated the membership lists and had Adam's private phone number on hand. Instead, she chose to call Enrico's number to speak with him. Adam assumed it was Movement business, since Adam worked for her as an Admi. "Yeah, she wants you to call her; I don't know what she wants," Enrico claimed.

Adam was not home at the time Enrico claimed M-C called for him, so he never heard the phone ring with his own ears. It was likely that M-C called Enrico directly to ask about Adam. Assuming it was about something structural, in the Movement, Adam returned her call.

« C'est drôle, on se connait depuis des années, et on dirait qu'on ne se connâit même pas » [It's funny, we have known each other for years and it's like we hardly know each other] M-C said.

Her comments reminded him of Renato's comment on his birthday card and appeared to be consistent with the spirit of the times and new camaraderie. Adam answered, « C'est vrai » [It's true.]

M-C continued, « Comme ça, je voulais connaître d'autres gens dans mon entourage immédiat, mais ce sont toujours les mêmes que je vois, soit Colleen, ou Fan. Donc, je me suis demandé : 'Qui donc que je connais, qui est une belle personne, qui donc pourrais-je connaître encore mieux', puis j'ai pensé à toi ».

[The thing is, I wanted to know other people in my immediate environment, but they are always the same people. I see either Colleen or Fan. So I asked myself, 'Who do I know who is a beautiful person whom I'd like to know better,' then I thought of you.]

Adam was surprised by this sudden outburst of emotion, but pleased. It was the first time in over four years that she had made an ostensibly personal overture. At no time did she visit him in the hospital, for example, nor did he expect anything from her, for they were not friends. Adam gave a general sentiment of agreement. She continued, « Ouais, donc j'ai pensé que peut-être on pourrait faire des choses ensemble, à part du Mouvement, comme aller au cinéma, écouter des disques, faire des choses ensemble, essayer de mieux se connaitre... » [Yeah, so I thought maybe we could do things together, aside from the Movement, like going out to the movies, listening to records, doing things together, try to get to know each other more...]

In effect, she was proposing a personal friendship, outside of the Movement. Adam was looking for new friends and had no reason to disagree, so he said « Oui » [Yes.] They agreed to go to a movie soon after. Their talk on the phone lasted about 30 to 40 minutes. Adam was very pleased to hear from her and he agreed to her ideas because he thought they were great, and above all, he thought she really meant them. After having tricked Adam into saying "I love you" just one month earlier and tricked him into hugging her the previous day, M-C had tricked him into agreeing to be her friend. For Adam, who suspected nothing, it was an honour to receive such an offer from an accomplished Admi like M-C — an absolute honour.

On Monday, M-C called him twice in the evening on the pretext of structural matters. The next day was the day they had agreed to have supper and a movie. M-C picked him up in her car before the café. It felt unusual to be in the car with her, given her status as the Central Administrator. From Frère-André, they drove south down Côte-des-Neiges past verdant cemeteries and turned onto Remembrance Road, embracing the north side of Mount Royal. "What kind of name is [-----]?" asked M-C, referring to his German-Jewish family surname.

"It's a German name," Adam said, wanting to avoid her anti-Semitic streak.

"But are you Jewish or German?" asked M-C, who already knew he was Jewish.

"Jewish," Adam said.

"Yeah, I can see that. You have a big, big Jewish nose with a big bump in it. Do all Jews have big noses like that with big bumps in them?" M-C countered.

Adam crumpled in his seat. Turning to the passenger door, he wondered how he could endure the evening with her if she continued with these anti-Semitic questions. "I really wouldn't know," he said.

"Do you think that maybe Petruchia is a Jew? Petruchia has a big nose," she said, referring to her General Delegate supervisor Petruchia, in Rome, Italy. "I really wouldn't know," Adam said again, getting irritated.

They had been together for less than five minutes. Adam asked himself if their new friendship could ever stand a chance if she was unable to overcome the enormous cultural, social and religious differences that separated them. M-C was Catholic, Adam was Jewish. M-C was French Canadian and French-speaking; Adam was English Canadian and English-speaking. M-C was born in Duplessis' Quebec and was nearly a decade older; Adam grew up in Trudeau's Canada. M-C was a single mom with a small child; Adam was a young guy with few responsibilities and no children. He wondered if she had thought about any of that constructively, and why she was trying to sabotage their new friendship.

The café she selected was on St. Lawrence Boulevard at Duluth, a short walk from the candy store his maternal grandfather had owned in the 1920s. At the café, Adam viewed them as starting over with a new personal friendship and tried to make a human connection with

M-C, despite her offensive comments. He made eye contact with her and told her she was his model as an administrator and that he looked up to her in the Movement. She abruptly broke off the eye contact and looked away, down to the floor, while breathing a huff. She looked very uncomfortable and even angry. The entire evening was tense: whenever Adam felt comfortable with her, he tried to tell her how happy he was to be with her and how he thought she was a good person, it made her uncomfortable. Adam felt that all her topics of conversation were contrived, including her choice of words. M-C conducted the supper like a job interview, asking Adam a series of questions. "Do you have any nieces or nephews? Did you have a lot of experience babysitting cousins? Do you have any experience with children?"

After the café, walking on St. Lawrence to her car, M-C said: « Ce n'est pas souvent que je sors avec les delégués de groupes ... Josh nous a dit 'mange pas, dors pas, mets toutes tes énergies dans le Mouvement...' »

[It's not often that I go out with group delegates ... Josh told us 'don't eat, don't sleep, put all your energy on the Movement].

Clearly, M-C still saw him as a group delegate, inferior to her status in the Movement. She still had not made the transition to "friend," as she had proposed on Sunday. They went to a cinema in downtown Montreal, 2001 University, in a neighbourhood where his maternal great-grandfather had once laboured in construction crews. While walking on University Street, Adam tried using the word [humorous] in French. M-C corrected him abruptly by yelling « humoristique! » in his face. After the film, Adam suggested they go up on Mount Royal to look out on the city. Once there, she parked her car at the Belvedere, where they pondered the skyscrapers of downtown, the St. Lawrence River and the South Shore hills of St. Bruno and St. Hilary.

Five centuries earlier, the Kingdom of France first felt the urge to branch out after the fall of Constantinople in the year 1453, which blocked its usual trade routes to the Orient. The navigator Jacques Cartier set forth from the port of St. Malo, France, in 1534 in search of a western passage to Asia. Instead, he discovered what became Canada and lost most of his men to scurvy and exposure to the elements the first winter. Cartier returned to France, but no Frenchman returned to

Prelude to the Abyss

Canada until Samuel de Champlain some seventy years later, in 1604. Champlain was better prepared than Cartier, having learned from the Natives how to camp in winter. He founded Quebec City and explored deep inland. French explorers like LaSalle ventured all the way South to the Mississippi, while de La Vérendrye went west and his sons were the first Europeans to see the Rocky Mountains. The rival British were also exploring North America and, following many skirmishes, British General Wolfe defeated French General Montcalm at a decisive battle on Quebec City's Plains of Abraham, in 1759. In treaty talks, France was given a choice to keep its possessions in the Caribbean or in Canada. The French chose to surrender Canada, and the French Canadians — at the time some 60,000 people, including M-C's ancestors — were left completely alone in North America, abandoned by their colonial masters and by most of the clergy. Huddled together, French Canadians clung to Catholicism and the French language.

Until the mid-twentieth century, French Canada had been a laboratory specimen of an arrested culture. This was mostly the fault of France, which had restricted variety by forbidding emigration to New France by Jews or French Protestants, known as Huguenots, who instead favoured the Protestant lands of Northern Europe and the American colonies and South Africa, thereby enriching those lands at the expense of Quebec.

Wolfe's liberating triumph over Montcalm opened New France to greater individual liberties, free printing presses and wider immigration policies, at last. Many of the British forces decided to remain and build families and were followed by merchants and their families from Great Britain. English, Scottish and later Irish names became common alongside those of the French. Aaron Hart became the first Jewish emigrant to Canada in 1759, and in time the Jewish community became a thriving success, reaching its zenith during the latter half of the twentieth century at one hundred and ten thousand people in the Province of Quebec, mostly in Montreal. While French Canadians tended to limit themselves to prayer and Church activities and a narrow range of male professions such as notary, lawyer, priest or farmer, successive waves of Italian, Greek, Slavic, Germanic and other immigrants became English Canadians and dynamos of burgeoning commerce alongside the Anglos and Jews. Like an urban metaphor of the double helix, whose two dominant cultures alternately blended and came together or else clashed and grew apart, by the 1960s Montreal was well established as the most fascinating metropolis in Canada. Since that decade, Quebec had been in a period of rapid social change and reflection. Relations between French Canadians and Jews had long been ambivalent and distrustful and remained so.

Adam and M-C sat in the car next to each other and later exited to get some fresh air. Although M-C had opportunity both in the cinema and on Mount Royal, at no time did she show any interest in him romantically or sexually, nor did she try to kiss him, put her hand on his body, or even hold his hand. Adam did not show any interest in her either; he was a perfect gentleman. Returning to the car, M-C asked, "Where will we be in ten years?" She told him her age; he thought she was a lot older than he was.

By the time she drove him home, he had felt uncomfortable with her most of the evening. He wanted to cover this discomfort so, like a gentleman, he said, « J'ai senti très à l'aise avec toi ce soir » [I felt very comfortable with you tonight.] M-C ignored this statement and seemed very uncomfortable that he had said it. He asked if she wanted to come up to his apartment for coffee or something. She seemed offended that he should say that and went home. Adam was afraid that perhaps his comment about being comfortable with her had gone in the wrong direction for their friendship and that the coffee invitation had compounded the matter. Nonetheless, he thought it unusual that she should act that way given that she had been in his apartment many times before, with him in it, most recently just three days earlier, when she hugged him the previous Saturday. The evening was a weak step towards friendship, more in line with a maritime disaster. Adam had a bad feeling in the pit of his stomach, as if he had just attended a reunion of the Donner Party survivors.

On Thursday, he got another message from M-C and called her back. "I want to see you tomorrow night after the Friday night gathering," she said. "I want to talk to you about something." He told her that indeed, he would be present at the gathering, and she could speak to him there. M-C replied that she wanted to see him *after* the gathering, at her house, to discuss something important. He asked her if she could tell him what the subject of the meeting would be. M-C refused to be specific, but used an ominous tone. Thinking it could be about something structural, that is, relating to the Movement, he had no choice but to agree. He let her know he would be available after the Friday night gathering. This created a mental void in his mind, since he had never been summoned to this kind of meeting before by M-C or indeed, by few people in his life.

He took a bath and wondered why she would want to talk to him. He thought it must be something structural, relating to the Admi sector. Perhaps M-C wanted to conduct an evaluation and synthesis of his work in the Admi sector? Given that he might be leaving the sector in the afternoon, the evaluation would be held the same evening, but in her house. He did not fear a bad evaluation from M-C, but he had never heard of any evaluation procedure being done. But still, if it were a structural meeting, he could not refuse. Or maybe it was structural, but quite different from an evaluation. Maybe M-C was angry with Adam for leaving the Admi sector; he was such a good Admi, she was going to plead with him not to leave. The purpose of the meeting must be to ask him to stay in the Admi sector and offer him an Admi position in another team. That would be perfectly timed with his leaving Raymond's team. But M-C could not offer him an Admi position. It was up to the Orientor of a team to approach him, and they should probably approach Enrico first. So then what?

Adam wondered if it could be something relating to their brand new friendship. Had he done something to displease her? Was she angry with him? Or maybe it was something in between the two? Maybe she had a terrible personal problem she wished to confide in him for the purpose of seeking his advice. If so, he would have accepted this as a great honour for himself to earn the confidence of such an accomplished administrator. He thought it unlikely that M-C would confide any such problem to him first, ahead of Colleen or Fan. He dismissed the idea of a personal confidence, thinking it just a fantasy.

Then he thought it was a combination of all these ideas: structural, personal and emotional. Perhaps M-C had a growing resentment to the personal attention he gave her. She felt that his enthusiastic behaviour over the previous months was inappropriate for the development of both their structural and personal friendship. His behaviour had been too friendly with her on Tuesday; his comment about "comfort" and his offer of "coffee" were too fast for M-C, and she was afraid it would mar their friendship. M-C was taking the occasion of his plausible departure from the Admi sector to tell him that she did appreciate his Admi work, but that, in the future, he should cool it and not hug her so much. If Adam did not follow her directive, she could use the meeting as a pretext to sexual harassment charges against him, just as Raymond had been victimized the previous autumn. But that didn't make sense either, because she had hugged him so vigorously just five days earlier. In the end, Adam dismissed all his ideas because none of them seemed to fit. Although he was very curious about what she wanted to discuss in this unprecedented late-Friday-night discussion, he had absolutely no reasonable idea about what it was; none of his ideas would stick. He drew a blank and tried to forget about it, without success. He did feel a lingering regret that M-C should get the wrong idea about him, and he hoped for a chance to explain himself, whatever the matter should be. Without any indication to the contrary, he would have to assume that it was a structural meeting and that refusal to attend the meeting would earn him discipline from Enrico.

Over the preceding year, Adam had undergone a radical personality change because of Enrico's accumulated psychological coercion techniques against him. Since the previous summer, Adam had had a part-time job in his field. Enrico laughed at his job and studies consistently for months, until his self-respect began to deteriorate. Adam no longer saw the value of his career and education in relation to the Movement and withdrew from the university. The same week, he made an application to the welfare office. His career was at a dead end; without a job, his money was running out quickly. His headaches, dizziness and disorientation were still persistent. Over the next twenty-four hours, the tension in his mind increased as the hour of M-C's special meeting drew near.

V — A FRIDAY IN MAY

[The "double bind" is a paradoxical communication where two opposing messages are conveyed in such a manner that if you obey one, you breach the other.]
—Isabelle Nazare-Aga

A FRIDAY IN MAY began much like any other day in the previous two years. Adam had dizziness and disorientation in the morning and had to take some time to get his bearings. His main personal challenge was to get through the day without headaches and to avoid new head injuries at all costs. In the afternoon, he attended a rescheduled meeting with Enrico and Raymond. Enrico was to address Raymond's upcoming departure for Japan and the reorganization of Raymond's team. Originally, Enrico had scheduled the meeting for July on a date just a few days before Raymond's actual departure. For Enrico's own reasons, which he did not explain to Raymond and Adam, he rescheduled the meeting and pushed it up to a Friday in May, in the afternoon before M-C's mysterious meeting with Adam. Enrico's meeting was held at four in the afternoon, in a café on Beaubien Street that was often frequented by the Great Antonio, a local eccentric folk hero and strongman who was known to pull city buses by a rope held between his teeth.

Raymond and Adam had become best friends; everyone in the council knew it. As such, Adam had wanted to avoid facing Raymond's departure. Different possibilities were discussed at the meeting: that Raymond could start a mission to Japan, that he could take a leave of absence, that Adam could become the temporary Orientor of his team.

By seven in the evening, Enrico decided that Raymond's team would be dissolved, even though it was his regular activity in the Movement. Raymond was refused a mission to Japan, since missions were granted only to General Delegates like Josh. Raymond would take a leave of absence for one year and would still pay the financial campaign if he wished to remain part of the Movement. He would re-contact Enrico after Japan, if he wished to fully reintegrate into the Movement. Group delegates still in Raymond's team could pass into Enrico's direct line of orientation. Adam would lose his status in the administrative sector and pass into Enrico's first instance and take orientation directly from Enrico. Adam would also start to become a regenerator, with a view to becoming a Team Delegate like Enrico. Enrico and Adam would meet in the coming days to discuss his project. Enrico would tell Adam what was expected of him as a regenerator and how to build a team in the Movement. There would be a meeting for regenerators in the coming weeks, and only people who had succeeded in bringing "new people" as nutrition to the weekly meetings would be allowed in.

These changes, on the day they came, caused massive uncertainty in Adam and instilled a sense of foreboding. Suddenly, the job he had loved as an Admi was gone, his identity within the Movement was morphing, and the reality of his best friend leaving was looming heavier and more ominously than before. Soon, he would have to take orientation directly from Enrico, whom he disliked and whose endless talks he feared. Soon, Raymond would not be around anymore to help him, to be his friend. His future had become uncertain.

Enrico's meeting had kept them until seven o'clock, at which time he drove Raymond and Adam to attend the Friday night social gathering at The Unicorn, a two-storey building on Papineau Street with a playhouse, bar and box office downstairs and a large meeting hall upstairs rented to the Movement. Adam's mind was occupied with thoughts of the future, what things would be like, how his life would be different. Enrico watched him closely in the rear view mirror, reminding him "…soon you will have to attend my meetings…" Adam felt his stomach sink and his adherence to the Movement waver for the first time since Chile. If Adam wanted to leave the Movement, *now* was

A Friday in May

the time, for later would be too late. There was much work to be done in his new important role as regenerator. Also, news of his departure right after Raymond's would make him look foolish and selfish, as if he had only been in the Movement to benefit from Raymond's friendship.

During the previous Sunday evening's weekly meeting, Enrico announced that their team was responsible for organizing the coffee counter at the social gathering on a Friday in May and that he expected everybody to volunteer and show up to work. Enrico's announcement reduced the likeliness that Adam would not attend the gathering on a Friday in May. Arriving at The Unicorn, Adam was apprehensive about M-C's special meeting with him. As a member of Enrico's team, he busied himself with their shared responsibilities for hosting the café, as Enrico had planned. M-C arrived soon after, and during the evening Adam saw her and Enrico talking to each other for several minutes. Enrico was with Adam every moment from four o'clock, kept him occupied and delivered him to The Unicorn until the arrival of M-C, who occupied him the rest of the evening. Enrico was talking to M-C while gesturing at Adam. Then both Enrico and M-C turned to look directly at Adam, while still talking to each other. Their conversation broke when M-C emerged from their tandem and walked directly up to Adam.

She said hello to Adam for the first time that evening. She asked if he was ready to go to her place that night and gave him a look that seemed to laugh in his face. Adam told her that he had arranged bus fare for his trip to her house and asked her to confirm her exact address so he could find it after walking there from the bus. He reminded her of how difficult it was for him to navigate her street, given his unfamiliarity with the neighbourhood. He asked her which bus routes went near her house so he could plan his trip there by public transit. He said he would probably take the 97 bus to Mount-Royal Metro, then the orange line of the Metro up to Jarry. He then asked how he could get to Waverly from there. He had started to ask about the extent of the 45 bus north on Papineau when she cut him off and said that they would go together in her car.

Adam was doubly surprised, because given that it was a structural meeting, he thought he was on his own for transportation.

Besides, she was uncomfortable with him around her daughter. Adam did not know M-C very well personally, so it never occurred to him to ask her for a lift. Suddenly, he was troubled and asked if they could go to a café in a public place, as they had on Tuesday, just three nights earlier. M-C said that she couldn't go out after hours with him because she had Rania, who had to sleep early. Adam understood that Rania was a child and felt that M-C was appealing to him to be considerate of her situation as a single mother. If he acted in an uncaring manner, it would be seen as insensitivity on his part during their first week of friendship. M-C used her own motherhood as a pretext to maneuver him into her apartment. He suggested they could have their talk another night, when Rania would be with her father, Vittorio. The details about Vittorio were sketchy and supplied by Raymond, who told Adam that Vittorio was from Chile and had fought with the Sandinistas in Nicaragua, where he had military training and had been tortured extensively prior to his sexual liaison with M-C.

M-C said that the "talk" had to be that night. Adam recoiled but did not refuse to go outright. M-C asked him the specific time he would go with her. Adam said he liked to stay at the gathering for a good two hours. M-C asked him to go downstairs with her. They entered a little bar on the first floor of The Unicorn; M-C asked for a glass of milk for Rania, who was suddenly with her but whom Adam had never seen before at the Friday night gatherings. They stayed at the bar while M-C smoked nervously, chatted with Adam nervously and looked at him nervously. They returned upstairs. At about 9:30, M-C asked Adam if he was ready to go with her. He was not willing but had already asked her to have the meeting rescheduled to another night or to hold it in public; she had refused both requests, and he did not have a structural option to refuse the Central Admi. With his wishes thwarted and his protestations exhausted, Adam agreed to go with M-C to Waverly, for the express purpose of *talking* about the undisclosed subject she said she wanted to discuss just one night earlier. After having tricked him into saying "I love you" the first Saturday in April, tricked him into hugging her in front of their team on a Saturday in May, and tricked him into her friendship the next

A Friday in May

day, M-C tricked Adam into going to Waverly this Friday in May. As they were leaving, Bliss saw them together and made a sexual innuendo about Adam and M-C, which made Adam very uncomfortable. He rebuked him quickly. Walking down the stairs, Adam paused and thought *What if Bliss is right?* Bliss, a group delegate in Colleen's team, was not a reliable person, so Adam dismissed his comments as disrespectful.

Adam left The Unicorn because he trusted M-C in her position as Central Admi. She showed him to her car, put her child in the front seat and told him to get in back. She drove the route from Papineau to Waverly Street. In the car, she looked at him pensively in the rear view mirror. Then she asked him about Raymond and how it felt to leave the Admi sector. Adam noticed M-C possessed the freshest news of the day about Enrico's team, even though she was not present at his meeting mere hours earlier.

They talked about Raymond's situation a bit. Adam told her that he was sad to leave the Admi sector and stated she was the highlight of his Admi experience, that he had learned so much from her. He told her he would be very sad if it meant that he couldn't see her anymore and added it was a good thing they had this brand new personal friendship. "We won't let you into the regenerators meeting next week unless you integrate at least one person into your team," M-C said, still regarding him as a group delegate. She seemed to know exactly what was discussed in the meeting with Enrico, as if she had read the transcript. Adam had the image of M-C and Enrico looking directly at him but talking directly to each other, just minutes earlier. He looked out the car window at the city lights and asked himself Josh's question: "Where are you going?"

He felt a twinge and realized he didn't know what he was getting into. Feeling that he was being squeezed out of the Movement, he became nervous and tried to change the topic of conversation, while drifting off into daydreams about the past and how they first met.

They had met five autumns earlier on the McGill campus when Adam was a teenager and quite liberal in the use of his time. A billboard poster from the unknown McGill Humanists caught his eye and invited discussion that same evening on "The State Of Democracy in North America." Adam looked in on the meeting hall but had no intention of staying. At the door, a man named Raymond greeted him and invited him inside for a meeting. Although Adam had no interest in attending, Raymond convinced him to stay. Adam sat in the audience with two reporters from the campus newspaper and two or three members of the public. Present from the Movement at the start of the meeting were Raymond, Gus, a woman named Trudy, and M-C, the principal speaker. In total, ten people in a room designed to hold over 300, an empty shell.

The meeting was extremely slow and confusing as M-C said hardly anything about the McGill Humanists, but she did point out they had a political party called the Humanist Party (HP). According to M-C, only candidates and political parties with the backing of large corporations could successfully run for elected office. Thus, all political choices were corporate-supported choices; all were ostensibly commercial in essence, dedicated to preserving the status quo in society. That was why all parties were superfluous, the political process was a joke, and that was why she was running for elected office. A mental haze Adam could not understand gripped him as she uttered her message of perfidious nihilism. The contradiction was massive, since she participated in the same activity she said was a fraud.

About halfway through the meeting, a pipe-smoking man entered the room. Adam got the idea he had arrived straight from work. The man had a special air about him; the whole atmosphere changed when he entered the room. He had a broad clownish smile on his face and looked around with a glazed pervert's expression. He exchanged some inaudible words with M-C, Raymond and Trudy. After a while, he took over the meeting from M-C and began to talk. He had an exotic accent; Adam learned that he was from Chile and his name was Enrico. Adam was struck by the profound ugliness of this man. His camel face looked like something you would see in a specimen jar, floating in formaldehyde on a shelf next to the pickled piglet embryo. His reddish-brown skin was taut and dry and full of pock marks, streaks, holes, scars and was dotted by the stain of long-broken blood vessels. His nose was remarkable: apart from being extremely large, the nostrils were turned up, revealing blood-red marks underneath. His eyes were large and black, with yellow eyeballs. His tobacco-stained teeth were crooked and broken in parts, brown, black and yellow in colour.

Enrico spoke in soaring, inspirational terms at length about "Humanism." He had a very special way of talking. Adam had learned about Humanism in college courses but was not aware that it had survived to the twentieth century in the New World. "Is there a link between the humanism of the McGill Humanists … or Humanist Party and the humanism of the Renaissance and the Enlightenment?" Adam asked Enrico, who flashed a broad smile, exuding a warm glow. His eyes made deep contact with Adam's own eyes, which remained transfixed. Adam felt Enrico glare right through him.

"What do you think?" Enrico asked while he gave Adam a look that said *Why do you ask such questions when you already know the answer?* Adam started to feel foolish for having asked the question; Enrico's eyes sparkled at that very moment of understanding. Adam seemed to understand exactly what Enrico meant to tell him as Enrico watched and followed his eyes attentively for several moments. Adam felt like Enrico was reading his mind and broke off the contact without noticing that Enrico had not answered his question.

When the meeting ended, Enrico asked Adam, Raymond and Gus to go with him in his Rocinante, so Adam could meet the rest of the people in the HP. Since Enrico represented the Humanist Party/McGill Humanists as a legitimate McGill student club, Adam accepted. He was told that both the McGill Humanists and the HP belonged to an international movement in forty-two countries headed by a man in Mendoza, Argentina, named Mario Luis Rodriguez Cobos, who was better known by his pen name, Silo. Enrico drove past the Movement's locale at the corner of Saint-Dominique and Duluth and then to his apartment on Alma Street and spoke further about the project of the Movement. In Enrico's kitchen, Adam asked, "What do you in the HP think about this?" or "What is your opinion of that?" Enrico said, "Don't say 'you,' say 'we.'" He pressured Adam to join the HP. Adam said that he did not want to join anything political at that time. M-C, who had arrived in a separate car at Enrico's apartment, was standing nearby and laughed in Adam's face. Enrico looked at her and said to Adam, "You're already in." From the first day they met, M-C saw how Enrico controlled Adam's will.

M-C had also been a candidate for the Humanist Party in the Quebec elections, and she served two terms as the official party representative while Enrico served one term. M-C was trusted with defending Colleen's leadership of the HP while her own leadership was being groomed, and she was endorsed as an Independent Humanist candidate for Mayor of Montreal by all her peers. Adam had a chance to speak further that same evening with M-C. Impressed by her bid to replace the inestimable Jean Drapeau, he asked her why she was in the election. While explaining her political platform, she attacked the other candidates, stopping long enough to criticize a Chinese-born Canadian man who she said should not be elected mayor because "… he's not speaking French." Adam found her attitude deplorably racist. She was definitely not Adam's type of person. Over the ensuing years, they could not and did not establish any mutual understanding or complicity until he began working for her in the Admi sector.

* * *

When they arrived at Waverly at about 9:50 in the evening of a Friday in May, it was Adam's first time there as her "new friend," and he was apprehensive. Adam went with M-C to help her put Rania to bed. M-C turned to him, still in the hallway and noticeably irritated. She said, « Peux-tu m'attendre dans la cuisine? » [Can you wait for me in the kitchen?] Obviously he could not participate in putting Rania to bed because he was not part of M-C's family life. He expected that once M-C was ready, they would go to the living room together and have their talk.

Once Rania was in bed, M-C marched briskly into the kitchen and offered him coffee, in the manner of an executioner who offers a last cigarette to the victim before he is shot. He declined, saying that it was too late in the evening for coffee and he didn't want to stay awake all night. He asked if she had tea instead, with honey and lemon. He told her he had a perpetual dry throat, which could be soothed by tea. He added that tea relaxed him late at night and helped him sleep. M-C made the tea for him, but coffee for herself. She deposited the tea on the table while she remained standing. She glared at him with the angriest eyes and tensest expression he had ever seen from her. Her eyes were coal-black and intense, like those of Maurice Richard, the Montreal hockey legend and hero to French Canadians who as a power forward had a reputation for skating hard and directly to the goal. She lit a Benson & Hedges 100 cigarette, blew the smoke out and asked him in English, "I suppose you're wondering why I called you here tonight?"

He wondered why she was speaking English to him. M-C had always spoken French since the day they met. It seemed like she did not know him or had confused him with somebody else. She had just said to him in the car, minutes before, that she did not understand his spoken French but, after five years of exchanges with her, this was a sudden revelation! It made him wonder if she had understood anything at all he had said in the previous five years! Also, if she persisted with this ominous tone, it would be difficult for him to communicate coherently, because the quality of his French was variable. If his confidence faltered at any point, his French would suffer and he would revert to an anxious teenager, searching for his words, self-conscious of verbs and with a suddenly thick English-Canadian accent. Despite the honey tea, M-C would have an advantage over him if his throat tensed up.

"Uh ... y-y-y-yes," Adam answered, very nervously.

M-C turned around and walked to her kitchen doors, which were French doors. In a swift gesture, she closed both doors and secured them. She turned around to face him with the same mean and nasty look on her face. Adam was extremely alarmed by her decision to close the double doors. He felt trapped without an exit, like he was about to be killed. His back was against her kitchen wall. There was no room for him to run out and escape. He was terrified; even if he had tried to escape, he would have had to pass her and risk being stopped, tackled or dragged to the floor.

M-C returned to the table and took a seat between Adam and the kitchen doors, blocking his exit. While she glared at him in silence, something terrible emanated from her body above her solar plexus. He felt its presence; it was cold, like a stinking draft out of a slaughterhouse. She breathed heavily as her body exuded fear, anger and hatred. Her anger nourished her hate. The room was filled with M-C's monstrous, terrible evilness, her consuming hunger, her hatred of happiness, her resolute hatred of men, her infinite hunger for evil and the abyss. M-C's force was stronger than any personal force Adam had encountered; it overpowered him and threatened to devour his life force and all light in the room. He was terrified.

Holding a burning cigarette in her hand, M-C continued to glare at him furiously. The terrible emanations from her chest grew stronger. As she was finally going to tell him the subject of the discussion, images flashed through his mind of what it could be. Adam knew she was very angry with him and asked himself what he had done.

Then she spoke angrily. "I noticed you're attracted to me. Every time you see me you're always nice to me, you hug me and kiss me on both cheeks…"

Oh my God! Adam thought. *Attracted? She's going to complain about sexual harassment. She objects to my admiration for her, and this is her way of telling me. I shouldn't have hugged her! I shouldn't have kissed her on the cheek!* Adam felt he had gone too far in letting her know how much he liked her. His attention was unwelcome and she was going to give him hell, as his superior. He was wishing ardently to explain himself, to tell her he had no sexual designs on her, when she said "…and so I thought we could … make love … here … tonight…" still in anger.

The instant these words escaped her mouth, his brain went into shock. His mind reeled and was overwhelmed by a series of bizarre and exotic images bursting on his consciousness: odourless colours, unseen shapes, engineering equations and mathematical formulae, all fused and blurred. Adam was flabbergasted, gobsmacked and dumbfounded; his mind was seized by a mental haze and paralysis. It was the most shockingly bad surprise of his life. M-C had said the words "make love" to him *in anger*! All the fragments of thought that had been gathering fluidly in his mind for the previous twenty-four hours immediately coalesced into a single ball of dark energy at the centre of his brain. This ball of energy absorbed his fears plus most of his memories, his self-confidence, his self-respect and most of the information he needed to extricate himself from the situation.

The ball of energy was extremely dense and could not be accessed by his conscious mind. The rest of his brain expanded to the size of the universe. Each neuron scattered to a different corner, completely devoid of all light. At the centre of this universe, his remaining mind tried desperately to access the ball of energy. Waves of energy and coloured light swirled on the surface, mingled with images from his life and the faces of people he knew. On its glimmering edge, he perceived refractive images of himself being abused as a child, and in the same glint of an instant knew he had not made any progress in the intervening years that could have helped prepare him for this. But deeper access was extremely painful, and he could not think straight when he tried.

M-C made no sense at all. Adam knew even though she demanded sex, she was *not* attracted to him. She could not have thought of this on her own, but must have been pushed or urged to assault him in this way by somebody else. Images of his domestic life and of the scene in Chile with Pigpen raced through his head. From experience, Adam knew it was the same kind of set-up. He knew there was more to this kitchen scene than just him and M-C; there had to be a third person who could manipulate other people to control Adam's own sexuality. He asked himself who the third person was. The ball of energy returned only one name. Stunned, Adam stared at her, seemingly asking if someone else was somehow involved in this. When she saw what Adam was thinking, she changed her glare to a smirk of amusement and confidence. She knew what Adam feared, and her tacit threat was understood.

Admi evaluation indeed! Adam thought. She followed with a sequence of subtle moves. She raised her eyebrows, tilted her head sideways at him, took a long, indulgent drag from her cigarette and waited for him to make a mistake. She blew the smoke out luxuriously, self-assured and in full control of the situation.

"I know it's not very romantic," she began in English and added in French « J'ai rien préparer pour ce soir... » [I have nothing prepared for this evening]. It was a weak excuse for bypassing the steps of courtship that should usually have preceded any sexual interest; her statement concealed something. She did not want any romance with Adam, but he had never asked her for any. So what were they doing? She hadn't prepared anything—like what? Why could she not wait until she felt romantic and had something prepared? What was the big rush to have sex without preparation or romance? There was a sense of urgency to M-C's demands, as if it *had* to be done, but her actions did not match the situation. « ...j'avais peur de me faire refuser ... je me suis déjà fait refuser dans le passé ». [I was afraid of being turned down. I have already been turned down in the past.] She made it sound like a *fait accompli* that justified cancelling any hope of romance or friendship. She had been refused in the past, but on this occasion, she had taken steps to ensure Adam could not refuse her. Included in these premeditated steps was her refusal of his reasonable request to have the talk another night and in a public place. Now it seemed clearer why she had said, "It has to be tonight! She was just thinking about her own sexual plans and not about his own best interests. Her statement did not allow Adam to refuse her advances, and her attending offer of a five-day friendship seemed inauthentic.

He rationalized her demands in an attempt to understand what she was talking about. The way she said it, it sounded like a cathartic exercise. First, she'd said that he was attracted to her; then she'd said they should have sex, as though one followed the other logically. It seemed like she was saying the alleged sexual attraction was distracting to their work in the Movement and that by having sex there that night, they could purge the sexual energy in one massive catharsis, then continue on with their Movement work, undistracted by this sexual problem. It made sense that the catharsis would be tied to his leaving the Admi sector the same night; this way, the alleged sexual attraction would be filed away in his memory of his previous position in the council, but his new position would be free of sexual tensions with

A Friday in May

M-C. It was as if she pretended to do him a favour he did not want, and this favour had to be done with utmost dispatch, the same night, without romance, and for his benefit!

But there were several problems with M-C's presentation of things. First, Adam was not sexually attracted to her; he merely liked her very much as his supervisor. They had achieved a good working relationship because he respected her, admired her and looked up to her. Second, the world does not work the way she suggested. Usually, a person will say, "I'm attracted to you," not the other way around. If every time a woman felt compelled to offer sex to a man who was attracted to her, it would be a very interesting world indeed! Third, her anger, rage and hatred did not match the sexual demands she made on Adam. Thus, her statement made no sense. That's why he said to her, in French and with a giggle, « Attends, Marie-Claude, avant que l'on fasse l'amour, peux-tu me dire d'ou ça vient, tout ça? » [Hold on Marie-Claude, before we make love, can you tell me where all this is coming from?]

She refused to answer; instead, she told him angrily that she had been preoccupied with sex for several months, that it was contaminating her thoughts. She said that her conversations, even at work, always came back to sex, that she was obsessed with sex, and she did not want the situation to continue. She said that she had suffered a severe depression the previous year, after she broke up with Vittorio. She said that she no longer knew what to do in life, that she no longer identified with the Movement or her own project; she added that she had no intention of going back to that state of depression. She said she had a need for affection, tenderness and sex and that she had a threshold of two or three months for going without sex before she started to become unbalanced. Now, she said she had gone without sex for so long, she was "going crazy." At the same time, she noticed Adam was attracted to her. She looked at him covetously; he flinched. Then she went on to say that she had made a decision, which she called « …un act unitif de laisser tomber mes désirs, et d'y aller avec mes besoins… » […a unifying act to let go of my desires and, to go with my needs…]

Adam recognized this vocabulary as Movement-inspired and felt the violence of her decision as a Team Delegate to isolate him in her kitchen on false pretences, after having maneuvred him there with delusive tactics so she could force sex out of him. He couldn't believe that she thought he was attracted to her. She must have confused his admiration for her as an administrator and a decent person with a sexual attraction. Since she had refused to answer his previous question in French, Adam switched to English and asked, "Attracted to you? In what way did you think I was attracted to you?"

She refused to answer that question also. She reiterated her need for affection, tenderness and sex, and added that she wanted someone nice to do it with. All of her comments about her own powerful sexual urges contradicted her initial statement that Adam was attracted to *her* and that she was merely "offering" him sex as some kind of public service. Adam felt there were other motivations at work.

While M-C again fumed in anger, Adam wanted to cancel everything and leave at once. Deep under his fear, he knew that he was being blackmailed sexually but could not in his conscious mind understand how. Adam felt that if he refused M-C outright and just left, she would report him to Enrico, who could, in turn, expose him to endless punishments and especially more intense ones, since he was now Adam's direct Orientor. The new decisions at Enrico's meeting were obviously made just to coincide with M-C's aggression against him, but he couldn't articulate how.

Without any preparation or warning, M-C was raping him, and Adam did not know how to defend himself. He asked himself what he would risk by leaving her without providing the sex she demanded from him. If Adam did leave the Movement on his own or was expelled by Enrico, how could they live in the same apartment? It would be very difficult to continue as Enrico's roommate if Adam was outside of the Movement. Enrico might even ask him to leave on his own initiative, within 72 hours, by Monday morning. If Adam had to give up his room in the apartment, where would he go? It would be difficult to start looking for an apartment without a job, without a degree or prospects for employment. Adam had just received his first welfare cheque eight days earlier and had withdrawn from school a few short weeks before that. He was still devoted to the Movement and did not want to leave. His options were extremely limited.

His mind oscillated between the two extremes for what seemed like a long time. He wanted foremost to leave Waverly without sex and still keep his place in the Movement without reprisals against him. But she did not offer that. She did not tell Adam how he could decline her demands and still leave her house in safety, while conserving his place in the Movement. If he risked it, what would people in the Movement think of him after he was expelled? What if Adam lost all his friends in the Movement? Would he become lumpen like all the other people who were denigrated for leaving the Movement? Most likely, yes.

Adam looked to the windowless wall on the south side of the kitchen. She turned to look with him. Turning the other way, he noticed there was a hand-made sign on her refrigerator. It said:

REFUSE LA SOUFFRANCE [REFUSE SUFFERING]

He recognized this message as being central to the ideology of the Movement. He looked long and ponderously at the sign. He wanted to believe the message, but he was in conflict. Of course, the sign was right: he was in a situation of potentially great suffering and had best refuse it. But what was the source of this suffering? M-C was causing it at that moment, and the suffering would get worse if he "made love" to her in her condition of hatred and anger. But how could she hurt him? M-C was his model and hero in the Movement! She was his supervisor in the Movement; and the Movement could do him no harm!

Marie-Claude could not hurt him! Marie-Claude would not hurt him! Marie-Claude was his friend!

To refuse suffering meant to refuse M-C; to refuse M-C meant to refuse the Movement. Adam felt like she and the Movement spoke to him through this sign. The message of the Movement was to reject suffering. Suddenly, he posited that his fears were just unreal imaginations, that he could dismiss all his misgivings just by applying the doctrine of the Movement and choosing to REFUSE SUFFERING. Was M-C testing his dedication to the Movement by placing this hand-made sign on her fridge? « Qu'est ce que tu regardes »?!! [What are you looking at?!] she challenged in an accusatory fashion and looked at the fridge herself.

Just then, his perception shifted and the sign seemed to become his only ally in the room. Adam was gripped by fear and took the message to be an omen of terrible evil waiting for him in her bedroom. He thought the best interpretation of REFUSE SUFFERING would be to refuse M-C for his own safety. He knew that was an unauthorized interpretation, one that she did not expect nor want; she would not have placed the sign there if she thought it would lead him to refuse her sexual demands. To refuse M-C meant to refuse the Movement, and Adam would have reasoned his way all the way out of it. Adam knew he was being tested, and he felt it was his last chance to decide for himself the true meaning of Silo's message to REFUSE SUFFERING.

"*Run, Adam! Run! Adam, get up and run!*"

Adam's plea echoed in his mind with the greatest urgency, but his voice remained silent and his body motionless. *Run where?* he asked himself. The kitchen doors were closed and fastened. M-C was between the locked doors and himself. If he tried to run, she could try to stop him and there would be a physical confrontation. Desperate, he looked at the closed kitchen doors, lowered his right shoulder and shifted his weight down to prepare for a jump. She saw this and countered with a forbidding mirror move of her own. What if Adam tried to escape right then and there through the double-locked kitchen doors? He was already terrified of her and scared for his life and safety.

Although he wanted to run, he could not chance being involved in a physical confrontation with M-C, because he was not a good fighter and she was still in a highly agitated state. If Adam hurt her in self-defence, he would suffer grave consequences in the Movement. He was terrified of getting head injuries, and she had an unknowable supply of weapons in her house. What if she won the battle and he lost his manhood? He did not want to hurt her in any case, because he considered her his friend. If he hurt her in self-defence, she could easily call the police and invent a story. Alternatively, Adam could escape through the fire escape, but the door was locked. If he succeeded in opening the back door, he had never been in her yard before and did not know where the fire stairs led or if the yard was fenced in, or if the stairs were wet and slippery. If he fled Waverly, she could still call the police, invent a story, and he would have been a fugitive on foot in a strange neighbourhood after dark, easy for the police to capture. There were witnesses who saw Adam leave The Unicorn with M-C.

For all these reasons, Adam was incapable of forcing the closed doors open and chancing an escape. He had to be mindful of all these possible pitfalls in order to protect his personal freedom. The genius of M-C's trap was that she could have him arrested as punishment for refusing her. He wanted to call the police on his own but was incapable, since it was not his home. He didn't know where the phone was, and it would have been especially galling to call the police on her in her own home. If he did, there would be consequences for him in the Movement. If she struggled with him while he phoned the police, it would look bad for him, not for her. She could create a disturbance, wake Rania and enlist her support against him. Once the police arrived, M-C would communicate with them in French better than Adam could. Since she was a woman with a (crying) child in her own home, she could easily pretend that Adam was an intruder, and the police would believe her and arrest him. She appeared to have anticipated every contingency in her detailed plan to frame him. In any case, the Movement had conditioned him not to trust the police, but to fear them.

« J'ai des besoins! J'ai un besoin d'être aimée, d'être touchée, d'être caressée, pis toi tu le fait tellement bien; t'est doux! Au début je pensais que t'étais comme ça avec tout le monde, mais là je vois que tu pourrais être utile pour moi ». [I have needs! I need to be loved, touched, caressed, and you do it so well; you're gentle! At first I thought you were like that with everyone, but now I see how you could be useful for me.] She did not speak about what Adam wanted, nor did she ask him. M-C did not ask him about his preferences or if he was interested in pleasing her. She just told him that he had been selected to have sex with her like a *fait accompli*, as if he were a drill thrall or a male drone to the Queen Bee.

Then she suddenly said, "I don't want to have sex with anybody." This statement bewildered Adam. She had taken the time to arrange this mysterious meeting where, just a few short minutes earlier, she revealed her intentions to be sexual violence. Now, she seemed to cancel her sexual demands and replaced them with nothing. His mind was left floating rudderless in a meaningless universe, without even a tormentor for company.

So can I go home now? he asked himself, and he wondered what kind of a woman would do such a thing. It was like she was playing with him, amusing herself by twisting and contorting his heart and mind in any direction her whimsical cruelty desired. Adam thought that at any moment she would burst out with the cackling, maniacal laughter of a sorceress who had planned a long evening of punishment for him in her torture chamber. This sudden shift in sexual demands was her way of punishing him for perceived sexual harassment, after all. As though, when she said that Adam was attracted to her, she had then offered him sex to excite him, just to pull it away, and say, "You thought I would have sex with you, Adam? I would never have sex with a loser like you!" while she watched his disappointment.

Adam hoped the whole evening was a Siloist simulation exercise — she would end the session there and he could escape the sexual harassment charges with a stern warning like "Now you know what it feels like to have your feelings played with!" And she would send him off into the night, having learned a lesson from the fright of his life. But M-C did not mention any sexual harassment charges, nor did she let him go.

Adam asked himself again, *Could M-C really be that sick*? He thought hard and reasoned that maybe the clue to understanding was held in her statement itself. He reviewed the statement and played with the words anybody and nobody and how would they be said in French. Suddenly, he understood that she was trying to use the English expression "just anybody" but had learned it imperfectly or was not completely able to use it the correct way. She had wanted to say, "I don't want to have sex with just anybody" as in the French « pas avec n'importe qui ». Instead of that, she said "anybody," which in French means the opposite « pas avec personne » and which Anglophones find confusing. Now it all made better sense to him, and Adam started to feel just a little relieved!

A Friday in May

He tried to explain to her his theory about somebody/nobody/anybody and she thundered, "No! That's not what I mean!" but refused to explain further.

The more he talked about his lack of willingness to have sex with her, the angrier she got. Despite this, he thought he should try to reason with her instead of asking questions, for his own sake.

« Sauf que je ne te connais même pas. Peut-être qu'on peut parler de ta biographie, de qui tu es… »

[Except I don't even know you. Maybe we can talk about your biography, of who you are…] he said, trying to eventually understand why she had said, "make love" without context and in anger.

« Qu'est ce que tu connais de ma biographie ? » [What do you know about my biography?] She asked him to talk about her biography, instead of her talking about herself, as he had asked.

« Je sais que t'étais avec Vittorio et vous avez eu un enfant ensemble; et là vous n'êtes plus ensemble. Mais àpart de ça, je ne te connais pas. » [I know you were with Vittorio, and you had a child together; and now you are no longer together. But aside from that, I know nothing about you.]

M-C nodded and smirked. Adam asked if she would tell him more about herself.

« Non! Je ne veux *pas* parler de ma biographie! » [No! I *don't* want to talk about my biography!] M-C screamed.

« Qu'est ce que tu veux? » [What do you want?] Adam asked, grasping for direction.

« Non! Je ne dirais pas non plus ce que je veux parce que je ne veux pas te faire rentrer dans mon moule. Dans le passé, mes tchums ont toujours voulu savoir ce que je voulais d'un homme pour ensuite essayer de rentrer dans mon moule, et ça *c'est une chose que je ne tolérerai plus*! » [No! I won't say what I want either because I don't want to force you into my mould. In the past, my boyfriends have always wanted to know what I expected of a man so they could try fitting into my mould, and that's *one thing I will not tolerate anymore!*]

When she screamed the part about "not tolerating that any longer," Adam felt like he was being held responsible for things that her previous boyfriends had done. At the same time, she held him forcibly in place at the outer threshold of her tolerance. All her past boyfriends were unknown to Adam, except Vittorio. Adam had no way of reviewing and evaluating her previous relationships. If he made one false move and went beyond the point where all her previous boyfriends had pushed her, M-C threatened dire consequences. She sat there for several minutes, screaming and yelling at him, shouting orders, making threats and interdictions. Adam could not scream back because his throat was already constricted, tense and dry, and he had trouble speaking for himself. She wouldn't let him talk.

« Ce n'est pas l'homme idéal que je cherche, c'est la *relation* idéale. Ça là, c'est juste en attendant... Quand je m'embarque dans une relation avec un homme, je suis *très* exigeante. Je demande beaucoup, et je demande rien de moins que la perfection; il faut que tout sois parfait, si non ça marche pas... » [It's not the ideal man I seek, it's the ideal *relationship*. This thing here, this is just while I'm waiting... When I start a relationship with a man, I am *very* demanding. I ask a lot, and I ask nothing less than perfection; everything must be perfect, otherwise it does not work...]

Adam did not understand exactly what she was talking about, though he did get the feeling this was just the beginning of her detailed plans to be extremely demanding of him, and if he was not perfect, things would not work and their friendship would be in danger.

« J'ai rencontré Vittorio le premier mai, puis on a eménagé en appartement un mois après ... j'avais tendance à me laisser aller dans des compulsions avec les gars ... à cause de ça, j'ai peur de faire fausse route. » [I met Vittorio the First of May and we moved in together one month later... With men, I tended to let myself get carried away into compulsions ... because of that, I'm afraid of taking the wrong path.] M-C said.

She's afraid of jumping into things and making mistakes? Adam thought. *But this is a mistake! What she's doing now is a mistake, a terrible mistake — can't she see that? Is she taking the wrong road on purpose?*

« Je ne veux pas un homme qui est dépendant émotivement sur

moi, ni financièrement. » [I do not want a man who is dependent on me emotionally, neither financially.] M-C said.

But I'm on welfare! he thought, grasping for meaning. *She doesn't want a guy who is financially dependent on her, so she deliberately picks a guy who is on welfare — what kind of sense is that?* It seemed like Adam was a character living inside M-C's mistakes, as if the whole course of her actions was to force him into serving as her latest mistake, to repeat her mistakes from the past, but for what purpose? Adam was stunned that she could sit there and tell him about her past mistakes with men while he fit the exact pattern of a man she wanted to avoid.

« Je ne veux plus être le sens de la vie de quelqu'un, je ne veux plus sentir que je suis responsable pour sa vie, pour sa souffrance, que si je m'en allais, que toute sa vie tomberait à terre. Et je ne le ferais *pas non plus! J'ai decidé de ne plus accepter ces choses-là dans ma vie!! J'ai des limites!!!* » [I do not want to be the meaning of somebody's life, I no longer wish to feel that I am responsible for his life, his suffering, that if I go away, his whole life would fall to the ground. And I won't do it either! Those are things that *I have decided I will no longer accept in my life! I have limits!!!*]

Adam didn't understand what she was talking about. He had never done anything to her to deserve this. However, when she screamed the last part about her limits, he felt that he was already farther past the threshold than he previously thought. She still felt the burning rage from injustices done to her by previous men, and Adam was being held directly responsible. As a result, all their guilt was being transferred to him. Without his even knowing how to act near her, he could easily transgress her limits and receive the full weight of her wrath. That was why he wanted her to talk about her past, but she mercilessly refused.

« Dans le passé, mes tchums ont franchi mes limites. *Tu ne franchiras pas mes limites!* » [In the past my boyfriends crossed my limits. *You won't cross my limits! I won't let you!*] she hissed.

Adam was petrified with fear. At this point, a crevice opened in her solar plexus, below the point of emanation of her murderous rage and hatred of men. Through this crevice, beams of light projected outward from her body. He could see into her soul, where miniature men languished and commiserated their lives away as prisoners. She had torn a strip off the soul of each man she had slept with and had kept these fragments as hostages and souvenirs inside her own soul. "Marie-Claude! Marie-Claude! Let us out! Let us out, Marie-Claude!" they called out to her in agony.

I don't want to go in there, Adam thought, frozen in fear. Not long after, the crevice closed up and she resumed shouting orders at him.

« Je ne veux pas que tu parles de ce qu'on fait avec les autres dans le Mouvement, par exemple. *As-tu compris!* » [I do not want you to talk about what we're doing with others in the Movement, mind you. *Do you understand!*]

He asked her why she wanted him to keep this secret.

« J'ai pas envie d'aller le crier sur le toit. » [I don't want to go scream it from the rooftops,] she said. Adam understood that she knew what harm she was doing to him and was ashamed, while completely unwilling to spare him. He was at her mercy and powerless to stop her. She had still more conditions to impose on him.

« Il ne sera pas non plus question de se toucher en public, de marcher la main dans la main ni de s'embracer. OK? *As-tu compris!* » [Neither will there be any question of touching in public, walking hand in hand, or kissing in public. OK? *Do you understand!*] She warned him not to tell anyone, but she had first taken the care to hug him where everyone could see. She demanded his submission. He objected meekly to her rules. "*It has to be that way!*" she insisted forcefully.

She told him that he could return to Waverly if he pleased her sexually that night and if he got the right idea about her conditions. « Je veux que tu reviennes içi pour faire l'amour… mais je ne veux pas que tu me prennes pour acquise… Je ne veux pas que ça devienne une cause de souffrance pour toi; la souffrance, c'est comme une toile d'araignée qu'on tisse et qu'on tisse et qui devient de plus en plus compliquée en la tissant. »

[I want you to come back here to make love … but I don't want you take me for granted… I don't want this to become a cause of suffering for you; suffering is like a spider's web that we spin and spin and that becomes more and more complicated as we spin it.]

She had made a conscious tripartite link between the sign on her fridge, the ideology of the Movement and their situation in her kitchen.

M-C had brought the sign on her fridge to life by making this conscious, verbal link. Adam told her it sounded like she wanted a simple sexual relationship with him, with no strings attached and no commitments. He suspected she wanted something like what Fan and Enrico had done only a few days earlier. Without referring to them, Adam asked M-C if he had understood her intentions correctly.

"No! That's not what I mean!"

He had failed to catch her meaning in both English and French. He looked at the fridge again.

« J'aime apprendre, mais je n'aime pas me laisser enseigner. » [I like learning, but I don't like being taught,] M-C said. Adam had not the slightest idea what she was talking about. He tried asking her about it, but she could not get him to understand. He tried to ask many questions so he could understand what had moved her to make such a violent demand on him and how he could escape the situation without consequences. He was rebuffed in every inquiry. She wouldn't let him talk; instead, she yelled at him. « Si tu savais çe que je vivais avant! Tu ne me poserais pas de questions comme ça! » [If you knew what I have lived through! You wouldn't be asking me questions like that!]

But he did *not* know what she had lived before, and he needed that information urgently to help him understand her and what he should do! She refused to tell.

Finally, he tried asking one more question. She angrily said that she would not answer any more questions. « Soit que tu le fasse… ou sinon…! » [Either you do it… or else!]

Then she shifted her weight sideways in her chair, and closer to him. She made menacing eyes at him with threatening grin. She flung the kitchen doors open and dared him to make a mistake.

Adam was not allowed to know the subject of the meeting before she sequestered him in her kitchen. She required him to have sex with her through coercion, duress and delusive tactics, but he was not allowed to refuse her. He was not allowed to leave Waverly freely. He was not allowed to be financially dependent on her. He was not allowed to be emotionally dependent on her. He was not allowed to ask about her life story. He was not allowed to ask her any questions that would evince painful or difficult memories. He was not allowed to say or do anything that reminded her of her previous boyfriends. He was not allowed to ask her questions that reminded her about what she had lived before or to ask her directly about it. He was not allowed to live with her in an apartment, especially not in less than one month. He was not allowed to please her or guess at how to fit her "mould." He was not allowed to understand what she said in French or English. He was not allowed to ask for clarification. He was not allowed to talk about his own needs, limits, preferences, wants or desires. He was not allowed to make her the meaning of his life. He was not allowed to make her feel that she was responsible for his life, for his suffering, or that his life would fall apart if she went away. He was not allowed to transgress any of her limits. He was not allowed to tell anyone in the Movement about what she did to him. He was not allowed to touch her hand in public, nor to walk hand-in-hand with her. He was not allowed to kiss her in public. He was not allowed to take her for granted or be possessive of her. He was not allowed to suffer. He was not allowed to teach her. He had to accept he was just a transient man for her before she found a "real" man. Finally, Adam had to act immediately based on her threats and all the previous conditions.

 Just an hour earlier, Adam had not even known that any of this would happen. Now he'd had to assimilate far too much information in a very short period of time. In order to exit the situation the same evening, his challenge was to figure out and admit to himself that he was in a dangerous organization that was harmful to him. Also, he had been in this dangerous organization for years, without noticing the harm it had done him. That M-C's offer of friendship was a ruse designed to lure him into her lair, to rape him. Moreover, he was being sexually assaulted by M-C, one of his *models* and *heroes* in that organization.

 Furthermore, people he considered potential good friends saw

A Friday in May

him as an easy victim to prey upon. Case in point, Enrico had been harming him for years. Considering to the previous six points, his judgement had failed him and was now questionable. He would have to leave the Movement, even though it held great meaning for him. He would fall into the dark abyss of lumpen life. He would have to give up his apartment or risk homelessness. He would have to seek a new place to live without a job, money or references. He would risk losing all his friends in the Movement including his best friend, Raymond.

Still not fully healed from his accident, his mind was fully occupied just with processing the decisions from Enrico's meeting. To fully understand these fourteen points the same night as M-C's myriad conditions was impossible for Adam. His brain was not capable of integrating all this information. There was no way he could have understood all of that in one sudden, compressed cognitive marathon. Human biology took over and his mind went into shock as a defense mechanism. Even when he tried thinking, his mind had already "shut down." The only way Adam could understand and make an informed decision was through gradual reflection. M-C did not offer him the luxury of time, however, and all the violence that she inflicted on him was pushed down, under the surface of his conscious mind. The defense mechanism prevented him from understanding until he could have to consider things on his own and understand the events gradually.

Procrastinating for his life, he asked if maybe they could sit in the living room for a while. M-C allowed him to sit on the living room sofa with her. Adam was extremely nervous and uncomfortable, his mind in deep shock, though conscious. By the time they sat on the sofa, Adam could no longer remember clearly what had happened in the kitchen, owing to his short-term memory loss. His thinking was chaotic and he could not analyze the problem without the full mastery of his faculties. He suggested they could listen to the evening jazz show on the radio, because it relaxed him. Indeed, since his accident he had taken to the habit of listening to the dulcet tones of Gilles Archambault on local French radio. He found it relaxing and needed to hear the jazz program every weeknight as part of his routine.

His anxiety grew progressively worse by the minute and

manifested in a case of nervous stomach, which started making extremely audible rumbling noises. M-C noticed the noises and asked him why he had them. Adam told her he was very nervous. He was also very embarrassed by the noises, which he called "borborygmi." She thought that was a funny word and asked him about it. Adam put on his "borborygmi" voice, hoping to relieve his own tension. It made them both laugh, except that Adam could not stop laughing nervously. He could not control himself, began hyperventilating and asked M-C for a paper bag. She became irritated by the endless laughter then blamed it on the radio, instead of letting him relax.

« Aïe! Si c'est la radio qui te fait rire, je vais la fermé! » [Hey! If it's the radio that makes you laugh, I'll turn it off!] She shut it off while he inhaled and exhaled into the paper bag. He was greatly distressed and his anxiety grew worse.

M-C showed no overtly sexual interest in him, though she did start kissing him on the mouth. Adam had tried everything he could in the kitchen to reason his way out of this. In the living room, his conduct showed his lack of willingness to engage in the sexual activity. M-C refused to recognize the gut rumblings, the nervous laughter, the hyperventilation and had silenced the radio. He had exhausted all his courses of appeal, but one. He still had one last chance to do some serious talking. He gathered his thoughts and told himself that this was not like talking his way out of an expired bus ticket or a late paper at school. He was fighting for his life now. He broke off the kissing and started to tell her about how afraid he was. She cocked her head sideways, put her fist on her cheek and gave him a look that said "Shut up and kiss!"

"What's that look you're giving me?" he asked her.

"What does it look like?" she said with the same look.

"It's a look that says, 'Shut up and kiss,'" he said.

« Bravo, Adam! » She resumed kissing him.

He understood that M-C was keeping his mouth occupied to prevent him from talking. But he still had a lot to say, so he broke off the kiss a second time.

« Marie-Claude, j'ai des tensions avec ça… » [Marie-Claude,

A Friday in May

I have some tensions about this…] She interrupted him and did not let him talk, just as she had all evening. She mapped out his tensions on his body. « Des tensions là, tu en a une là et une autre là ». [About tensions, you have one there, and you have one there.] she said.

At the first "there", she touched his chest near his heart. At the second "there" she brought her hand up to his head and touched the centre of his forehead — the exact point at which the Force entered his body during the Experience of the Force, which he had mastered in recent months and which now bore such importance for him. She lingered with her finger on his forehead while she stared into his eyes. Adam got the idea that M-C wanted him to understand something about the tension in his head. Such tension would be an impediment to his ability to experience the current situation with M-C, his new personal friend. She had taken the words right out of his mouth and he was speechless. She was exactly right: he had a tension in his heart and he had a tension in his mind. She smirked. She knew exactly what tensions he had and their exact location, but did not care a whit for his problems.

Adam did not know what to do. However, within seconds of her touching his forehead at the point of entry of the Force, Adam made a link between the message on her fridge, REFUSE SUFFERING, and her flippant disregard for his tensions. The point of entry for the Force in the forehead is also the intellectual centre or the "seat" of the mind. He deemed that her exercise was in testing his devotion to and understanding of the Movement's doctrine, and that this test was planned to coincide with the day's events. It was as though he had passed the "group delegate phase," but if he wanted to be a regenerator and eventually a Team Delegate, he would have to suspend his fears, ignore his tensions and accept the pretence that M-C could not hurt him. (In so doing, M-C imposed her twenty-seventh condition.)

Otherwise, if Adam failed her test, there would be no room for him in the Movement. Since she had refused to explain herself or answer his questions, he was left only with that esoteric explanation. This entire test experience, in turn, had been planned and executed by M-C as an initiation ceremony without her having informed him first. He was thus completely unprepared to deal with the situation. M-C told him he had to make his decision immediately. She was forcing him out. The only way to remain in the Movement was to submit to her sexual demands.

Adam had to decide right then and there if he loved the Movement and if he really *loved* the Movement. He wanted M-C to explain to him how he could leave Waverly in safety and they could still be friends and he could stay in the Movement; she made no such offer. He looked around and asked her what if Rania should come down in the middle of the night to see her mother having sex in front of her, on the living room sofa? M-C said they should go to her bedroom instead. Dejected, he followed her to her bedroom, but he did not consent; he was a defeated man. Once in her bedroom, he still did not co-operate with her violent demands for sex. They lay down on her bed. He was on the right side, she on the left. He thought, *I am in bed with the Central Administrative Sector. What am I doing in bed with the Central Administrative Sector?* He told her about his concern and added he would write a book about it one day titled *Love in the Admi Sector*; she said the book should be titled *Sex in the Admi Sector*.

They still had their clothes on, but loosened a bit. M-C asked him if he had much experience with girls and sex. He told her "No, I've had sex with only four girls" and that his longest relationship was with his first girlfriend, when he was seventeen, though they never had full relations. He started to tell M-C about his other experiences but she said she didn't have to hear any more. « Moi là, j'ai une liste longue de même. » [As for me, I have a big long list.] she said about herself. She mimed the shape of a scroll and, with her other arm, unrolled the scroll so that the sheets cascaded down over the bed and onto the floor. The scroll sheets would have recorded the passage of hundreds of men she had slept with; she offered no names. Adam felt he was out of his league and was intimidated by her experience. She asked if Adam had ever been in love. He said he thought he was once, when he was seventeen and his girlfriend was sixteen; he called it "puppy love." M-C said that was good enough experience for Adam not to confuse his feelings and ordered him not to fall in love with her. (In so doing, M-C imposed condition number twenty-eight.)

A Friday in May

M-C touched his side and his mind lost contact with the present. He went off into daydreams and memories of the past, of what he had lived in the Movement, of many diffuse images flashing before his eyes. He stared off into the window at his right and took in the room, including her spinning ceiling fan, which mesmerized him with the motion of its blades. He forgot where he was and did not know what he was doing. He thought about all the friends he had in the Movement. What about Dwight? Would Dwight ever talk to him again? Would Tara? How about Renato, Suzette, Karim, Marie-Lyne, Bassam, Mina, Popo and all others? Adam was, after all, part of the group in the council. Raymond had just, for all practical purposes, left the Movement that same day; nobody knew if he was coming back. If Adam left the Movement and Raymond left Montreal, when and where would they ever meet again? It was no longer certain that Adam could keep Raymond as a friend. He was in deep anguish. Would Adam lose all his friends if he made the wrong move?

"I'm going to explode!" Adam was called back to reality by M-C's voice. He was terrified she was going to scream at him because he was still not undressed, still not having sex with her. His mind could not conceive her meaning, when she explained. "This is called diffuse sex."

Curious, he asked, "What is?"

She asked him if he was not aware of what he was doing? He asked her what he had done so wrong that she should explode at him? She said that he was tracing a figure eight on her side with his finger, over and over again, and that it was very annoying. She said that it was called "diffuse sex" and was a form of sexual violence because it excited her tremendously, but could never bring her the true sexual satisfaction she required from him. She asked him again if he was not aware of it.

Adam looked down, and his hand was still tracing the figure eight on her side, above her child-bearing hips. He continued tracing the figure eight, the symbol of infinity and the first symbol of the Movement he had ever learned when he was a teenager in the Humanist Party. The loop went in, the loop went out. The loop went in, he was in the Movement. The loop went out, he was out of the Movement. The loop went in M-C — he was in the Movement. The loop went out of M-C — he was out of the Movement. If Adam entered M-C — he was in the Movement. Adam stayed out of M-C — the unthinkable. Adam wondered who these people in the Movement truly were and what the real meaning of the figure eight was.

"Stop it! It's annoying!" she screamed. It was the first time a woman had ever screamed at him in bed and he already wished it would be the last. He again felt self-conscious; M-C had caught him thinking heretical thoughts. Adam said sorry and erased the loop from M-C's side by rubbing her skin a little bit, like an eraser on a blackboard.

M-C went down between his legs, undoing his pants button and fly. She pulled his pants down. Exposing his genitals, she started to perform oral sex on him. She took a long time performing oral sex, but very little happened to Adam. He felt no sexual excitement with her at all. Eventually, she tried a different method and he got a semi-erection. After a while with the semi-erection, she removed the penis from her mouth for a while to play with it. When she tried to reinsert it in her mouth, Adam used an old boy's trick to prevent her from taking it in her mouth. He reached down subtly and tweaked the skin at the base that held the penis in place, to the left. The penis swayed far to the left and she completely missed her attempt at reinsertion, mouth agape. She was surprised and made a move to try again. Adam tried the same trick again, this time to the right. It worked perfectly while he played innocent. She was mystified by what was going on, but after a while she figured out what he was doing and he admitted to it. Although this was clearly his attempt to avoid sexual contact with her, she paused long enough to order him in a loud and angry voice « Fais plus ça! » [Stop that!]

She then reinserted his penis in her mouth, sucking on it hard and angrily. "You're hurting me!" Adam said as her teeth ground into his penis. M-C stopped briefly to adjust the intensity of her assault. Her prolonged sucking yielded only an unconvincing erection. She stopped after a while, saying her jaws were tired. The penis went limp almost immediately and she rolled over, disappointed and frustrated.

« Qu'est ce que tu veux faire maintenant? » [What do you want to do now?] she asked, referring to his failed erection.

« Faire semblant de dormir. » [Pretend to sleep.] Adam said, playing dead and indicating his lack of consent to continue.

« Bien merci beaucoup! » [Well thanks a lot!] M-C said, insulted and on the verge of tears.

They lay there a while, motionless and silent. He understood that it would not be enough for M-C to hold him to service; she expected him to satisfy her. He had to perform, or else. He recalled what had excited women in the past and got the idea that if he could stimulate her with his fingers with sustained intensity, maybe he could bring her to full orgasm and avoid having to penetrate her altogether! He suggested to her that it could help her have an orgasm. She finished undressing and he performed digital sex on her. She seemed to enjoy it, so he thought he was doing his job as a group delegate. After a while, he asked her if she wanted another finger in her vagina. She enthusiastically said yes. He inserted a second finger and continued to stimulate her. She was growing increasingly excited by his strategy to avoid expulsion from the organic structure of the Movement.

Adam thought the strategy was working toward orgasm when he inserted a third finger and her vagina expanded to accommodate it. He continued with his strategy of bringing her to full orgasm, hoping she would let him go home after that. With her favourable response, he took the chance of inserting a fourth finger from the same hand, leaving the thumb out. Her reaction was hesitant but curious. She allowed him to continue like this for a while, then sat up, put her hand on his and said, "Don't put your hand inside me." That was it. That was the end of his strategy. Adam had taken it as far as it would go. M-C's request not to have his hand inside her was understandable, and he could not think of any other way he could satisfy her and still avoid having full sexual intercourse with her. She wanted his penis inside her, just as she had made clear in the kitchen.

Then M-C took out condoms, which she had already waiting for him. She ordered him to put on a condom. Adam tried resisting the condom as a form of rebellion, then she said that if he didn't wear the condom, she would send him away into the night and he would never come back to her house ever again, and they would never be friends.

He understood he was being threatened again, that he had used the condom rebellion strategy as far as it would go. He panicked when he realized his strategy did not have a backup plan—it had delayed penetration only a few seconds while provoking her. He asked her to put it on. He languished between her legs for a while, trying to avoid the inevitable. She told him to get on with it. He got on top of her and just lay on her. She fumbled around between his legs and inserted his penis into her vagina.

Once penetration was achieved, M-C continued to sexually assault him for hours, well past midnight. Despite hours of sexual contact with her, Adam had no excitation and the ejaculation was delayed indefinitely. Unfortunately for him, she enjoyed this prolonged sexual contact tremendously and interpreted his lack of desire to be assaulted as a good night of rape for her. After he finally ejaculated, he removed the condom while standing on the floor and noticed that the condom had burst — there was a hole in the tip and all the sperm was gone. He told her about this and she was alarmed. She said she would go to the clinic the next day to have a "morning after" pill, to prevent pregnancy. They fell asleep soon after, wrapped in the sweaty embrace of each other's arms. She was soft, warm and womanly. He was the perfect victim for her crimes.

VI — THE SUN, THE MOON AND THE TRUTH

"A great deal of intelligence can be invested in ignorance when the need for illusion is deep."
—Saul Bellow

ADAM AWOKE a Saturday in May; it was the first time he had ever slept in a woman's bed. After that point, he had no previous experience to guide him and was in uncharted territory. M-C did not talk to him much at breakfast with Rania and did not seem very happy to see him or have him in her house. Outdoors, they walked on Waverly toward Guizot Street and she told him how he could get up to St. Lawrence, then to the Metro. Adam asked if they would ever see each other again.

« On verra » [We'll see,] she said and added that it would depend on how well he had understood the conditions she had imposed on him the previous night.

He felt betrayed, and it impressed on him the feeling he had been assaulted. A phrase rang out in his mind: "*Under the spreading chestnut tree I sold you and you sold me,*" but he couldn't remember from where he knew it. He reminded her he still wanted to be her friend. She remained silent, frowning, and treated him like a stranger. He didn't know it yet, but he would never again feel a sense of belonging at any meeting or event of the Movement.

Adam left and walked very slowly to the de Castelnau Metro Station, with disturbing sensations, doubts and misgivings. The world seemed different and strange; a foggy haze had descended on Montreal. On St. Lawrence, Adam started to think about what he would do if in the end her offer of friendship was a ruse, just to extract sex from him. To his own great surprise, he asked himself what recourse he would have in the Movement. How could he fix the situation if she didn't call him back? Adam reasoned he could appeal to Josh, since he was the General Delegate. The Council of Team Delegates would probably be involved for making a complaint against a Team Delegate. He was thinking heresy!

Adam resumed his train of thought and reviewed the possibilities of lodging a complaint to the Council of Team Delegates, asking Josh to chair a Tribunal. Any such Tribunal would have been *ad hoc* in his mind, unsupported by the *Norms*. Which of the Team Delegates would actually support Adam if he made a complaint against M-C, their beloved peer? Out of the Team Delegates, Adam knew both Colleen and Fan were good friends of M-C and would never take sides against her. Enrico would probably not support him, though it was difficult to say. Gus would probably vote with Enrico. M-C herself could not support him, but as the accused she would probably not have voting rights anyway. That left only Renato.

Adam felt that of all Team Delegates in Montreal, Renato was probably the most sensitive to his situation and the most likely to lend his support. That meant only one vote out of five in Montreal against M-C. The rest of the council consisted of Team Delegates strewn over North America, such as Pigpen, Yorgo and Ned in Ontario, Nestor and Felipe in California, maybe Roberta or Heath — Adam wasn't sure, plus Josh himself. Of those, Adam had bad relations with some, or else they were all better friends with M-C and would not support him. It seemed that of the entire council, the only potential sympathizer was Renato; luckily, he was in Montreal. If only Adam could talk to Renato before Enrico got involved in this.

Adam boarded the blue line of the Metro at the de Castelnau Station and headed for the Côte-des-Neiges Station, where he disembarked. Walking up Côte-des-Neiges Road to Frère-André, Adam thought maybe he could just ask Enrico an innocent structural question but not mention M-C's name. He shrugged off that thought and tried to just play it cool with Enrico, until he could reach Renato hopefully the same day.

Adam entered his apartment less than an hour after having left

M-C. Enrico had a female victim still in his bedroom. He emerged and said he had "got lucky" the previous night; it was obvious he wanted Adam to compete with his latest conquest. Adam played it cool, not saying who he had been with, nor did he mention M-C's name or what happened at Waverly the previous night. It seems Adam's sense of prudence and privacy were utterly irrelevant since Enrico already knew everything. Enrico followed his usual pattern, as on moving day a year earlier. He took mere minutes from the time Adam walked in the door to redefine their new structural relationship as an extension of his dominance and virile masculine hegemony. Without pause or further questions, he told Adam where Adam was the previous night, who Adam was with and most importantly, what they *did*:

> Yeah, so this could be a good thing for you, if you learn how to take it the right way. Easy come, easy go. Know what I mean? Don't start flying with colours. Yeah, for sure. You're gonna have to learn not to fly away with images of your whole life with her; she's not the meaning of your life, Adamito. Learn how to give and let go. Learn how to give without expecting anything in return. You'll learn that you can be with other women, and she can be with other men, don't get possessive of her. It's sort of "you scratch my back, I scratch yours" kind of thing. But you'll have to realize, you know, that she has her own life there, and she has a little girl too, and who are you to interfere with that? No, but you let her live her life there, and you have your own life to live; you have your project, you have your own friends. And she also has her own project and her own friends, and this is why there has to be a lot of communication between the two of you, so that you have an understanding, Adamito! This could be a really good opportunity for you, know what I mean? But don't start flying with colours, okay, man?

With Adam's mind still in shock and very hazy from the previous night, it reeled again and descended further into shock. The word "CONSPIRACY" cut through his mind at warp speed. How did Enrico know all that? Had he been the victim of a plot by both Enrico and M-C? His mind could not fathom the implications of this. Enrico had already anticipated all his doubts, questions, concerns and courses of action and replaced them with his own specific instructions about what Adam was expected to do with M-C. Any idea of appealing to the Council of Team Delegates evaporated on the spot. Adam urgently reviewed the events of the previous evening in the new light of how it affected his status in the Movement. Enrico and M-C had been speaking to each other at the gathering, less than twenty-four hours earlier. In a flash, he reviewed the events from the time he left the social gathering with M-C, this time asking himself what words she could have already exchanged with Enrico before she trapped him in her home and threatened him in her kitchen.

As though Adam were not confused enough, the very first orientation Enrico gave as his new Orientor was the imposition of his conspiracy with M-C to sexually assault Adam, and the reinforcement of her twenty-eight conditions imposed the previous night. More troubling still, Enrico's words, their sentiment and direction bore a striking similarity to M-C's own words the previous night in her kitchen. Enrico's instructions were festooned with phrases and expressions that Adam had heard in a slightly different way. Adam felt his will had been annexed by Enrico and resold to M-C. He was supremely frustrated at this shocking turn of events.

His mind shifted back and forth between M-C's twenty-eight conditions and Enrico's macho show in his face. Enrico's comments revealed a deep level of planning and co-ordination between himself and M-C to control Adam's life and sexuality. This was extremely distressing to Adam. M-C had let Enrico know she wanted Adam to adopt that "easy come, easy go" attitude with her, and Enrico's task was to ensure Adam respected M-C's conditions.

Where was Adam's will in this? When did he decide on anything? What if he did not want to "give and let go?" M-C and Enrico had decided between themselves in advance what would be best for Adam, who was expected to give without expecting anything in return. Their terms were that M-C would not be bound to Adam but could see other men; Adam could see other women and not be bound by M-C, though he was still required to provide her with sex. Who was Adam to interfere with M-C's home life, indeed? Between Enrico, M-C and Adam, the third person on the outside looking in was … Adam! Enrico and M-C decided everything for his sexuality. Any departure from their plans would be interference on Adam's part. Enrico stated clearly that M-C and Adam were not intended to be friends; he knew it in advance of her assault. These were the governing principles of Adam's relationship with M-C, decided upon without his participation, foreknowledge or consent. M-C imposed her conditions on Adam and assigned Enrico to enforce them. Adam's acceptance of these principles was in itself made a condition of his further advancement in the Movement.

At noon, he turned on the television and watched *Star Trek*. Even though he knew the episode thoroughly, he could not concentrate. He was completely disgusted and turned off the television in less than five minutes. In the afternoon, he went to a Movement event in Lafontaine Park, an expansive green space at the juncture of the Plateau and Old Montreal, across from which was the Central Library of Montreal, where Pierre Trudeau had been pelted with rocks the day before he was elected prime minister. There, Adam met Curly, a group delegate in Fan's team, and asked his advice on his problem. Since Adam could not tell Curly any details of who else was involved, Curly could not help him very much. Adam felt uncomfortable at the event. There he also saw Raymond, his former Orientor, but could not tell him what happened because of M-C's law of *omerta*. Adam looked forlornly at the pedal boats where, as a child, he had played on the man-made lake.

At the evening's potluck supper, Adam felt a growing discomfort and a huge wave of emotion building inside him. He experienced a massive feeling of profound contradiction, but could not put his finger on what it was. After supper, he had a discussion with Popo, the Admi in Gus's team, about what happened, though he could not tell him who was involved.

Popo was a strange bird who could be observed without

binoculars yet was not so easily approachable. A fan of Diamanda Galás and satanic operas, the young man of seventeen was a gifted cartoonist, illustrator and political essayist with a knack for adjectival phrases and biting satire. The product of a French Canadian mother and Serbo-Croatian father long since gone from Popo's life, a pair of John Lennon glasses, a trusty notebook and an odour of cigarette smoke were his constant companions. Clad in black from his Dr. Martens boots to his long greasy hair, quick-witted and verbally gifted, Popo had already learned at his tender age the art of reflecting before speaking and was blessed with a hesitant speaking style that made his witticisms even funnier. Popo was a free thinker, suspicious of traditional society and its *idées recues*, and had a talent for perceiving deeply inside human nature and motivations. When Adam tried writing a letter to M-C that evening, he invited Popo to join him at his desk and help him, though without an addressee. In the letter, Adam pleaded with her to save their friendship.

On Sunday afternoon, Adam walked up to Mount Royal and tried to write in his journal. There, refugees of winter tossed Frisbees, some played pitch and catch or badminton, while others played hacky sack by Beaver Lake, a cherished spot for relaxation, leisure and play for all Montrealers. Adam always liked Beaver Lake because he could see the sky above, the lake area and the forests surrounding, but not the city below. He wanted to take control of his thoughts and understand what had happened to him, but his mind was still in shock and his thoughts and emotions were blocked. He reviewed the previous two days but could not bring himself to review Friday. Despite his best efforts to help himself, the events of Friday were stuck in that ball of energy and remained that way until he had an extended period of time to review them gradually and in a different setting.

Returning to Frère-André, he questioned Enrico about how he knew where and with whom Adam was, and what they did together. "That's intentionality, man; that's what happens when you put your energy in a certain direction. People can see that, man, and they're attracted to you," Enrico said. By caressing Adam's ego, Enrico tried to make it look like Adam was the initiator with M-C. At the weekly meeting, Enrico discussed Silo's theme of suffering and contradictory actions that produce suffering. Adam was preoccupied with something else and could not concentrate. He ran back and forth between the meeting and his phone. Suzette noticed this and asked him what was going on. Adam could not tell her. He was like a ghost of the Movement, already excluded *de facto* but not yet able to understand well enough to leave the structure, still turning up at Movement events.

On Sunday evening, M-C phoned him; she said she had been to the clinic and had the morning after pill, adding that if she had not gone to the clinic, she would have certainly become pregnant with his child. Adam felt a little emotional bond with her. She also said that Rania had an incident where the drawstrings on her hooded jacket became entangled in the window of the car, and if M-C had not acted quickly enough, the girl could have been strangled. He felt another emotional ping inside him and was distracted from confronting M-C about Friday night. Adam had been hoping for a reassurance that she hadn't sacrificed their friendship for sex, that she still wanted to be his friend.

« J'ai bien aimé notre vendredi soir. Tu peux venir ici cette semaine. » [I really enjoyed our Friday night. You can come back here this week,] M-C said and added, "I was going to teach you about the craft, but it wasn't necessary because you did it so well." Adam asked her what she was talking about. M-C said, "The craft is something in the Movement that is passed on from woman to woman and then from woman to man. The woman is usually obliged to teach it to the man because the man is so unskilled and inconsiderate sexually that he doesn't know what to do — how to please a woman. But in your case I didn't even have to tell you what to do because you did it all so well."

Adam was so relieved that M-C called to invite him back to Waverly that he missed the obfuscation of the friendship and discarded the letter Popo had helped him write. "J'ai bien aimé ça quand tu m'as appelée 'Sweetheart'. " [I really liked it when you called me 'Sweetheart.'] M-C cooed after telling him not to fall in love. He started to tell M-C about his fears for what would happen to their friendship, but she did not let him talk.

« Des peurs là, on n'en a pas besoin. Je ne veux pas que ça

devienne une cause de souffrance pour toi ... la souffrance c'est comme une toile d'araignée qu'on tisse et qu'on tisse et qui devient de plus en plus compliquée en le tissant » [As for fears, we don't need them. I don't want this to become a thing of suffering for you ... suffering is like a spider's web that we spin and spin and becomes more and more complicated as we spin it.]

In her comments about fear, M-C made a conscious link to her own comments about tensions from just forty-eight hours earlier, repeated her statement about suffering, and linked it to her fridge sign, REFUSE SUFFERING, and how their situation was related to the doctrine of the Movement. Fresh from Enrico's meeting about contradictory actions that produce suffering, Adam recognized and understood the significance of M-C's links at the time. He was previously unaware, however, of how the Movement's doctrine of suffering involved the metaphor of the spider's web, and this served to confuse him more. Though he tried to tell M-C he was afraid of what would happen to their friendship in the near future, she had dismissed his fears without withdrawing her sexual demands in time for their next visit.

On Monday, Enrico had his orientation meeting with Adam, in which he told him what was expected of him as a regenerator in the organic structure of the Movement. Adam could be promoted to the Council of Team Delegates if he succeeded in building a team. Enrico again raised the points he had made on Saturday, this time mentioning M-C by name. He described how Adam's relationship with M-C would fit into his project and how to keep things straight. Adam no longer felt comfortable in the Movement, but he could not identify the reason why. Although he had big problems with M-C, he did not want to leave at that point. Thus, he could not think of a valid excuse for not attending Enrico's meeting. Far from helping, Enrico's detailed meeting occupied Adam's mind and distracted him from resolving the situation with M-C.

* * *

From that Saturday in May onward, Adam spent the rest of the year running around, trying to pick up the loose pieces of the conspiracy puzzle wherever they may have fallen. First, Enrico had spoken to him about M-C without M-C's presence. Then, Adam returned to M-C and spoke to her about Enrico, in his absence the next day, Tuesday. In both cases, Enrico and M-C gave partial information about their activities, but never fully answered his questions. This pattern continued throughout the summer, with M-C and Enrico amusedly playing ping-pong with Adam, always sending him from one Team Delegate to the other, the three of them never in the same room at the same time to discuss the matter and address his concerns. Adam always had to reach and struggle for the missing information, as in the "monkey-in-the-middle" game.

On Tuesday, Adam arranged to meet M-C at her workplace on Esplanade Street, at a quarter past four in the afternoon. By this time, she knew she still had not answered his questions or addressed his objections from that Friday in May. In her car, she told him she was nervous and felt very uncomfortable being with him. Adam was also uncomfortable with her, since he intended to discuss Enrico's privileged knowledge of the events since Friday, and all previously unanswered questions.

« J'ai des doutes. » [I have doubts.] M-C said and asked, « Qu'est ce que t'as compris de vendredi soir? » [What did you understand from Friday night?]

« Pas grand chose » [Not much] Adam said and confronted her with news of Enrico's reaction to him on Saturday. He said he would like an explanation of what was going on. "Enrico seemed to know where I was Friday night and who I was with. I guess he has very good powers of observation..." Adam speculated.

"No, that's not it. It's because I called him before I asked you to sleep with me; I wanted to make sure it wouldn't fuck you up in your process," admitted M-C.

Adam was stunned by the implications of this. M-C had just confessed to his face of having conspired with Enrico to sexually assault him, but she acted like there was nothing to it. Adam was in shock again and his mind still could not fathom the implications. "And … I guess … you chose Enrico because he's your old peer and friend and you wanted his advice?" Adam asked after a thoughtful pause in her car.

"No. I called Enrico because he's the Orientor of that team…I didn't want to hurt you!" answered M-C.

She said she called Enrico and asked him whether it would "screw" Adam up in his process if he were to have sex with her. The negotiations that went on between M-C and Enrico were entirely behind Adam's back and without his consent, and he was not made privy to the details of their discussion. M-C concluded an agreement with Enrico on the terms of Adam's sexual relationship with her. What authority did Enrico have, or what authority did M-C think he had, to grant or refuse permission to have sex with Adam?

Far from wanting a friendship with Adam, it seemed M-C found him completely unapproachable and the prospect of getting to know him as a human being so revolting that she chose the shortest possible route to get sex from him, in order to accommodate her busy schedule. She was not at all interested in any friendship with him. On the contrary, she saw him as a person who was not in control of his own life, his own decisions, his own sex life — a person not too far from the hospital's intensive care unit and in need of constant supervision from older adults. She wanted sex from him, and she abused her position in the Movement to get it. The consent came from Enrico! It bothered Adam that M-C did not see Raymond as his Orientor, but a guy like Enrico. It did not make sense, so Adam reminded her that Raymond had still been his Orientor up until the Friday in May, at seven o'clock.

"But Enrico is the Orientor of that council. That's why I called him," she said.

How could M-C know *in advance* that it would be more appropriate to call Enrico instead of Raymond? Furthermore, how could M-C have known in advance the exact date and hour of his transition from Raymond's team to Enrico's team without having spoken to Enrico in advance? Even Raymond and Adam had not known in advance the outcome of their meeting with Enrico. Why would the outcome even matter, unless M-C was trying to purposefully avoid Raymond? M-C had known Raymond seven years and never had a reason to avoid him, until now. She admitted to Adam that she called Enrico in advance and spoke to him about Adam's sexuality. How convenient for her that she had planned her assault mere hours after his transition from Raymond's team.

« Est-ce qu'on peut être plus honnête ici ? » [Can we be more honest here ?] Adam asked, believing she was filtering something.

« Aïe ! Sont pas des mensonges que j'te raconte ! » [Hey! These are not lies that I'm telling you!] she yelled.

Adam had taken his best chance at asking M-C about the situation, without confronting her directly with accusations. He still wanted to be her friend and tried to give her the benefit of the doubt and a chance to explain herself. When she screamed at him in the car, however, he was crushed and his doubts were pushed back down under the surface.

When Adam returned to M-C's home, it was his first time there after having slept in her bed; everything seemed unknown to him and strange. M-C was very uncomfortable and told him so again: « J'ai des doutes » [I have doubts.]

At one point, he got up from the sofa to walk from the living room to the kitchen. « Aïe ! Tu changes ! T'es en train de changer ! » [Hey! You're changing! You're in the process of changing!] cried M-C.

Adam froze in his tracks, terrified of moving a single muscle. Did she mean he was changing shape or colour in front of her eyes? Why was he not aware of this change? He felt like he was in a science fiction movie. Moving only his mouth, he asked her what she had meant by that.

« T'es pas comme t'étais il y a trois minutes » [You're not like you were three minutes ago,] answered M-C.

Adam didn't know what to say about this, though it did make him very uncomfortable. She explained further by saying that her sexual experience with him last time had been so good. She was afraid that he might change, and if he did anything different, sex wouldn't be the same for her. Her comment put pressure on him to both remember and limit his performance to the same quality as before; otherwise, he risked displeasing her and losing the friendship. The situation got progressively more complicated with each new assault.

In the kitchen, they had rice and vegetables for supper. While she was at the stove, Adam was seated at the table and tried broaching the subject of Enrico again, hoping this time that he could wrest some information from M-C without her screaming at him. This time, he started by telling how Enrico told him every detail about what Adam should do with her and how he should act, and what M-C expected from him and so on. Adam concluded this summary by pushing his line of questioning through to its logical conclusion, asking "So, I was wondering if you would know how Enrico knew so much about our relationship even before I did?"

M-C slammed the wooden spoon against the pan and shouted, « Enrico-là, il est paternaliste! » [That Enrico! He's so paternalistic!]

Adam knew M-C's statement was true, but he felt something was left out, because she had not answered the question. There was just the slightest hint in her comment, however, that M-C was disappointed in Enrico's handling of the information he possessed. As though she had indeed asked for Enrico's permission before she sexually assaulted Adam, but that Enrico was not supposed to tell Adam about it. During this exchange, she never denied that Enrico was speaking about her in his comments. It was like the Movement had a transmitter atop Mount Royal and only Team Delegates like Enrico and M-C had been given receiver-decoders.

There was a growing tension between the two poles of her argument: her alleged desire not to hurt Adam and her potent desire to extract sex from him at any cost. Which was more important to her? More disturbingly, why would M-C even think that sex with her would screw him up in his process? If she was *planning* "consensual" sex with him as mutually respecting and non-violent adults, then what was the problem? If she wanted to know his true thoughts and feelings about having sex with her, why did she not get to know him first and ask him herself? Why did she go against her own stated wishes for friendship five days before the Friday in May? What was the rush?

M-C went over to him and put her arms around him while Adam was seated on the chair. "I didn't want to hurt you, sweetheart," she repeated. Since she reassured him so warmly, it was hard to confront her any further on the matter. He did get her to agree, however, not to involve Enrico in their affairs anymore. When she agreed to that, it renewed Adam's perception of Enrico as a meddler in his affairs with women and he felt protective of M-C, thus further discouraging him from confronting her about her previous violence. Adam had completely misread the situation.

Adam was faced with the same double-bind conundrum as before. There was a growing body of evidence that M-C had sexually assaulted him as part of a conspiracy with Enrico. But Adam never put his finger on the key. He could not put it all together; there was always some information missing. The missing part left doubt in him, which he had to consider when contemplating his departure from the Movement that meant so much to him. His challenge was the same as in May: leave the Movement based on suspicions and doubts, or try to ask reasonable questions in the hope of getting information. Being a reasonable person, Adam could not allow himself, based solely on doubts and fears, to sever his relationship with M-C. It was by exploiting these fears that she abused her position in the Movement.

After supper, M-C told Adam to join her in her bedroom. Sitting on her bed, she told him that she had « les genous de fer » [iron knees] and that she used her iron knees to intimidate men into giving her whatever she wants. She told him she would use her "iron knees" against his testicles if Adam did not submit to her sexual demands, as she claimed to have done to many other men in her past.

Given the threat of physical force, he had no choice but to undress and comply. He did not furnish the sex she required, but rather searched for delaying tactics as he had the last time. She was already undressed and on her back with her legs open; she beckoned him to perform oral sex on her. He looked between her legs and was completely grossed out; he did not want to go anywhere near her dark continent. With her legs open and knees raised, Adam tried crawling under her left knee to avoid them entirely, looking up at the ceiling. She lowered the underside of her knee onto his throat and angrily ordered him to stop fooling around. She performed oral sex on him until ejaculation while she sat on his face. After that, she was still sexually aroused and violent, so she assaulted him a second time the same evening, ordering him to make love to her. Adam had not consented, but Enrico had. This was her "iron knees" assault.

The next morning, she charged at Adam with a toothbrush in her hand. "What the hell is this?" she asked and accused him of taking her for granted. Adam said he didn't like going a whole night or morning without brushing his teeth, as had happened last time he visited. M-C said such moves put him on thin ice and their friendship in jeopardy as it demonstrated that he expected sex from her every time he placed his toothbrush in her bathroom!

When Adam returned to Frère-André, Enrico paralleled M-C with sexual harassment of his own. Enrico said that after M-C had finished with Adam, he would be assigned to servicing Gus's mother sexually. Enrico acted out a disgusting scenario in the kitchen, in which he played both Gus's mother and Adam: "¡Oh más profúndo, Adamito! ¡Más profúndo!" [Oh deeper, Adam! Deeper!] Enrico was rubbing his chest and breathing heavily while taunting Adam with cries of "thrusting and releasing, thrusting and releasing" and feigning the comments of Gus's mother, an elderly and heavy-set Chilean immigrant woman with whom Adam had nothing in common.

On the last day of May, Adam felt uncomfortable at the weekly gathering. During the evening, M-C saw Vittorio talking to Adam and she decided to snoop around, watching and listening, observing and following them. At her insistence they left by stealth (without Vittorio), this time to Adam's apartment. She never said she asked permission from Vittorio's Orientor (Colleen) to have sex with Vittorio. In the car, she told Adam she had visited Enrico for a structural supper in March. "Where's Adam?" M-C had asked Enrico. According to M-C, Enrico said "Oh, he's out now. He'll probably be back later ... you know, he really *likes* you." Adam had arrived home in the middle of it, when they were having a pasta supper.

In the present, Adam needed to know what came after that, i.e. what happened and what was said between them after that meeting in March until the Friday in May. Adam asked M-C, but she would not tell him. When she and Enrico were in the same room, they were like matter and anti-matter. She said she had felt uncomfortable with Adam after Enrico made that remark in March. It did not make sense that she could have been uncomfortable with Adam while still demanding sex, as she did on the Friday in May. Somebody must have urged her to do it. Adam wanted to know more about the origins of her designs on him.

At Frère-André, Adam tried to get M-C to tell him more about the events between March and May. She resisted talking about it. She said it made her very uncomfortable to be in the room knowing that Enrico was in the next room. Her private discomfort never prevented her from praising Enrico in public, calling him by the nickname "Maestro" or adopting his expressions like "Know what I mean, jelly bean?" as her own. She sought Adam's support for her unresolved feelings about Enrico. Adam held her in his arms and supported her in her feelings. She was extremely responsive to this and she started kissing and groping him. M-C engaged in a long and active night of sexual assault against Adam. First with her mouth, then full penetration up to and including ejaculation. They were still awake at five thirty in the morning when people in the lane started making noise. They fell asleep soon after.

That day, they were both uneasy being near Enrico. This was the start of the annual summer festival season, the high point of outdoor fun and social rituals to which Montrealers looked forward after the long winter. Adam told her he wanted to see the fireworks and enjoy the weekend with her, as friends. She refused everything, saying that she wanted to stay in bed with him and have more sex. Adam returned to his bedroom with her so they could talk about it in private, away from Enrico. M-C cut the talking short and began touching and kissing Adam. "What I'm trying to say is I love it when you tell me you love me. I know I told you it's not good for my process if you show it too much. Well, I changed my mind," she said. She liberated his penis from his pants and performed oral sex on him until an erection was achieved. She undressed herself then undressed him; she guided his penis inside her and assaulted him. This was M-C's "reproduce-her-domestic-mistakes-with-Enrico" assault.

During that weekend, M-C asked Adam about his images of her. Musing out loud, he got carried away and innocently said he wanted to live with her, but he did not mean for her to take that idea seriously or act upon it. M-C knew this and said so in a letter sent by Bulletin Board System the first Tuesday in June:

> Quand je t'ai dit que je voulais vivre avec toi ... Ta reaction m'a decontenance, je me suis sentie rejete ... j'ai percu une prudence, un recul que je n'avais pas senti avant ... voila que je percevais des barrieres chez toi ... tu voulais te rehabiller ... tu voulais reculer un peu, patienter, ne pas brusquer les choses.
> [When I told you I wanted to live with you ... Your reaction took me aback, I felt rejected ... I perceived a caution, a step back that I had not felt before ... now I perceived barriers on your side ... you wanted to get dressed ... you wanted to step back a little, to wait, not rush things.]

M-C dishonestly manipulated his feelings and pushed him towards living with her as a symbol of his devotion to her. As she had always intended, she repeated with Adam her own stated error of living with Vittorio after only a month. She made no attempt to give Adam his freedom. The same weekend, he pointed out that their plans to see the fireworks had been thwarted.

"I don't feel it's necessary to saturate ourselves with each other so much. We could do things with other people also, do things outside, include a circle of friends," he told her. She agreed to this in principle, stating emphatically that she wanted to have fun. Later in the day, she told him by phone she had vomited after returning to Waverly and that she vomited when she was in profound contradiction. Adam understood her profound contradiction to mean that she was not serious about their friendship; rather, the prospect of being his friend made her physically ill.

On Monday, they had many issues to discuss which had never been properly addressed, including how and why she was demanding sex from him. Hesitant to call her, Adam needed to confide in a closer friend than Curly or Popo, so he contacted Raymond and chose to share with him part of the sexual transactions since May. Raymond was

The Sun, the Moon and the Truth

very surprised and could not picture the two of them as a couple. He helped Adam prepare for his phone call to M-C as best he could. Given her habit of screaming at him, Adam tried talking to her very gently. He got no answer from her at all; he sensed that she was depriving him of her contact in order to punish him for having made their friendship a top priority. She admitted that the next day when she finally broke her silence and sent him a letter. In her letter, she confirmed she did not accept his vision of their friendship. She admitted the friendship had not gone according to plan from the outset:

> Je me croyait forte…et je croyais que si quelque chose se passerait, ce serait toi qui tomberais en amour et que moi non; et comme je ne voulais pas te blesser, je me suis assure d'etablir des limites tres claires des le depart.
> [I thought I was strong … and I thought if anything happened, it would be you who would fall in love and not me and as I did not want to hurt you … I made sure to set very clear limits from the start.]

About the weekend they had spent together, she said:

> Je me suis sentie mal quand tu ma dit…que ce serait exagere d'tre [sic] avec moi hier soir quand on a passe toute la fin de semaine ensemble.
> [I felt bad when you told me … that it would be too much to be with me last night when we spent the whole weekend together.]

M-C also amused herself by manipulating his own feelings:

> Je me suis sentie mal quand tu ma dit que tu exagerais, que tu allais faire attention de ne pas trop dire 'Je t'aime'…
> [I felt bad when you told me you were exaggerating, that you would be careful not to say 'I love

you' too much...]

    M-C then reversed her own terms, mixing French and English: Ca me fait du bien de sentir que tu fais attention a moi, [It's a good feeling to know that you pay attention to me] 'that you care.'

With Machiavellian skill, she tricked him to her give her even more affection, without answering how or when they would be friends outside of the Movement. She forced him to fall in love with her as an efficient means to keep him in her orbit, to prolong her assaults against him as she pleased. Adam was left more confused than ever while M-C's increased sexual pressure on him continued to accumulate.

VII — NOTES FROM CUBA

[The water is like that of tall mountains, glacier water. I gaze without quenching my thirst completely and this beauty is like a wound … I can almost feel the pain!]
— Marie-Claude Desrochers

ON THE THIRD weekend in May, Josh was in town for a planned meeting with some Team Delegates from Ontario. As Josh's executive secretary, M-C knew she would be busy that weekend, because she planned the visit herself. Thus, that Friday in May was her best chance to trap Adam when he was most vulnerable and she was most available. Colleen arrived at the gathering well before M-C.

« Scuse-moi, Frank! » [Excuse me, Frank!] Colleen said to Adam as she burned her lit cigarette into his hand.

He wondered if this was Colleen's way of showing her disapproval of his being close to M-C in a sexual way. But he asked himself how Colleen could know anything about that if M-C had told him not to tell anyone in the Movement about their sexual contact. Could Colleen have already known something about it before him, just like Enrico? Colleen and M-C had been close friends since their childhood in Laval.

When M-C arrived with a bag from McDonalds, this was the first time Adam had her seen with people from their council after their first night together. She instilled an atmosphere of secrecy and put a great deal of pressure on Adam not to say anything about the sexual incidents, not to act amorously toward her and not to touch her in any way. Adam very much resented the repression. Despite this, she made passionate eyes and sexual innuendos to him. "Conserve your energy for later…" she said between bites of her hamburger. By these gestures, she made it clear that she expected sex from him later that night. Adam was being dishonestly maneuvered into a compromising position once again. Indeed, she was doing to him what she forbade him doing. Her acts carried the risk of public exposure and were in open defiance of her own stated wishes. Her many threats and interdictions applied only to him, not to herself. They were surrounded by her Team Delegate peers Colleen and Enrico, both seemingly aware of the situation.

They had agreed earlier in the week that Adam would go to Waverly with her on Friday night. There was talk of M-C attending private social meetings with the Council of Team Delegates, given Josh was in town. Despite their agreed plans, she offered Adam's bedroom at Frère-André to Josh as a result of the adjusted sleep quarters, while "forgetting" she had left a personal letter for Adam on his bed. Josh found the letter, read it and kept it for himself. In addition to Team Delegates Enrico and Colleen knowing and approving of M-C's sexual abuse of Adam, Josh was now also aware. The same evening, M-C said to Adam, « J'ai toujours eu tendance à attirer des gars qui étaient dépendant émotivement sur moi ». [I always had a tendency to attract guys who were emotionally dependent on me.] She walked over to him, put her arms around him and continued, « Mais je sais que çe n'est pas le cas avec toi » [But I know that's not the case with you] and added plainly, "Don't fall in love with me," thereby contradicting her earlier amorous overtures that same evening.

Adam was to go with M-C in her car to Waverly. Before she got in, however, she asked Fan's permission to give him a lift. From his place in the back seat, he felt ill at ease with Fan because she also ordered Adam from the front passenger seat to massage her neck during the ride. Worse, Fan made a sexual joke aimed directly at M-C and Adam: « Vous autres-là, quand vous faites l'amour, est-ce que vous buvez du Pepsi? » [You guys, when you make love, do you drink Pepsi?]

Adam froze up with fear and stopped massaging her neck at once, while M-C and Fan laughed together at his surprise and alarm. Fan had a high-pitched girlish voice and a jarring laugh like a hyena whose genitals have just been slammed in a car door while watching a particularly funny movie. Adam wondered how Fan could have known so quickly and who told her. Just as Colleen, Enrico and Josh already knew, could M-C have told Fan also, once again in open defiance of her own conditions? The two Team Delegate peers laughed together at how nervous Adam was.

Short days earlier, Adam had wanted to enlist the support of the Council of Team Delegates against M-C. Now, the situation was exactly the opposite as M-C lined up her allies: Josh, Enrico, Colleen, Fan. After they dropped Fan off, M-C continued to Waverly.

She asked him if he would be capable of having sex with her without falling in love. Adam said that no matter what happened he would try hard not to fall in love with her, since it seemed so important to her and he wanted to remain friends.

« Déjà là, y'a un petit quelque chose qui commence à se former. Je le resens chez toi. » [Already, there's a little something starting to grow inside you. I feel it in you] she said.

Adam was very surprised and unaware he had any love for her, and equally surprised she could feel any. By her own terms, she had to release him from the sexual obligation, given that she saw him falling in love with her and she claimed to want to prevent his suffering.

On Saturday, Adam felt uncomfortable at the council meeting given by Josh. Nor did he approve of M-C's plan to simply "disappear" from the meeting without saying goodbye to everyone, as he usually would have. She insisted they leave by stealth. He wondered if people would not notice that he and M-C had vanished together at the same time, betraying the secret she had required him to keep. In her car, she told him about the importance of stealth to prevent creating "noise" in the structure. "Out of all the men in the council, I chose you," she added. He asked her why they had to keep the sexual contact secret. "It has to be that way! There's no other choice!" she insisted so emphatically that he could never raise the topic again.

M-C said she had an affair with a man in the structure, several years ago. They were also stealthy in their relationship. He used her for convenient sex after the meetings and treated her badly. Adam again asked her to review the events leading up to that Friday in May and to clarify her intentions. M-C told him she met the previous December with Colleen and her boyfriend Dennis, and they said M-C should get involved with Adam. M-C doubted whether it would work then asked herself, *Why not with Adam? Why not?* At that point, if she wanted just his friendship, why hadn't she called him well before? Allowing for the holidays and his return from Chile in January, she had four months to get to know him.

« C'est pour ça que je t'ai invité d'aller au cinéma avec moi: d'habitude j'aime connaître un gars avant de coucher avec. » [That's why I invited you to see a movie with me: I usually like to get to know a guy before sleeping with him,] M-C added during the same exchange, revealing the *true* reason for their Tuesday evening meeting eleven days after the fact. At the time, she said it was for coffee and a movie.

During the same conversation, they reviewed the events of the Tuesday in question, when she drove him home and Adam offered her coffee. She said to him in an accusatory tone, « Çe soir-là, quand je t'ai reconduit chez toi, tu pensais que j'étais pour monter? » [That evening, when I drove you home, did you think I would go upstairs?]

She insinuated that the situation was not safe for her, even though she had already planned to sexually assault him. While she declined coffee in his apartment, she offered him the same drink in her place only three evenings later. A mere eight days after that Friday in May, Adam visited her at Waverly and brought with him a recording of instrumental music, since they had agreed to develop their friendship. Instead, M-C set the tape aside and sat with him on her sofa, kissing and touching him all over while pulling down his pants; he felt immobilized. She assaulted him with her mouth and, unexpectedly the Force started to rise in his chest. The experience of combining sexual assault with the tingling expansion and contraction of the Force was incredibly powerful. On her carpet, she continued assaulting him with her vagina while the pain mingled with the pleasure up to and including ejaculation. Adam was left spiritually sexually and structurally confused. This was Marie-Claude's "coffee and stealth" assault.

Notes from Cuba

* * *

Sunday morning, M-C left for Cuba on vacation. She knew in advance that she was going. Thus, when she said, "It has to be tonight!" she knew that was her best chance to trap Adam. He was most vulnerable, and she was most available. When Adam returned home, Josh had slept in his bed, but there was no sign of the note from M-C. It was suspicious that she left such a note for Adam when she had personally arranged for Josh to occupy his bed. It was very unsettling to have the General Delegate know his sexual business, and Adam was also fearful that Josh would discuss it with Enrico. On Monday, Adam called Josh in Toronto and asked about M-C's note. "It was a kind of 'last farewell,'" Josh said. Adam asked Josh if he could have it back. "I don't know what I did with it," Josh said. History does not record what Josh did with the note.

Less than two weeks after M-C threatened him not to tell anyone, Team Delegates Enrico, Colleen and Fan, in addition to Josh, now seemed to know more private information about his sex life than Adam expected. Just as Adam was "monkey in the middle" between M-C and Enrico, so was he kept seeking answers between M-C and Josh. On the last Sunday in May, Enrico got a phone call, during which he discussed Adam in the third person. "Guess who's coming to see you? Somebody who really likes you..." Enrico said after hanging up. Adam asked Enrico to tell him who it was, but he did not think it could be M-C, because she was in Cuba. Enrico made a sexual comment about M-C but would not say who the mystery caller was. Mere minutes after Enrico hung up, M-C arrived, much to Adam's surprise.

The first words out of her mouth were: « J'ai peur que tu changes. J'ai peur que ça devienne mécanique. » [I'm afraid that you change. I'm afraid of it becoming mechanical.]

Adam was alerted by the statement [I'm afraid that you could change], since it was the second time she had said that; he asked her to explain. In his bedroom, she told Adam she was very uncomfortable with Enrico around, but she did not say why. She gave a long and complicated explanation, which Adam found hard to understand. She did say, however, that she loved Adam's sexual performance, but feared that if he changed and stopped being himself, it would risk becoming "mechanical."

Adam asked himself why she should be afraid of him changing. How much could he change in the space of a few days or weeks? He reasoned she was not truly afraid of him changing; she was afraid of her *image* of him changing. It made sense that her image of him would change at that time, because they were in closer contact and learning about the other. Thus, the experience of becoming friends and learning about each other was a threat to M-C's fixed, perfect image of Adam as her ideal sexual slave. The direction of her pressure, since her "iron knees" assault, had been to duplicate the pleasure she had on that first night. This new development pressured and confused Adam more.

A few days after this, M-C sent him a letter titled "Notes From Cuba". It contained observations she had made during her recent vacation. Adam read it several times because it was in French and there were many layers of meaning and vocabulary he did not understand. Several passages were very disturbing and he made a point of discussing the letter in person with M-C the next time he saw her. In one of these passages, Adam was surprised and alarmed when she compared the "beauty" of the Cuban waters to a "wound," the sensation of pain it gave her — and the ease with which she moved between beauty and pain.

> L'eau est comme celle des hautes montagnes, l'eau des glaciers. Je regarde sans pouvoir m'abreuver totalement et cette beaute est comme une blessure … Je sens presque la douleur!
>
> [The water is like that of tall mountains, glacier water. I gaze without quenching my thirst completely and this beauty is like a wound … I can almost feel the pain!]

With the letter in hand at Waverly and Adam's homemade pizza in the oven, Adam asked M-C to explain two other passages that confused him. First, they reviewed M-C's problem with her image of him, and the meaning of « floue ».

> Il me semble que tu es irreel. Ton image est floue …
> J'ai meme regarde ma petite photo prise a Kitchener pour voir a quoi tu ressembles vraiment. Ca m'a un peu surprise. [sic]
> [It seems to me that you are unreal. Your image is blurred ... I even looked at my little picture taken in Kitchener to see what you really look like. It was a little surprising.]

M-C explained that she had not known him before their first night together. In getting to know him since then, she had learned that Adam was completely different from his image and reputation in the Movement, and this was a great shock. She said that Adam was a beautiful person and went so far as to say that the other people in the council did not even know him the way she did, that she saw things in him nobody else did. M-C said « floue » [blurry] was like when the image on the television screen was distorted or lost completely. Then he asked her about the problematic word « graver ». Everything turned on « graver ».

> On dirait que mes souvenirs des douces et longues nuits passees avant mon depart n'ont pas suffit a graver ton image.
> [It seems that my memories of the sweet and long nights spent before I left were not enough to (engrave?) your image.]

There were many explanations, but she could not get him to understand « graver »; there was talk about "engraving" and other processes. Eventually, Adam understood « graver » to mean "replace her previous image of him with a new image." He asked what was wrong with her previous image of him. She avoided that question, saying she hadn't known him back then, and her new image of him was entirely positive. At first, her comments seemed to be a compliment, especially considering her laudatory comments on page 3 of the same letter:

> Ou as-tu appris a aimer comme ca? Ces gestes qui semblent te venir si facilement, ces caresses, ces baisers, ces mots doux murmures a mon oreille, ces gestes lents, precis qui font monter en moi le desir jusqu'a ce que j'ai l'impression que je vais exploser. Comme un volcan qu'on finissait plus d'eteindre...Ce soir, je me tortillerait surement dans mon lit en pensant a toi.
> [Where did you learn to make love like that? Those gestures that you seem to come by so easily, these caresses, kisses, gentle words whispered in my ear, these slow movements, precise and that increase the desire in me until I feel I will explode. Like a volcano that could no longer be extinguished ... Tonight, I shall surely twist and turn in my bed thinking of you.]

Despite this stunning vote of confidence, he wasn't doing anything special, and her explanations did not reassure him at all. Rather, he was forced to question himself again about her intentions, in this new light. If, as M-C claimed, she discovered Adam was such a beautiful person only after their first night together, how was she able to tell him specifically he was « une belle personne » [a beautiful person] five days earlier?

If she really wanted to be his friend, why had she been so surprised to learn that Adam was a beautiful person? What was her interest in becoming his friend? Why was it so painful for her to get to know him, to see her image of him change, since the events of her "iron knees" assault, especially? If her experience of getting to know him as a person and a friend was so painful for her, why did she bother? Why should M-C be so surprised that he "made love" as she described above, if she already saw him as a beautiful person? Did not one follow from the other? If she feared that any further changes in her perception of him would diminish her enjoyment of his sexual performance, would that put their friendship on hiatus? If Adam had to hold back or conceal his true personality from M-C just to satisfy her sexually, did that not make him her slave and she his mistress? Would Adam be able to withstand the tremendous pressure on him to live up to and duplicate the glowing service rating she gave him on page 3 of her "Notes From Cuba?" Could Adam repeat the same quality sexual experience for M-C using a production line mentality, while suppressing his own personality? Would the conflicting forces tear him apart? What were the implications of the previous ten points for his participation in the Movement — an organization that placed the Human Being as the central value in its philosophy?

How could the Movement continue to advocate "Humanizing the Earth" to make the world a more human place to live, while it opposed violence and discrimination in all its forms? How could it still favour open communication between its members in such a Movement where M-C had been and still was his model?

The homemade pizza Adam made for the three of them at supper was so delicious, Rania started to like him more. Adam slept while M-C tippy-toed to the kitchen at two in the morning to savour the last slice from the fridge.

VIII — THE SPIDER AND HER PREY

*"The victim is caught in a spider-web,
held captive at another's disposal, bound psychologically,
and anesthetized. He is completely unconscious of what has happened."*
— Marie-France Hirigoyen

M-C FIRST started insulting herself and her body during her "iron knees" assault. That particular afternoon, she was ashamed of showing Adam her body in daylight, afraid of what he would think of her stretch marks after childbirth. Adam was a young man with a very big heart. Emotionally, he was still like a teenager and absolutely detested hearing a woman insult herself if he had already had sexual contact with her. Despite his best efforts to avoid falling in love with her, she succeeded in getting him to get closer, to comfort her, to see her as vulnerable, to forget about what she was doing to him. Her sophisticated techniques of emotional and sexual manipulation, compounded by her sexual assaults, gravely damaged his emotional health. She used self-deprecation to plant in Adam the seeds of Stockholm syndrome and cultivated it all summer to control him.

With each subsequent assault, she insulted another part of her body: her breasts were too saggy, her knees too bandy, her mouth too triangular or her vagina too loose. Each time, she tricked him into comforting and reassuring her about her womanhood. During successive sexual assaults, she insulted her own intellectual abilities saying, « Je connais rien, moi » [I'm a know-nothing.]

She also insulted her career success, her lack of ambition, her abilities as a mother for Rania, her chameleon personality and her lack of personal warmth. M-C continued with more insults against her body; Adam augmented his efforts to be sensitive with her and to show her that she was feminine and sexy. For each self-deprecation, he felt compelled to comfort and reassure her. On each separate night, he took her in his arms and told her she was a good person, a good mother for Rania, a smart woman with lots of administrative skill, a nice person, and a likeable person.

M-C told him about previous men who had been rough with her; men who expected her to support them financially; boys who rejected her; men who had done every kind of nasty thing to her including sodomize her without permission or even lubricant. She told Adam about a boyfriend with whom she shared an apartment owned by her grandmother on de Normanville Street north of Beaubien in the La Petite Patrie neighbourhood, an impoverished and less interesting colony of the Plateau. Since the apartment had sentimental and patrimonial value, she objected when the boyfriend renovated it contrary to her wishes. To aggravate matters, the boyfriend lost his way in the renovations, ran out of money and completely destroyed the kitchen; she was reduced to washing dishes in the bathtub. By impressing these sad stories upon Adam, she got him to see her as a victim and further distracted him from confronting her about the genesis of their relationship. Adam felt bad for her that she never had a good relationship with a man and tried to be extra gentle with her. Throughout it all, he always saw her as his friend and cleaved to their Movement solidarity.

During one of her early assaults in May, M-C yelped in pain. Startled, Adam asked her what was wrong. She became more agitated, telling him that his penis had gone all the way to touch a sensitive spot, and this produced a sharp pain. He didn't know what that meant, but he felt bad for her. She acted like he had hurt her on purpose. He withdrew completely and tried to console her. He told her he didn't mean to hurt her and would never hurt her on purpose. She said she didn't think he had done it on purpose, but she never seemed to believe him. After that, he tried to be careful and extra gentle with her, as she explained to him up to what level he should penetrate her, but not beyond. He tried to make her experience as pleasurable as possible, so she should never feel pain. The more gentle and caring he was with her, the better her sensation was and the more she enjoyed sexually assaulting him. In so doing, he was conditioned to please her and never confront her on the important issues they still needed to discuss. Once he was emotionally dependent on her, she shifted tactics away from self-deprecation and began insulting him with increasing frequency and meanness.

M-C spoke like a common whore and spoke of sexuality in a crude, vulgar way, unlike any girl he had ever been with. She took her temperature every morning even when she wasn't sick and kept detailed accounts of sexual acts performed.

"Stop it, it's disgusting!" he told her, since this offended him greatly. He convinced her not to talk that way, but to treat herself with more respect and allow him to respect her also. She absolutely adored his humanistic approach to sexuality, and she fell even more deeply in love with him! She continued her self-deprecation by insulting her vagina, saying that it was inadequate to satisfy a man since it had been stretched out of shape from childbirth. « De penser qu'un enfant est passé par là. » [To think that a child passed through there.]

When she said that, he felt crushed and crooked. He was still concerned for her self-image after her recent insults against her body during the recent assaults. He tried so hard to reassure her there was nothing wrong with her vagina. M-C rolled the covers down off him and handled his penis. He felt frozen. She assaulted him first with her mouth, then with her newly revivified vagina. She exploited him masterfully and manipulated his behaviour. This was M-C's "self-deprecation" assault.

* * *

M-C asked Adam to spend the third week of June with her so she could have the experience of living with him. She allowed him to bring his own toothbrush. Just as Adam had warmed to her personality the previous year, he began to see Waverly was not such a bad place either. The best thing for Adam was that Enrico was never there. She lived upstairs from the landlord in a spacious apartment that Montrealers called a "five and half." From the front door, her bedroom was at immediate right and Rania's the last door on the right, after the linen closet. The kitchen was dead centre after the interceding lobby. The living room was on the immediate left, the bathroom next and her computer room/office the last door on the left. There, M-C excelled at her paperwork, for which Adam admired her administrative efficiency. Unlike Frère-André, Waverly was bright, clean and had a feminine touch.

The preceding weekend, he had tried to clarify the situation with her by reviewing events since their first night together. They talked about starting from zero, though no progress was made. On Monday, she was talking with Josh on the phone while Adam brought out a surprise — a new jar of cocoa butter cream to rub on her feet, which she enjoyed with great pleasure; sometimes she fell asleep swiftly when he massaged her feet with regular hand cream, and he later used that as a strategy to evade sex with her. When he showed her the jar of cocoa butter cream, she thought it was a gun he had brought to shoot her. She started crying and was completely hysterical. She begged him never to surprise her ever again. Adam agreed not to surprise her anymore but asked himself how and when he had picked her as his mate. He could not remember and it troubled him; he blamed his lack of memory on the accident.

Other times that week, he leaned out the bathroom door to talk with her while flossing his teeth; she thought the dental floss was a rope he would use to strangle her. He hugged her from behind and asked her about her day; she began trembling and appeared terrified. He shifted his weight on the sofa and she jumped out of her skin. It seemed he was a stranger in her home and she did not know him. Half the time, she was like a small, lonely, pathetic wild animal, shivering in the cold rain. Otherwise, she was an aggressive sexual predator, hurting him at will with great pleasure and cruelty. These radical fluctuations in her personality made it exquisitely painful for him to be near her, destabilized his own personality and distracted him from his own problems. Indeed, close exposure between them was sudden and overly intense, as per her wishes. It was not the friendship they had agreed to. Adam's reaction was like that of Gulliver in the Land Of Giants. M-C seemed larger than life to Adam, and all her defects were magnified to the point where he could see nothing else in her. Adam felt Lilliputian in comparison as his life became dominated by trying to solve *her* problems!

On the third Tuesday in June, she called in sick from work so she could do her administrative work for the Movement, relating to the preparation of the council's census report. For background music, she played the instrumental tape Adam had given her, a New Age collaboration by a Greek musician and a British vocalist, and she especially liked the saxophone solo, saying it was "like music to my clitoris." She was in conflict, since she felt guilty about calling in sick when she was not really sick; she also felt excited and under pressure from Josh to write her census report. She was also sexually aroused and looked to Adam to give her sex. She decided that she would have sex with him and this sensation excited her greatly when she knew that her work mates were at work while she was at home having sex. That way, she claimed she could use her sexual energy to convert her guilt into pleasure, then be freed to write her report.

She asked Adam to rub her back while she lay on her bed. He said they could play a game called "blackboard" and explained that he would write out letters on her back with his finger and she had to guess what the letters spelled in words; an open palm lay flat on her back would be a blank space between words. She had a feminine back worthy of an expensive dress. She agreed to his rules of play and was hoping for an easy word like "cat" or "bird" when he spelled out "ANTI-NUCLEAR SHELTER" and protested it was too easy when she couldn't guess right.

He tried a second time, this time tracing "NEBUCHADNEZZAR KING OF BABYLON" but she was stumped. "Oh, I hardly think you're trying, Marie-Claude," he said and they both had a good laugh. In these spare moments of domestic fun when she was not being tempestuous and irascible, the question "Marie-Claude, you remember that Friday in May? Did you happen to rape me that night? Because

I kind of got the feeling you did" came to his mind, but he thought better of asking it. She claimed the game had stimulated her already heightened libido when she liberated his penis from his pants. She assaulted him with her mouth, then lay crossways on the bed and beckoned him to perform oral sex on her. She had several orgasms and told him that he could penetrate her any time. He did not want to — she would have to be satisfied with her orgasms. She asked him several more times to penetrate her: « On dirait que tu sais exactement quoi faire pour faire plaisir à une femme » [It's as if you know exactly what to do to please a woman]. She pleaded with him to lay on top of her and he refused her, after which she inserted his penis inside her vagina and assaulted him. This was M-C's "guilt-into-pleasure" assault.

* * *

At Waverly he always told her, "I wouldn't hurt you. I just want to be your friend," each time she was sexually aroused and during her assaults. The morning after, he did not understand the rush of emotions and had trouble dealing with them. He started to cry, not knowing why. He wanted her to comfort him, to hug or console him but she would not or seldom for more than a few seconds. He had shortness of breath with tension in his chest, followed by several staccato exhalations. On one such occasion, he was in turbulent emotional straits and called out, "Help me!"

She started dry heaving instantly and her body convulsed at her solar plexus. "I can't even help myself!" she cried out. During these moments Adam told her he felt weak and needed her to be strong for him, as his new friend. She found his crying, his hard breathing and sharp exhalations of breath, his weakness and pleas for friendship, sympathy and understanding an emotional burden, but refused to release him. For her part, M-C also had frequent emotional scenes, often on the same topics where she had refused to help Adam; now she expected him to comfort her. She exploited his sympathy and tricked him into becoming emotionally dependent on helping her with her own emotions. Adam could not be financially dependent on her but she indulged in his emotional support for dealing with her career. She was distressed because her job was being eliminated and she would be reassigned to data entry. She accepted all his comfort but justified her refusal to help Adam, saying about herself, "I'm not a loving person."

Adam's efforts at communication with M-C were lost in the vortex that swirled around her like a tornado around the Tower of Babel. Beginning in May, he tried many times to find quiet moments when he could talk to her about what had happened since they first had sex and where they were headed. She did not let him talk about it; she always wanted to leave the room, or she ordered him out with a stern question, « On y va? » [Ready to go?] Adam resisted and she quickly transformed her question into an order, « On y va! » [*We're going!*] He still wanted to talk while she pretended there was nothing to talk about. He could not go along with her order; she accused him of being insubordinate. The same thing happened at night when he wanted to talk to her about the situation and she said angrily, « *Bonne nuit!* » [*Good night!*] He had not finished talking and no progress was ever made.

Each time that she had screamed at him, it made him more withdrawn, more afraid of her and less able to express himself freely. Every time he initiated a discussion, he was more careful, quiet and cautious and spoke to her in a very gentle and soft voice. She asked him to speak louder; he was hesitant as he tried to bring up the subject of that Friday in May without offending her. Invariably, the phone rang just then, and M-C engaged in long conversations, and their quiet talk was put on hold. Alternatively, she was paged with an audible ping through her computer to respond to a request as system operator of the BBS. When her phone call or BBS business was over, she grew impatient with Adam and asked him to wrap up his points quickly. She had to tend to Rania or Movement business. Yet, he still had not said anything!

She screamed in his face that he was too gentle with her, he talked too low, he whispered. She ridiculed to his face his way of talking to her gently; it destroyed his small remaining confidence. Adam's efforts at communication with M-C were further impeded by the spectre of Vittorio and regular phone calls from mysterious and anonymous men who sought her emotional support for reasons she did not disclose. She often had angry phone calls with Vittorio, with whom she had much unsettled business including his on-again membership in Colleen's team and off-again departures, which M-C claimed he did to spite her. She told Adam that Vittorio had become alienated by her work in the Movement because it took up so much of her time and she was never available for him. Vittorio complained that every time he tried talking with her, the phone would ring or she would attend to the BBS or other business.

By the third Wednesday in June, Adam was extremely hurt and wounded by M-C. He found verbal communication with her impossible, so he wrote a poem for her. His feelings were contorted, and he felt she did not have the right idea about him. Adam had a morning alone in Waverly and took time to reflect about how he could communicate to her in writing, since she would not let him talk. The result was the poem "Marie-Claude" below. In itself, the poem was a desperate plea for understanding since "desire" does not truly rhyme with "pleasure." The entire poem demonstrated the small, meek and wounded self-confidence with which Adam approached M-C on a daily basis, letting his poetic talent speak for him when his own voice failed.

> Feelings like never before
> Your heart an open door
> Through which perceive universe of pleasure
> Love, strength, friendship, desire
> Weakness, too, and health, humour and leisure
> Wisdom and kindness, all in good measure.
> Luck, learning, our blessings we bestow
> Through life's river we flow
> Together we grow, our souls we show
> A grander meaning may we know.
> For every day a helper, a healer, a beauty deeper
> Forever a lover, a hugger, a dreamer, a feeler.

He left it on the kitchen table and she found it upon her return from work. She loved the poem. They poured drinks and sat in the living room. He played Beethoven's Ninth Symphony on her stereo. He had loved this music so much ever since Raymond introduced it to him as the anthem of the Movement. He enjoyed listening to it, especially the crescendo "Ode to Joy" chorus, the lyrics of which Raymond had sung in German, much to Adam's delight. Adam thought he was finally starting to reach her as a friend. He looked her in the eye, apparently with a glimmer. She leapt to her feet and said angrily, "*Don't fall in love with me!*" She turned off the music, extinguishing the Movement's anthem. Adam was stunned. She kept the poem for some unknown reason, leaving him completely confused. After that, she cancelled their "friendship time" in the living room and ordered him to the bedroom, where she declared they would have sex, then she sexually assaulted him. This was M-C's "Ode-to-Joy" assault.

* * *

M-C was not receptive to the message Adam intended for her in his poem the previous day. After several weeks of these violent, artificially engineered sexual encounters, he was quite frustrated, inarticulate and at a loss what to do. Poetry had not worked the previous night, so on the afternoon of a Thursday in June, he tried prose. He wrote some notes to himself in the form of a draft letter and showed it to her when she came home. In the letter, he specifically said that he did not want to have sex with her if it meant that they could not be friends. After she read the letter, she handled the paper like it was a large turd and folded it with great disdain. M-C told him, "I do not want to see you tomorrow after the Friday night gathering. I want to be alone. I don't want to see you Saturday night – I want to be with my friends. I was invited to Colleen's for Saturday night. I never get to see my friends anymore because of you. You take up all of my time. Now will you let me see my friends?"

In excluding Adam from her list of "friends," namely Fan and Colleen, M-C showed that she was embarrassed and disgusted to know him. If she wanted to be his friend, why did she not invite him to meet her other friends? She never satisfied any of his written personal preferences to have a friendship without sex.

The following Saturday, at his request, they had another conversation, this time in Jarry Park, where the Montreal Expos had become the first Major League Baseball team outside of the United States and where Adam had enjoyed pleasant afternoons with his father. The discussion addressed her changing image of him; she reminded him that she had not known him before that Friday in May. She told him she did not suspect he would have "the new sensibility" or such a strong sensibility of any kind. She then restated that the people in the council did not know what was really inside him. She specifically said that kind of sensibility she expected to find in Team Delegates. It was very rare in a group delegate. With tears streaming down her cheeks, she cried out forcefully, « T'es *plein* de sensibilité! » [You're *full* of sensitivity!] The statement resounded as though M-C had underestimated his level of sensitivity and now it presented a problem for her. He wondered, "What is the problem?" Why should she regret that he was sensitive? Behind these questions lurked the questions he had asked himself after her "Notes from Cuba." These questions formed a barrier between his current conscious mind and the insanity of M-C's mind. Adam feared that if he thought the questions through and resolved them completely, the barrier between his conscious mind and the violence of M-C's mind would dissolve and he would be overtaken by it, just as he had feared with increasing intensity. She wanted to attend an Expos game with him. It never happened.

Then she gave her appreciation of their time together during the week. She said that he had been very nice to her. He made breakfast for her before she went to work, had lunch waiting for her when she came home, washed the dishes during the day and offered to run errands and make supper. She added, however, that he was far more emotionally dependent on her than she had expected, that she had become the meaning of his life, and that he was like a big baby, following her around everywhere, trying to please her. She specifically said that Adam had become as emotionally dependent on her as some of her previous boyfriends and that she felt he would fall apart if she disappeared from his life. Her statement hurt his feelings very badly and he started crying. M-C let him cry for a good long while then reached over and took him in her arms to comfort him for a few seconds. "I have an idea," she began. "Why don't we make love now?"

"What? I'm crying and upset. No, we can't do that!" Adam protested, still in tears. M-C took him home and ordered him to sit in the living room. She played the Kansas song "Dust in the Wind" on her stereo — purposefully picking that one from her record collection. She told him that their lives were transient and their relationships even more so. She said friendships are made and broken every day and their own would be broken very quickly. She would not think twice about hurting his feelings. M-C said the only way Adam could evolve as a person was to have as many meaningless relationships as possible in rapid succession, each one including meaningless sex. Enrico and Gus had also told Adam the same, as had Pigpen, Yorgo, Fan and Josh, who remarked to Adam about his friendship with M-C: "Enjoy it while it lasts."

M-C told Adam that he fooled himself by seeking meaning in friendships and in so doing enchained himself to a search for meaning. There could be no doubt remaining about the lesson the Council of Team Delegates wished Adam to learn, starting with the Swiss girl in Chile. M-C danced, sang and acted out the lyrics, then went much closer to rub the following lyrics in his face, to tell him her friendship was as much a fraud as herself:

> "Don't hang on
> Nothing lasts forever, but the earth and sky
> It's there always
> And all your money won't another minute buy
> Dust in the wind … all we are is dust in the wind."

Once the song was over, M-C went over to him on the sofa and mockingly sang "Dust-in-the-Wind" in his face while she undressed him and pulled him down toward the floor, on top of her. Adam was crying profusely and begging her to stop, saying, "No, no. I don't want to."

M-C shook her head, said, "Yes, yes," interspersed with the lyrics of the song. She pulled him on top of her and guided his penis inside her. She continued her "Dust-in-the-Wind" assault on the living room carpet up to and including ejaculation.

On the last Friday in June, M-C was on vacation. Adam was very sick owing to an aggravation of his sinus problem. His doctor had prescribed decongestant for the condition. Adam bought the extra-strength variety, which induces sleepiness. He had taken too large a dose, not knowing that a smaller pill of the regular strength would have worked. When M-C arrived at the social gathering on Querbes Street in Outremont, she was extremely disappointed and angry to learn that Adam was sick, blaming him. « C'est plate! T'es toujours malade! » [It's no fun! You're always sick !]

They stayed only briefly at the gathering, long enough to play games, then went to see a movie together. M-C didn't understand the cultural landscapes and Adam had not the energy to explain. During the movie, he felt his body being completely consumed by the effect of the decongestant; he was falling asleep in the cinema. During the car ride home, he explained to her what was happening to him, that he was falling asleep because of the medicine and that he would go straight to bed after arrival. Once inside Waverly, he went to bed very quickly. M-C climbed on top of him and assaulted him with her vagina.

The next day, they went for a meal at his favourite restaurant in Montreal's Chinatown, where he had had a memorable meal with Raymond early in their friendship and Raymond demonstrated his fluency in Mandarin only to be laughed down and pointed at by the Chinese waiters who scoffed at his McGill education.

There, M-C looked at Adam with the exact same expression in her eyes as she forbade him from showing her only ten days earlier during the events of her "Ode-to-Joy" assault. « Qu'est-ce que tu vois dans mes yeux? » [What do you see in my eyes?] she asked with deep love in her eyes.

Adam felt very uncomfortable because of her interdiction against the same look in his eyes, while her own seemed extremely sincere. "I don't want this evening to end," M-C said longingly, passionately, holding out romantic love as a privileged substance of which Team Delegates could enjoy freely but group delegates could partake only if they were offered.

Driving home to Waverly, Adam told her that he was exhausted, still feeling the effects of the decongestant. When they got home he staggered into bed at once to sleep. She leaned over him and, faking concern asked, "Are you okay, sweetheart?"

Nearly asleep, Adam was barely able to answer. "I'm okay sweetheart, I'm just very, very tired." Half-asleep and just milliseconds from slumber, he then felt her all over his body; she mounted him and assaulted him by inserting his penis in her vagina. M-C deliberately made certain that Adam was tired before she had sex with him against his will. Just as Enrico was an incubus who hypnotized and had sex with women, so M-C was a succubus plaguing Adam with her nocturnal twinned "sick not an excuse" assaults. At some point during the assault, she said she needed to "fill up on sex" with him, because she would not see him for several days.

The day after this assault, M-C left to Mexico for an international meeting to "Humanize the Earth." Before leaving, however, she warned him she could meet, fall in love and have sex with any man in Mexico and she would feel no loyalty to Adam or their relationship, just as she had warned before her trip to Cuba. In both cases, she reminded Adam that their friendship would be transient until she found a real man, and Adam was not to take her for granted or become possessive of her. She also gave him his own key to Waverly in case he missed her and wanted to sleep there in her absence. She returned in July, where she saw Adam at a social gathering of the Movement. Popo also attended, having also returned from Mexico. M-C listened in on the edges of their conversation as Popo related to Adam how Gus had urged teenaged Popo to "sleep with every girl" in Mexico. M-C asked Popo if he had success following through on Gus's advice. Popo shot back to her face, « Pas de tes crisse d'oignons! » [None of your damned business!] Adam wished he could be more like Popo.

M-C enlisted Adam to tag along with her and Rania during their vacation in the Lanaudière Region of Quebec, north of Montreal, for three days and two nights in mid-July. "You're part of my life now," she told him in her car en route via the county of her paternal ancestors. Although he had no job, he welcomed the vacation. He felt calm, though his mind always harboured a doubt about her intentions. When they arrived there were family games and activities like horseshoe toss, the beanbag toss and nature trails, swimming and a sandy beach where children built sandcastles and destroyed them just as pointlessly. At the archery field, fellow vacationers referred to Adam as Rania's father, and he was quick to correct them.

The fresh country air gave Adam an appetite as he finished Rania's and M-C's suppers after polishing off his own. Their room had two bunk beds in it, one for Rania, one for M-C and Adam. With Rania asleep after dark, they went out to contemplate the tall pines and starry sky of their native province. Adam recited a poem by moonlight for M-C that contemplated giving new names to the stars, which she found beautiful. It was a perfect evening; the air was still and the deep Laurentian forest utterly silent. He pointed out the Big Dipper, but she didn't understand how a saucepan could be in the sky. The excitement of a shooting star rescued him from having to explain it further.

Their beds were nothing more than thin, foam mattresses, not very comfortable and quite cold. M-C told him that she wanted to have sex with him. He said they should not have sex because Rania was there, sleeping. M-C said that didn't change anything, that she could have sex with her child in the same room, as long as Rania was sleeping. Then Adam resisted again by saying the mattress was too uncomfortable to have sex on. She refused that answer also and grew angrier with him with each passing second. She told him the true reason why she had brought him there was to have sex with her and restated angrily she expected it now, or she would be insulted. Adam had to submit because she recapitulated all the previous threats she had made to him during her previous assaults. The second day, M-C demanded sex from Adam again and this time made it clear from the outset that she would not tolerate any kind of stalling or delaying tactics as she had the previous day. She ordered him based solely on her position of power over him in the organic structure of the Movement.

Lies My Guru Told Me

These were M-C's twinned "vacation-toy-boy" assaults.

On a Sunday morning in July, Adam awoke in M-C's bed, after a night during which she had sexually assaulted him. He was a caretaker for a cat in Laval and had to visit the house twice a day and see to the needs of the cat. He got up from the bed and started to ready himself for his trip. M-C called out to him that she wanted him to stay in bed. She asked where he was going. Adam explained and said he would just take an hour.

M-C made several statements to prevent him from leaving freely. « Mais pourquoi ne l'as–tu pas nourri hier? Pourquoi est-ce qu'il mange tellement? Reste avec moi. » ["But why did you not feed him yesterday? Why does he eat so much? Stay with me."] « Mais il doit lui rester encore quelques grains dans son bol... »

[But he must still have some kibble in his bowl...] « Tu me laisses pour un chat? » [You're leaving me for a cat?] M-C made it sound like he was eloping with the cat, and she started to cry. Adam told M-C the cat didn't eat so much, but he just needed to be fed. She didn't buy it.

As a condition for his leaving, M-C made him promise to have sex with her upon returning from Laval as proof that he loved her more than he loved the cat. Adam did not consent. He was coerced and he was never truly free to leave Waverly at any time. This was Marie-Claude's "pet shop" assault. Soon after this, she told him she wanted to get a dog for Rania and asked for his approval. When he hesitated, she made him feel guilty for being mean. When he eventually caved in, M-C said she had just been testing him to see what kind of father Adam would be, and she would not get a dog after all.

M-C demonstrated what kind of mother she was for Rania with her telling of the turtle incident. She related how she and Vittorio drove Rania to a lake in the countryside, where they decided to dispose of Rania's pet turtle by releasing it into the lake. "Good thing it wasn't winter," Adam said.

"It *was* winter. Turtles don't mind a frozen lake because they are cold-blooded creatures," M-C replied. Even so, what kind of mother would expose her three-year-old to that horror? Adam felt a normal mother would not include the child on such a trip and would invent a white lie to comfort the child's concerns for her pet.

Earlier that week, she had sent him a few lines from a poem in French.

> Comme les cailloux que font danser sur l'eau calme les enfants des pecheurs et qui font parfois deux sauts et parfois vingt… Ainsi je ne sais point jusqu'où mon coeur lance par ta main douce se rendra palpiter sur l'eau grise des jours que j'ai cesse d'appeler ma jeunesse…
>
> [As the pebbles that the fishermen's children cause to dance on still water and skips sometimes twice and sometimes twenty times … Thus I know not just how far my heart cast by your soft hand will throb on the grisened waters of the days I have ceased to call my youth…]

When he read this poem on the BBS, he was touched, though did not fully understand her meaning. It was so much like her — dark, sombre, macabre, French, seductive, regretful, noncommittal and mournful.

Adam was at Frère-André without M-C at about one in the morning on the second Sunday in July when she called him. She said she was going over to scoop him up because she didn't want to sleep alone. When he met her outside, she was trembling nervously, and he was concerned for her. She said that she missed him terribly and just did not want to spend the night without him. She asked him if he would go with her to Waverly. Outside his apartment, he held her gently in his arms to warm and soothe her. He asked her why she was trembling. She claimed that passing ruffians had called out to her from Queen Mary Road and treated her like a common whore, asking her how much it would cost them for her services. Adam asked her why they did that. M-C said it was because she was wearing her white Indian-knit cotton blouse, the same blouse he often said was so attractive on her, so feminine. He felt really bad for her and suddenly protective. He gave her a warm, soft hug to reassure her, and noticed she was covered in goose bumps.

He asked if she wanted to come upstairs so he could make tea to help her relax. She said she would not feel comfortable if Enrico were home, and she used that as a pretext to maneuver Adam towards her own apartment. Adam specifically said he didn't want to have sex; she said he wouldn't have to, that she just wanted to sleep with him in the bed with her. Adam agreed to go with her on that condition.

Once at Waverly, they got into bed and Adam held her in his arms to calm and help her stop trembling. After a few minutes like this, she seemed calmer and told him « Je n'ai jamais vraiment eu de relation avec quelqu'un qui me stimule positivement ». [I have never really had a relationship with someone who stimulates me positively.] She rolled the covers down and said that he was the first man ever to ask how her day was, and she loved him for it. While she sexually assaulted him with her mouth, he felt his soul detach from his body and rise above the bed slowly to the ceiling, where it co-mingled with hers. He could see deep inside her and deeper inside their relationship than he had in her kitchen. Marie-Claude Desrochers was a beautiful person, and although she had forced him to fall in love with her like a mining engineer drilling for precious metals, his love came from within him and was his own genuine emotion, despite the pain of extraction. He loved Big Sister.

He flinched and instantly his soul fell all the way into his body lying on the bed below. The same instant, she mounted and assaulted him with her vagina and whispered in his ear, "I'm so happy my guide put you on my path," until his ejaculation. This was Marie-Claude's "Bastille Day" assault. The next morning, she revived their defunct moving plans and used the subject to manipulate him for the rest of the summer, much to Enrico's gleeful approval. "I knew it! I knew it!" Enrico exclaimed, adding "Now you will be a Daddy."

IX — THE SISTERHOOD AND HER WAR AGAINST MEN

"I am a man more sinned against than sinning."
—King Lear

IN THE AFTERNOON after her "guilt into pleasure" assault, M-C criticized her father Moritz's ability to please her mother Maureen sexually, saying, « Mon père est tellement nerveux tout le temps, je ne sais pas comment ma mère a fait pour le *tolérer* pendant quarante ans ». [My father is so nervous all the time, I don't know how my mother managed to *tolerate* him for forty years.]

She ridiculed Moritz's sexuality then walked around her kitchen imitating his gait and especially ridiculed his low-hanging testicles. She had also ridiculed her father in her "Notes from Cuba" letter. M-C ridiculed her brother Hugo for being dreamy and lost in the clouds and told Adam she did not like her brother Jean-Vivien because he used to pin her to the floor with his knees on her chest when she was twelve and he was sixteen. She also complained of being demeaned for being a girl, and she was still bitter over a family trip to Niagara Falls where she had been left behind for being too young, her parents preferring only the older children. M-C also related how she was raised in a racist atmosphere where Jews were despised and her father made anti-Semitic comments in their home. Moritz, it seemed, was a character who sometimes let fly with a loud fart at the supper table, then blamed M-C for it in front of everyone.

Her best childhood memories revolved around family outings like a fall day in her recessed mind when the entire family went apple-picking in Quebec's rich apple heartland. With six children and both parents plucking apples all day long, they had so many apples upon returning that Maureen's kitchen was overflowing with every type of apple dish for weeks: apple sauce, apple pies, apple cakes, baked apples with cinnamon, apple torts, apple crumble, oatmeal with apples, delicious sweet fresh McIntosh apples!

* * *

The eve of St-John-the-Baptist Day, M-C took Adam to her parents' house in Laval, where her family planned to celebrate Quebec's provincial holiday in the same home where she had grown up and where she had discovered her clitoris under the drip-drip of a leaky bathtub faucet.

They were both concerned about how she would introduce Adam to her family. After arriving, she introduced him as « mon muffin anglais » [My English muffin]. There, Adam met her two elder sisters, Goneril and Regan, for whom M-C had nothing but kind words, the two brothers Hugo and Jean-Vivien, whom she had criticized, and her parents. Goneril was a conservative and reserved homemaker, and Regan an illustrator of children's books who Adam found esoteric and disrespectful of tradition. Goneril had been educated at a convent where the Catholic nuns made her feel ill at ease about her sexuality and the discovery of her clitoris. Regan, as the next eldest daughter, was also expected to acquire Catholic values at the same convent where her parents had sent Goneril. After the end of the Duplessis era, M-C had narrowly escaped the same education as her sisters, and she imagined herself running across the open field of liberated sexuality wearing her slut sneakers with the nuns in hot pursuit. M-C wanted to reminisce with her sisters about code words such as "red alert" they had used as teenagers to discuss menstruation in mixed company. The eldest of four sisters, Goneril put her foot down and vetoed any such menstrual anecdotes.

Adam found Jean-Vivien abrasive and politically hyperactive; he seemed peeved when Adam compared him to noted French racist Jean-Marie Le Pen and asked Jean-Vivien why his parents gave him not one but two girl's names. Jean-Vivien nearly came to blows with

Adam. Hugo was indeed a dreamer yet much nicer than his brother and excelled at the same career as Moritz, one at which M-C had failed, which caused her to resent him. Her younger sister Desdemona had married outside of her gene pool and learned to speak Yiddish in the process. Being the youngest child, Desdemona was the last to leave the family home and the only one to live with their mother, Maureen, while Maureen suffered a severe depression.

Desdemona told Adam that she was the only sane person in her family and that all others were *meshugeh* [*crazy*], including M-C. Adam took an instant liking to Desdemona. Rania played and delighted on the floor with her many cousins, including Sofia and Casper. A free spirit, Hugo had engaged in geographical humour when he named his son Casper after the Caspian Sea, following Desdemona, who had named her daughter Sofia after the city in Bulgaria. Moritz and Maureen were nice to Adam and did not make any anti-Semitic or disrespectful comments to him at all. Moritz gave Adam a ginger ale and made him feel at home. Decorated with photographs of their children and grandchildren, the Desrochers' large home seemed filled with love. They had raised several children there, the fifth being M-C, who had no reason to be bitter or angry. During the visit, Adam pointed out a spider crawling on the wall. Moritz leapt to his feet and crushed the life out of the spider with a Kleenex. "What did I tell you? He's so nervous all the time," M-C quietly said to Adam, in sympathy for the spider. Of her entire family, M-C most resembled Jean-Vivien and Moritz in personality, despite herself.

Returning to Waverly, M-C told Adam how her family had a hard time accepting and understanding Vittorio because of his background and Spanish accent. Adam asked if her family would react the same way about himself because he was Jewish. She called him "judio mio" [My little Jew] in Spanish and also « mon p'tit Juif » [My little Jew] in French. She used this as a pretext to get sexually provocative with him, turning "judio mio" into a kind of dramatic mantra. Arriving in Waverly, she became aggressive and put him down on her bed. She opened his shirt and caressed his chest; she called him "judio mio" over and over. She opened his fly and, removing his penis, assaulted him with her mouth. Adam felt immobilized and did not know how to fight her. She mounted him and continued her "judio mio" assault with her vagina.

The next day, there was a barbecue at the home of Gus and Lethe in Montreal's mostly French-speaking working-class East End. English Canadians were hesitant to venture into the neighbourhood, which occupied half the island, and they did so with trepidation, scarcely knowing their Gallic countrymen and only the East Enders knew what they thought of English Canadians. Adam arrived without M-C to discover everybody there was in the mood to tease him about her. He was uneasy as both Gus and Renato made disparaging comments about M-C and Adam, insinuating they were a couple.

"Oh come on! You leave together, you arrive together … Adam has a girlfriend!" Renato said.

"She's not my girlfriend!" Adam told them, upholding M-C's condition. Despite M-C's stated wish not to be seen together and her condition of not touching her or acting amorously toward her in public, everybody had already observed them leaving and arriving together, just as Adam had feared. People drew their own conclusions about the sexual nature of the relationship, and the rumour that Adam and M-C were a couple spread rapidly in the council. Soon after, M-C went against her own wishes and dropped any public pretence that they were *not* a couple. Everybody had a good laugh at Adam's expense. "So, did you have a good fuck last night?" Gus asked him disrespectfully.

When M-C arrived, all comments and laughing stopped abruptly, as though everyone in attendance was already afraid of her, but not of Adam. Driving away with her afterwards, Adam told her what they had said about her and how he tried to defend her honour.

"They don't know what we have!" M-C took her turn insinuating they were a couple after all.

Terribly confused, Adam began crying. M-C said that she had slept with nearly all the men in attendance and they were all sexually inadequate and sexually insecure. She added that Renato, Gus and Enrico taken together still did not have Adam's sexual prowess and that if ever they bothered him again, Adam should tell them what M-C said about their sexual performance, and she would back him up. She added that she had not actually slept with Gus but that being married to Lethe was punishment enough for him. Adam got the idea M-C had a lot of power to embarrass a man sexually and destroy his self-esteem and reputation in the Movement. He thought about how dangerous her sexual anger and public retribution could be if turned against him.

Arriving in the doorway of Waverly after the evening was over, M-C embraced Adam, kissed him passionately and implored him to have sex. She used the spectre of her sexual control over men and the joint offence from certain men in the council as a pretext to celebrate the close ties between them. He felt himself being drawn deeper into an entangled situation with her from which he could not extricate himself. His will was like a liquid dissolving inside her. He was in conflict but did not know how to fight her, given her previous threats. She started assaulting him with her mouth, then her vagina, exclaiming "I feel alive and wonderful when you're close to me, and I want to share a lot of things with you," all the way through to ejaculation. This was her "St-John-the-Baptist" assault.

The next day, she revealed to Adam her hatred for Renato. She had an affair with Renato when he first came to Montreal six years earlier. She never said that she asked Renato's Orientor (Josh) for permission to have sex with Renato. « Renato là, y'avait un pénis minuscule; c'était tout p'tit tout p'tit, on ne le sentait même pas! Quand il me la mettait, cétait 'hein! Quessé rentré?!!' Je ne sais pas comment Fan a fait pour le *tolérer* pendant toutes ces années-là ». [That Renato, he had this tiny penis, it was a little teenie-tiny teenie-weenie, I hardly even felt it! When he put it in it was like 'Hey! Is it in yet ?!!' I don't know how Fan was able to *tolerate* it all those years"] M-C equated Renato's tiny penis with the problem of male inadequacy to women, just as her own father had failed to please her mother sexually. She made Renato's allegedly little penis sound like a provocation to women.

Renato was the sweetest guy in the whole council and best exemplified the ludic style. He had catlike body language and mannerisms, with sandy blonde hair, a slight build, a melodic voice and a gentle social manner. Men, including those who were completely at ease with their masculinity, wanted to pick Renato up, caress his soft fur and dangle string over his nose if he wasn't lapping milk from his bowl.

Alternatively, Renato could imitate a bird and have Adam laughing in stitches. Sometimes Renato would buzz about busily, wearing his shirt with thick horizontal stripes alternating yellow-and-black with black-and-yellow. People would call after him "Bumblebee! Bumblebee!" Like Enrico, Renato had been trained as an engineer in Chile and like many immigrants to Canada, he found the adjustment difficult as he tarried between Montreal and Toronto, finding only mixed success in his field.

Renato had been Fan's regular boyfriend for four solid years, after which she still had not learned to pronounce his name. Fan was a particular species of Francophone not so easily understood by the English-speaking world, but who flourished in Quebec. Raised in the hinterland of the province's homogenous Abitibi region, Fan had never met a Jew before she came to Montreal. A parlour revolutionary and embittered feminist innocent of history or geography, she was to ride the crest of bourgeois-bohemian favouritism that propelled racists like her to the top of leftist society. She maintained friendships with people from Vietnam, Slovenia, Iceland, Chile, Iran and Senegal without making distinction for the names of their countries, preferring to lump them together into her solid disdainful unit of "Allophonia."

It became progressively clearer to Adam throughout the year that Fan had disliked him for years and would never have accepted him in her circle of friends with M-C and Colleen; M-C knew it perfectly well. Many such incidents brought this to the fore. In January at Toronto's Pearson Airport, Fan threw a projectile in Adam's face, but she never admitted to it.

After a Friday social gathering in April, Renato invited Adam to sleep over at his place on the sofa. The next morning, Adam thanked Fan for her hospitality. Fan said hatefully, « Non! Ça tu diras ça à René! » [No! You can tell that to René!] (René was Fan's disrespectful name for Renato.)

At a social gathering in Outremont in July, the rumour Adam had a girlfriend in the Movement blossomed and reached the farthest-flung corner of the council, including Fan and Lima, Renato's Peruvian Admi. Lima was ecstatic for Adam and pressured him to reveal the woman's name. Adam made Fan guess to test a certain intellectual curiosity he had. Neither Lima nor Fan could guess correctly, and when he said Marie-Claude, Lima was happy, but Fan seemed dejected. Adam asked if she was surprised or dejected, and Fan said she was neither. After the gathering, M-C invited Adam to stroll with her through the charming streets of Outremont — Champagneur, Bloomfield, de l'Epee, Lajoie, Saint-Viateur and Laurier — and ruined the evening by telling Adam that Fan was surprised, sickened and worried at learning of her relationship with him.

The end of July was Raymond's last night in Montreal before leaving for Japan. Adam was fed up with Fan, especially in light of her recent two-faced attitude toward him and M-C. He wanted to settle his business with Fan and keep their future contact to a minimum. He saw her at the social gathering and asked her if she had money she had borrowed the previous week. When the gathering dissolved, M-C said goodbye to him, but then he asked her for a lift to Frère-André. In the car, Adam asked if they could go to Waverly instead, telling her he had just lost his good friend to Japan for a whole year and would really feel like being with a supportive friend. Upon their arrival at Waverly, M-C said she wanted to drive him home so she could be alone. Adam asked why, but she claimed nothing was wrong. After prying, signs came out that something was wrong. She said that Adam had been cheap to ask Fan to repay her small debt, and she didn't like cheap people. Now he was getting angry.

M-C related how Enrico had received a complaint from Fan, then relayed it to M-C, who then used that information against Adam without shame. Adam told M-C his opinion that while some people may think it cheap to ask for the return of a small debt, it was equally cheap to withhold or object to the payment of a small debt for the same reason that it was such a small amount. Adam referred M-C to the Movement's own ideology, paraphrasing from Silo: "The same number may appear larger or smaller depending on whether you must give or receive."

M-C started to see his point and seemed to question whether Fan was justified. Adam started to see Fan as a hypnotized robot under Enrico's control. They got into Rania's bed to sleep, since M-C wanted a change while Rania was with Vittorio. Adam still wanted to talk with her; he asked why she kept things from him and let problems get worse instead of talking to him. To remind him of the extent of her power as the System Operator and Central Admi, she uttered his BBS username and password out loud while reclining on a pillow. Adam had not finished talking to her when she rolled down the covers, mounted him, and assaulted him with her vagina. Given she had already said she did not want to see him in Waverly, that she wanted to be alone, that she did not like cheap people like Adam, it was impossible for her to find him sexually appealing or to be aroused by him that night. Rather, she sexually assaulted Adam as punishment for displeasing Fan, for having tested her loyalty to the Council of Team Delegates, for having insinuated that his friendship with Raymond was as important as her own with Fan, for having quoted the Movement's doctrine to her, and as anti-Semitic violence. This was Marie-Claude's "pot-calls-the-kettle-cheap" assault.

On the second Friday in August, Fan interrogated Adam at the Friday night gathering about his occupation and lack of purpose in life, humiliating him in front of everybody. M-C said to him « Quessé qu'on va faire quand Fan vient pour visiter? C'est vrai! Quessé qu'on va faire? » [Whadda we s'pposed to do when Fan comes to visit? It's true! Whadda we gonna do?]

Later in August, Fan came over to work on M-C's computer. They both ignored him. The three of them could never be together at the same time. In front of Adam, M-C rejoiced with Fan about the fact that she was « enfin libre » [finally free] from him that weekend. She then made plans with Fan for a corn roast with their shared friends, only because Adam would be absent. To this day, Adam had never attended any event in M-C's home as one of her friends. In the end, the sum total of M-C's newfound feelings for Adam was to temporarily push her about one percent off her original course. M-C's loyalty to the Movement, her status as a *vieja*, coupled with her friendship with Fan and Colleen, prevented her from ever becoming his friend, just as she intended.

Throughout the summer, she had shared with him still more hurtful stories from her youth. As a teenager, she had taken to hanging out at a recreation centre on Curé-Labelle Boulevard in Laval. There, and at parties, she tried to become more popular with teenage boys, but they rejected her offers to kiss, sometimes pushing her face away and calling her ugly and by certain untranslatable colourful nicknames.

Also, when she was fifteen she got together with girls in her age group. They listened to records in their basements. One day, M-C brought a recording of classical music and played it for her girlfriends. They had listened to only popular music before. M-C was in tears because the music was so beautiful and so deeply meaningful to her, but her friends laughed at her and ridiculed her.

After high school she studied bicycle path design in junior college, where she had been a member of the Communist Party and the Women's Committee. She intended to follow in her father's career path of landscaping but failed to yield positive results in all three ventures in her early twenties. A short time later, Colleen drew her into the Movement.

On the first Friday in August, M-C had the day off. She had been harassing Adam for months with insults, demeaning remarks and verbal jabs. They had lunch at a Vietnamese restaurant on Mount Royal Avenue East; on the sidewalk afterwards, she bumped into a man she knew from the co-operative housing complex where she had formerly dwelled. He was friendly with her but she was frosty and sharp with him and visibly uptight, later telling Adam the man brought back many bad memories of disputes in the militant committee. It seemed even her socialist ideals could not free her from bad experiences with men who were her ideological equal, brothers in "The Cause."

In her car, she began to pester Adam about his clothing, personal hygiene and personal appearance; she insulted him and got very nasty and degrading. His self-esteem had been declining progressively since that Friday in May, but the tipping point came when she criticized his pants, comparing him to Pigpen and calling him a slob. She said Adam was not sexy and did not satisfy her; she wanted him to fulfil her fantasy of "getting fucked by a young dumb stud." Her scenario was for Adam to wear a new pair of tight jeans and a simple white cotton short-sleeve shirt. She said it was the sexiest thing, like a construction worker. M-C induced in Adam a feeling of extreme emptiness and sorrow, mingled with indignation.

Adam couldn't take any more of her insults. He began to cry in the car. She reached over and feigned concern for him, saying she "didn't want to hurt him." He had heard the same thing from her three times on the Tuesday following that Friday in May and also in her letter of the first Tuesday in June. Not persuaded, he batted her hand away and told her, "Fuck off. Get away from me."

It never occurred to her that men had feelings and it still didn't. He looked at M-C and thought about her very carefully. Who was this surly, mean, evil woman who had stood a chance to become a cabinet minister? Her insults reminded him of some previous event. He searched his memory and recalled an incident when he was in junior high and a girl had said the same thing to him. Just then it hit him — M-C had the same behaviour as a girl twenty years younger. He lost control when he couldn't remember how and when he had ever picked M-C as his "girlfriend." His teeth began chattering uncontrollably, and he had cold shivers in the warm summer air for several minutes — long enough for M-C to finally shut her mouth.

Arriving at her home, he thought about a course of action. He decided he would leave the apartment but without asking permission or telling M-C where he was going. She was washing the dishes when he got ready to leave. He intended to act perfectly casual, in order to test a long-standing suspicion. "Anyhow," he began "I'm going out now. See you around sometime." He waved lightly in her general direction and started out the kitchen door without offering a kiss or any explanation. She turned quickly from her sink, chased him to the door, grabbed him by the arm, turned him around swiftly, violently pulled him back into her kitchen and kissed him roughly on the mouth, making dental contact and reasserting her sexual jurisdiction on her slave. She impeded his free movement. It was the first time he ever tried to leave her kitchen on his own, and it failed miserably. Just as he had always thought, Adam was never truly and entirely free to leave her house unencumbered.

Subdued, humiliated and pensive, Adam walked to the Wise Brothers' store on Plaza St-Hubert, a covered outdoor shopping complex. He bought a new pair of well-fitted blue jeans and a short-sleeve white cotton T-shirt, with a design on the front that said "Blue Moon Café." From there, he made his way on his own to the Friday evening gathering at a community centre straddling Querbes and Fairmount Streets, which had been a private school Pierre Trudeau attended as a schoolboy in the 1920s and 1930s. Trudeau's classmate was a little boy named Pierre Laporte. Some forty years later, Trudeau was prime minister when fanatical revolutionaries kidnapped a diplomat and Laporte; the terrorists advocated a separate homeland for French Canadians and the political separation of Quebec from Canada. Trudeau invoked the *War Measures Act* and called out the army. The terrorists responded by strangling Laporte with his own necklace and leaving the corpse in the trunk of a green Chevrolet that was left abandoned on the South Shore of Montreal. To rub it in, the terrorists chose the date of October 17th, the day before Trudeau's birthday. Adam could not help but notice how the psychological effect had been carefully engineered to remind Trudeau of his childhood and make him feel maudlin, weak and sentimental, childish and powerless when thinking of his old friend.

Adam was at the bar when M-C entered and approached him from behind. She did not know that he would be wearing new jeans and told him « Ouais … t'es pas mal cute dans tes jeans » [Yeah … you're pretty cute in your jeans]. When she got near enough to his back, Adam stuck his behind up in her face, right in her nose, rather than saying hello face-to-face. Obviously, this was a show of hostility on his part that precluded sex. She pretended not to notice that and talked non-stop during the car ride to Waverly about how sexy he was and how she would finally get to live out her fantasy with him!

When they got to her bedroom, she ordered him to strip. She hugged his jeans on the bed and would not let them leave her sight. When he tried putting his jeans away, she called them back to the bed where they remained for the evening. She was in love with his laundry. She touched him all over his body, groping his penis extensively. She pulled him on top of her and ground her pelvis into his own on the bed with her head pointing to Waverly Street. During this grinding action, she inserted his penis inside her vagina and assaulted him, whispering in his ear "you're my young dumb stud" repeatedly until ejaculation. This was Marie-Claude's "construction-worker" assault.

Progressively, the enormous forces M-C had imposed on him had a cumulative effect and his system began to break down. Adam got more headaches, a sore back and a cold. When he returned to Frère-André with the cold, Enrico observed him for a while then remarked he had a cold. Adam said yes.

"M-C has a cold," Enrico said; it excited him to insinuate they were in close contact at a time when he already knew they were. He waited until Adam was bent over the kitchen garbage, in a vulnerable position, to approach him from behind. He leaned over Adam, wrapped his arms around him from behind, and calling out "thrusting and releasing," started touching Adam's chest in a sexual way, making lewd sexual advances. Adam straightened up very quickly and all in the same motion told him: "*Don't touch me like that, thank you!*"

Throughout the summer, Enrico made unsolicited parallels between Adam's situation and his own experiences with Lola. Over time, Enrico compared everything between M-C and Adam to Enrico and Lola and "the problem of sex and death."

M-C was less pleased with Adam's sexual performance. « Tu me touches pas assez! Je veux que tu me touches plus! D'autres gars dans le passé, aussitôt qu'ils avaient fini, ils ne me touchaient plus, ils tournaient sur leurs dos, pis ils s'endormaient. Pis moi j'étais là pis, 'ouais, c'est platte pour moi!' J'veux que tu me caresses même quand t'as fini, je n'aime pas comment tu le fasse maintenant! »

[You're not touching me enough! I want you to touch me more! Other guys in the past, as soon as they're finished they stopped touching me, turned on their backs and fell asleep. So I'm there all alone and like, 'Yeah, it's boring for me !' I want you to caress me even when you've finished, I don't like how you do it now!] After that, Adam tried touching her more. She accused him of touching her too much. « Tu t'accroches! T'es tout le temps en train de me toucher! » [You grab on to me! You're always trying to touch me!] she yelled at him repeatedly.

Adam had to find the right balance of how to touch her enough, but not too much. He never found it. Extremely nervous, he could no longer deliver the sexual performances that she expected as duplicates of that Friday in May. Despite his best efforts to keep his standing in the Movement, he ejaculated too quickly for her liking and could not remember the sequence of techniques she required him to make. His performance became contrived and visibly forced. During one of her assaults, Adam ejaculated too quickly and she screamed in his face, "How many times can YOU come?"

The Sisterhood and Her War Against Men

The next time Adam returned to Frère-André, Enrico appeared out of nowhere and told him about how women are multi-orgasmic and need to "come" more than men. Enrico said Adam had to learn how to prolong his sexual performance. Enrico gave him tips on how to please women; Adam tried ignoring him. During one of M-C's assaults later in the summer, Adam ejaculated too quickly and M-C screamed in his face, "Did it ever occur to you that *I might want to come!*" The next time Adam returned home, Enrico appeared out of nowhere slightly out of breath, as if he had just returned from mailing a birthday card to Dr. Hannibal Lecter. "Yeah, you know, man," Enrico began, "When I have sex with a woman, they *love* it, man, and it always lasts *at least three hours.*"

On the second weekend in August, Tara hosted a picnic lunch at her parents' home in the LaSalle neighbourhood which, like its neighbour Verdun, was one of those places in Montreal relatively unknown to Adam, since he had no family or friends there and never visited as a child. LaSalle had been named for the French explorer who established French colonies near the Mississippi River but who was murdered by mutineers following a ruse involving the safety of his nephew.

Where LaSalle's colonies could have succeeded, the whole continent might have been tipped in favour of the French. Tara was the Support in Renato's triangle; she and Adam played Frisbee with the gang under the hot sun. It was supposed to be an entirely friendly get-together until M-C made vicious, humiliating, and vindictive sexual insults against Renato, in front of everyone. M-C was sitting near Renato, who was across from Adam. During what Adam thought was good-natured joking, somebody made a little joke to the effect that Renato was « Le Roi du Hot Dog » [The King of Hot Dogs]. It was a reference to a restaurant of the same name on St. Hubert Street in Montreal. It was harmless and meant as a joke.

M-C immediately recognized this as an opportunity for humiliation. « *Avec une saucisse minuscule!!!* » [*With a tiny sausage!!!*] she blurted into Renato's face, referring to his astronomically small penis, just as she had threatened to do since her "St. John-the-Baptist" assault.

Everyone laughed, but not M-C, for she was dead serious. « *Hein! Tu te fais-tu dire ça des fois! Hein?* » [*Eh?! You ever been told that! Huh?*] M-C continued to taunt Renato. She slammed herself back in her chair in a vicious rage while poor Renato meekly tried to defend himself.

« Je ne sais pas, des fois... » [I dunno, sometimes…] He looked down at his feet.

Afterwards, in her car, Adam wanted to say a word of defense about Renato but was terrified of speaking up and confronting M-C, who had her silence rule in effect and was breathing exclusively through her nose. Adam began thinking of what kind of abusive harassment Renato must have endured from her in the previous six years since the end of their affair. What would Adam have to go through to qualify for joining the Council of Team Delegates and what quality of life could he look forward to in the coming years?

Increasingly, Adam felt like a character he had seen in a movie titled *Misery*. It is about a woman who kidnaps her favourite author and forces him to write subsequent novels based on her own fantasies about her favourite characters and how she would like to see the stories turn out. Crippled and bed-ridden, the man has no freedom of his own as he is exploited to satisfy the woman's imagined scenarios, which she reinforces with violence and confinement. The film's soundtrack is punctuated by Buddy Holly singing "Oh, misery, misery ... what's going to become of me?" While the woman drives her Jeep to town, the man is strapped into the passenger seat, longing to call out for help, but not daring to do so.

With M-C steaming in man-hating rage, the feeling was overwhelming. Adam started singing Buddy Holly's "Raining in my Heart" out loud, but softly to himself, lingering on the line, "Oh, misery, misery ... what's going to become of me?" Adam particularly enjoyed the scene in *Misery* where the imprisoned man lifts his typewriter over his head a thousand times a day to build strength. When he is ready, he surprises his captor by braining her repeatedly over the head with the typewriter and screams hateful words at her with each blow: "*You twisted! Sick! Fuck!*" M-C looked at Adam sideways, wondering what he was up to.

M-C's anger did not dissipate for the rest of the day. By nightfall, Adam was exhausted and tried to get into bed to sleep. She went up to the bed and intoned, « Il ne te resterait pas un peu d'énergie,

Sweetheart? » [Would you have a bit of energy left, Sweetheart?] in a mocking and sugary cajoling voice.

Why? Energy for what? What's she getting at? he thought, nearly asleep. Before he knew what was happening, she was all over him, touching, sucking … she was having her way with him. He had protested her aggression, and she knew he was practically asleep when this happened. This was M-C's "tiny-penis" assault. A few days after these events, M-C told Adam, "Lima came over for our Admi meeting last night; Renato came with her. I think he might have thought he was *welcome* here; isn't that funny?"

On the second Tuesday in August, M-C went to a movie with Fan, without inviting Adam. M-C never invited Adam to any private event with either Fan or Colleen, both her "important" friends. After midnight, M-C wanted to have sex with Adam, but he told her they should not for her sake, because it was already half past midnight and she had work the next day. He wanted her to get her rest.

« Non! Quand je deviens cochonne, il n'y a rien qui peut m'arrêter! Ça sera comme ça quand on vivra ensemble! » [No! When I get horny, there is nothing that can stop me! It'll be like that when we live together!] She said, « Même s'il est minuit vingt-neuf, il n'y a rien qui peut m'arrêter! » [Even if it is twenty-nine past midnight, there is nothing that can stop me!]

She had her way with him, first going down on him, then mounting him with her vagina, up to and including ejaculation. She sexually assaulted him with anger and after he had protested he was almost asleep. This was M-C's "friendship-for-Fan" assault.

On the third Friday in August, they were in her bed, quiet and alone. The darkness of her bedroom submerged them in a feeling of intimate closeness. She turned away from him, staring at her window blinds.

"I don't deserve you. You deserve better than me," she said.
"Don't say that!" he said, and added, "Stop putting yourself down."
"I'm not nice to you. I do things to you," she continued.
"You do?"
"Yes!" she whispered desperately.
"What kind of things?" he asked curiously.

"I do *things!*" she shouted into her pillow and added that she was afraid of keeping him, but she was afraid of losing him also.

"Well, I don't know what to say," he said, adding "I'm here now."

« Fais-moi l'amour » [Make love to me] she said.

"I don't feel like it," he told her and offered to rub her feet with regular hand cream, secretly hoping she would fall asleep.

She assaulted him with her mouth for a long time but could not get much more than a semi-erection. With violence and anger in her eyes, she mounted him and assaulted him with her vagina. After a while, she pulled him closer to sexually assault him in various positions. During the assault, he could tell that he was failing to please her. He had already passed a point where his system had broken down and he could not perform sexually, not even to save his position in the Movement. This was his worst sexual performance ever and M-C did not enjoy it at all.

After the assault was over, he retreated naked to the kitchen, she to the bathroom. He had placed some bagels in the toaster-oven and she retrieved them, toasted. She sat naked at her kitchen table, sliced the bagels and called them « pain juif » [Jewish bread], adding that the bagels were nicely toasted in the oven. She added that bagels didn't complain when you put them in the oven and asked him to laugh at her joke, calling the bagels « de bons petits Juifs » [Good little Jews].

She then proceeded, still naked, into a vicious diatribe about the Holocaust and how Jews take it too seriously; she told him he should learn to laugh at the Holocaust. Jews like Adam complained too much about the Holocaust, but the bagels did not mind being burned alive in the oven and Adam should see the bagels as models of obedient Jews. In fact, Adam had never discussed the Holocaust with her. Looking at him with the same hateful eyes she used in the same kitchen on that Friday in May, she thrice urged him to laugh at the Holocaust and the term [Jewish bread.] Waving the bagel in his face, M-C invoked Josh and said "even Josh laughs" at the Holocaust.

Adam felt there was a big difference for a person who has overcome trauma in their personal or family history to see it in a different light some day after reflection, meditation, rebirth, community and healing. It was quite another for somebody who had never shown themselves to be a good friend to do so. What were M-C's qualifications? Adam asked himself what was she thinking during the assault, just minutes earlier. Did this verbal assault mean that while he was languishing and failing to please her sexually, she was fantasizing about sending him to a concentration camp and seeing him incinerated alive in a German oven, while she laughed and smeared cream cheese on a toasted bagel? Was this his punishment for having failed to please her sexually? Or had she had this fantasy for some time? Adam was profoundly wounded, under attack by this evil woman. His mind was still in deep shock from the violence of what she had said to him when, naked and with millions of Jewish sperm still in her vagina, M-C screamed at him « Moi-là, je suis POUR le OLP!! Trouves-tu ça drôle, toi? Hein! Peux-tu rire de ça!!? T'es-tu capable de rire? » [As for me, I am FOR the PLO! Do you find it funny, you? Eh! Can you laugh about that!? Are you capable of laughter?]

His mind reeled from her violence as he strained to remember what OLP meant. He reasoned it was the French acronym for PLO, and the PLO is the Palestine Liberation Organization. *I'm in a right-wing extremist group*, he thought. *This is serious. How did I get into one of those? I don't remember the Movement being that.* There was another word for it, but he could not put his finger on it. The common link between the PLO and the Nazis was that they both actively murdered Jews. It was not enough for M-C to wish him dead at the hands of the Nazis. She declared her support for a genocidal anti-Jewish terrorist group still active in killing Jews, including potentially all his cousins in Israel, his family in Canada and himself.

M-C's statement could no longer be seen as a misguided or misinformed statement about the past: she had made a death threat against Adam and his entire extended family. Her own family was normal and had no discernible defect that could have caused her to act this way. Desdemona was being polite when exposing the insanity of her family. M-C was to blame: she had lied about Moritz's anti-Semitism. In fact, she, M-C, was the anti-Semite. Desdemona had previously rejected the Movement after M-C had tried recruiting her; perhaps Desdemona knew the unpronounceable word that eluded Adam and with it, the true identity of the Movement. After many anti-Semitic incidents, this was Marie-Claude's crowning shame and her "Genocidal-Maniac" assault.

x — MARIE-CLAUDE AVENGES HERSELF ON THE MALE SPECIES

"If one wished to carry the psychological point of view to an extreme, one could consider every person's life a 'drama' that develops in the midst of accidents suffered by the central character."
—Luis Ammann

ON WEDNESDAY, after M-C's return from Cuba, Adam was in bed at Waverly when M-C started to tell him about why she was uncomfortable with Enrico around the previous Sunday. She said they had an "affair" when Enrico first came to Montreal, seven years earlier, and that *he* was the man who told her to wait for him after the meetings and who treated her badly. She never said, however, that she asked Enrico's Orientor (Josh) for permission to have sex with Enrico. M-C became pregnant by Enrico and had an abortion. Therefore, there was a long-standing emotional and sexual bond between M-C and Enrico, who had his finger in every pie. She added in passing that she had a miscarriage with another man. She started to cry as she recounted her experience with Enrico. Adam comforted her by taking her in his arms and soothing her until she was calm.

She reached for Adam's penis. He told her not to but she assaulted him orally notwithstanding. During the assault, he touched her shoulder. She stopped everything and spiralled into a lengthy emotional scene, with convulsive crying originating at her solar plexus. Deeply wounded, she ran away to isolate herself on the fire stairs, leaving Adam alone in her bedroom. Concerned for her, he went to console her. She refused his help and ordered him to wait for her indoors, without any explanation. He stayed inside while she smoked several cigarettes and listened to the sound of summer crickets, which always had a soothing effect on her. He wondered what he had done wrong, why was she so hurt? He started to feel bad, even though he didn't know what he had done. Adam's mind explored in some detail the full inventory of things he might have done wrong. She continued to give him the silent treatment for some time, until the crickets and nicotine did for her what Adam could not. She finally returned to the bedroom and told him why she was upset.

When M-C was eighteen, she had a boyfriend with a motorcycle in Laval who forced her to perform oral sex on him at an open site in his house, visible from the street. She didn't want to because she protested they were practically in the street; she felt exposed and vulnerable. He manhandled her and forced her to perform oral sex on him, grabbing her head and placing his hand on her shoulder. She had never told anyone and concealed her pain for fifteen years.

At this point in the story, she started crying again. Adam felt so bad for her. He wanted to spare M-C the pain of having to continue with that sad story. Interrupting her, he told her he understood the bad thing that the boyfriend had done to her, and that when Adam had touched her in the same way, without knowing it, he reminded her of that awful incident. He told her she didn't have to finish that sorry story, that he understood her. He held her gingerly in his arms as she cried and cried on his shoulder. He cradled her and he rocked her gently, whispering soft words in her ear and caressing her gently for hours until she calmed down completely.

She then resumed sexually assaulting him. She took his penis in her mouth and assaulted him until there was an erection. "You're so nice to me, sweetie, and you say such nice things to me. I don't deserve you," she said while guiding his penis into her vagina and assaulting him until ejaculation. This was M-C's "motorcycle" assault.

By morning, Adam was exhausted; it was the most sexual contact he had ever had with a woman. His slight experience could not help him. She blamed him because she forgot to take her temperature and could not record it on graph paper. « Je veux pas que tu viennes ici juste pour faire l'amour, pis c'est tout! Je veux que tu sois attentif avec moi! Comme ce matin, j'ai oublié de prendre ma température! Au lieu de rester couché t'aurais pu me faire penser! Sont des choses qui m'aident pas! » [I do not want you to come here just to make love, and that's all! I want you to be attentive with me! Like this morning, I forgot to take my temperature! Instead of lying in bed you could have reminded me! These are things that don't help me!] she screamed.

If her plan was to get pregnant, she never breathed a word of it to Adam, who suspected nothing. The next time Adam returned home, Enrico buttonholed him and said, "Adam, you have to be sensitive with a woman. You don't just fuck her and that's it. No, you have to show a certain sensitivity to her needs. And you ask her questions, man, about what she wants, and you listen to her…" Thereafter, Adam tried to be more attentive and caring with her. She accused him of getting too involved in her personal life and of making her the meaning of his own life, as she had feared and warned him not to.

On the third Friday in June at Waverly, Adam was lying in bed with M-C, talking. Without notice or permission, she rolled the covers down and began assaulting him, first with her hands, then her mouth, then by mounting him and inserting his penis into her vagina. By this time, she had already read his printed letter from the previous day, stating that he wished to stop having sexual contact with her. After the assault, she again raised the subject of her and Enrico's aborted child, as she had done with increasing frequency since her "coffee-and-stealth" assault, her "unresolved-feelings-about-Enrico" assault and her return from Cuba. Whenever Adam was with her, Enrico was never far from her thoughts and her pain. She spoke emotionally about the abortion, then her body convulsed at her solar plexus and she started crying. Until the abortion, M-C thought she was pro-abortion; she never knew what kind of searing emotional pain she could experience during and after an abortion, her pro-abortion position was entirely political — she had no experience to guide her. At the time of the abortion, Enrico and M-C were luminaries in the Canadian portion of the political Humanist Party, whose slogan was "The Human Being is Being Born." They kid you not.

She related to Adam the details of how Enrico had never supported her emotionally during her pregnancy and the abortion. She said that Enrico jettisoned her after she became pregnant and did not want to talk to her about it. Enrico no longer wished to have sex with M-C, the playtime thrill of her body being too risky; he thrust $100 at her to have the abortion done, but he would not involve himself any further. She felt discarded, like garbage, she said to Adam seven years after the event.

As she cried on his shoulder, Adam became the first man in whom she ever confided her abortion ordeal. She said she never wanted to have an abortion again and she felt guilty that she had been a bad woman for having one. She had concealed her pain and kept it repressed inside her soul for seven years. Even though Adam was already morally opposed to abortion, he calmed her and told her at length what a good person she was. He whispered to her a cyclical theme he had learned in French class: « Les ondes de l'océan se composent et se décomposent sans cesse » [The ocean waves flow together and flow apart continuously without cease], and repeated it several times, since she felt its soothing action compelling. She started to say it out loud herself and it began to work for Adam also as he imagined himself sleeping in a cabin on the shores of Lake Memphremagog, where the swish-swish of the glacial water had given him the most restful sleep of his life. He rocked her gently in his arms, stroked her long dark hair and soothed her until she was like melting butter in his arms. The next day, she resumed screaming insults at him.

M-C told Adam throughout the summer that she wanted to have sex with him during her menstrual period. Adam said that he did not. She went on to say that she wanted to overcome the image of menstruation as a dirty thing, and the stigma of menstrual blood as unclean and not at all sexy. He said he wanted to keep it that way, with "extra stigma for me, thank you kindly." She said that they would try having sex while she was having her period, and he resisted her wishes each time. She also said several times that she was jealous of her neighbours because they seemed to have happier lives than she, as she watched them enjoying themselves on their lawns. She added how she wished her neighbours could see her having sex with Adam, because she wanted to show off. She was sure this would offend and irritate her neighbours greatly.

One bright day late in July, M-C said that she was ready to have sex with him on her kitchen table, with the kitchen curtains open. She wanted to make sure that her neighbours on Waverly Street and across the backyard, on De Reims Street, could see them having sex in broad daylight. Adam said he did not want to be exposed like that and in any case, she was having her period and this was not a time to have sex. She became angry with him. She said that they would take a shower together, but that after, they would have sex together on her kitchen table, and there was to be no more resistance from Adam. After the shower, she compelled him to penetrate her while she lay down on her back on her kitchen table. Adam was afraid of her and felt he could not refuse, lest he face the consequences of all the accumulated threats she had made to him all summer. He asked her if he could wear a condom at least, to protect himself from her blood; she refused the condom, saying she wanted him to overcome the stigma of sex during menstruation.

Having been refused all other options, he penetrated her without a condom while standing on her kitchen floor and she lay on her kitchen table. Her eyes rolled back in her head and disappeared. The intrusive sunlight revealed the imperfections of her face: a few pock marks and creases, though none as unattractive as Enrico's. She beckoned him to continue, since she found the action extremely exciting. His penis started to draw blood while she was completely stimulated. After several minutes of this non-consensual sex, Adam felt completely grossed out. More than wet, his penis was dripping with blood. He couldn't take it anymore and tried withdrawing. She encouraged him to keep going and called out mockingly to her neighbours, as though they were watching. Lyrics rang out in his head from a song he knew: "Lying on stained wretched sheets with a bleeding virgin; we could plan a murder or start a religion."

He freaked out and could not continue any further. Trembling, he withdrew completely and in so doing smeared blood on her kitchen table, much to her disdain. M-C was extremely disappointed in him but said the session on her table had done her some good. She was pleased with the prospect that some of her neighbours may have seen her in that position and been offended as a result. This was Marie-Claude's "bloody" assault. Earlier in the summer, she had told him that when visiting Enrico at Frère-André, she would often eat her brown-bag lunch first at the nearby St. Joseph's Oratory. There she sat on the outdoor steps and performed oral sex on bananas for the purpose of offending the Catholic pilgrims who climbed the stairs on their knees beneath her.

In August, M-C still had not finished dumping her unresolved feelings about Vittorio on Adam. She re-enacted the events of their lives together related to their break-up eighteen months earlier, though Adam could not follow the story or the emotional sub-plots. She also told Adam more details about her miscarriage. She related how it had occurred only a year earlier, when she and Vittorio were in the process of reconciling. She sobbed that she had wanted that baby because it would make her feel young again and rekindle her marriage plans with Vittorio. She was in such grieving agony when she lost the baby. When Vittorio told her to "get over it" instead of supporting her or consoling her emotionally for it, she was in the deepest grief of her life, worse than her abortion with Enrico. As she told her story, her body convulsed sharply at her solar plexus and she began to cry. "*I wanted that baby!*" she screamed hoarsely.

M-C could barely talk because she was in the most pain of any woman Adam had ever seen. She was a completely naked woman, totally vulnerable. He relied on his instincts about what to do and, as with similar events all summer, he comforted her. He offered to take her in his arms and give her all the love he had left in his heart. She plunged into his arms and told him Vittorio would not do even that for her. Adam was the first man ever to console her for her miscarriage, and she had kept all her feelings inside and repressed since the ordeal. She got him to console her, even though she was never pregnant with his child — as though the miscarried child had somehow become his own. He tried to give her the best emotional support he had ever given her. He rocked her gently, he whispered in her ear, he kissed her softly on the cheek, he talked to her with unprecedented wisdom; he encouraged her. Without any experience in the matter, he reached down inside himself and told her why her body could not accept that baby at that time: her body had rejected it.

"There, there now," he said and sang softly to her from a French Canadian lullaby: « Fais dodo Marie-Claude à Maman. Fais dodo Marie-Claude à Maman » [Go to sleep Mama's little baby, Marie-Claude], substituting her name for the baby's. He became her mother. He changed the lyrics or made up lyrics to make her laugh. He consoled her with the greatest patience and concern for what seemed like hours. When she was nearly entirely calm, she turned her head, kissed him and thanked him. He told her it was nothing. She rolled the covers down and began to sexually assault him. He protested gently, whispering in her ear, "No, sweetheart. You don't have to do that. You're all confused now. Go to sleep." Persistent, she went down on his penis, assaulting him.

They dozed off on her futon and she told him to take the whole blanket for himself, since she would find it too warm. He wrapped himself in it but left half for her, suggesting she might be cold. She murmured she wanted none of the blanket and drifted off to sleep while Adam became enveloped in a warm comforting air pocket. Soothed and somnolent, he was nearly asleep when he heard a tiny, meek pathetic voice from her side of the bed « J'ai froid » [I'm cold.] In one motion, he lifted the edge of the blanket, lowered it across her body like the retractable roof on Montreal's Olympic Stadium and pulled her a little closer to him, whispering "Islanded in warmth" in her ear. She nestled into him, kissed him sweetly once and whispered « Merci » [Thank you] in his ear. He just wanted to be her friend. This was M-C's "unmourned-miscarriage" assault.

On the first Sunday in August, M-C told Adam about the incidents of the previous January, when Fan and Renato had broken up in Chile. M-C had called Enrico and asked him to be supportive of Renato when he got back. She also called Colleen and asked her to be supportive for Fan upon her return. The five people involved were the five Team Delegate peers in Montreal, and M-C saw herself as the banker in this pentagon. When one peer had a personal need, M-C translated it into structural terms so that her own personal needs could be satisfied when she wished to "cash in" the council's debt to her. Over the years many such sexual transactions had transpired between Team Delegates who treated the Movement as their own personal brothel. Where no Team Delegate was available, a group delegate would be supplied. Enrico slept with M-C and M-C slept with Renato. Renato slept with Fan and Fan slept with Enrico. Colleen slept with Felipe. M-C had a sexual need and, like Fan, felt the council owed her a favour. From the council, she identified Adam as the man to supply her with sex and Enrico as her peer responsible for making the arrangements. It was at that moment that their previously separate evil plans for Adam merged.

 M-C was busy with her own sex life in January as she "helped" group delegate support Dwight move apartments, then "made love" with him after a long and friendly chat. M-C told Adam the strange story of how she "selected" Dwight Daneker, a Scandinavian-American philosophy student and aviator from Baltimore and New York, to have sex with. When she separated from Vittorio in July three years earlier, she and Rania went to live with her parents in Laval. One night, she asked her internal guide a question: "Should I reconcile with Vittorio or should I continue on my path?" She slept on it and heard a voice that said: "Continue on your path: you will meet a German." The psychic shock wakened her. She was convinced the voice came from her guide. After that incident M-C asked herself, "What should I do? Should I go to Berlin and wait to meet my man?" For years she went looking for this German man and never forgot her guide's prophecy. When she had opportunity to "make love" to Dwight in January, she thought that since Daneker was a German name (which it is not), maybe Dwight was the man of whom her guide had spoken.

 M-C used her guide's prophecy as a metaphorical third hand, with which she reached out and grabbed Dwight, while she denied her own responsibility or even the very act of grabbing him, by taking the attitude "I didn't seduce Dwight, my guide placed him there before me." Although Daneker was ten years her junior and a group delegate in the council, she never said, however, that she had asked Dwight's Orientor (Renato) for permission to have sex with Dwight. Daneker's consent was irrelevant to her because he was in fulfilment of a prophecy — it *had* to be. Just as she reassigned responsibility for her actions with Daneker to her internal guide, so she asked Enrico to absorb her own responsibility for Adam — to be her conscience. In the same way, she also pretended that Adam might be the foretold man because of his own German-Jewish name.

M-C also told Adam how she used one of her group delegate Admis, then twenty-year-old Mike Aldunkel, to absolve herself of her own responsibility for cheating on Vittorio. Mike and M-C were in France the previous summer for an international meeting of the Movement to build a "Universal Human Nation" based on the five central principles of Humanism. While returning to Canada by plane, M-C found it more convenient to sexually interfere with Mike by liberating his penis from his pants. She never said, however, that she asked permission from Mike's Orientor (Pigpen) to sexually touch Mike. She selfishly claimed that when she subsequently fondled and groped Mike's penis, this was the signal that proved to her she was finished with Vittorio and there could be no reconciliation.

M-C had made a business trip to Madrid in the spring of that year, to attend a special conference for Admis. She told Adam she had stayed with a local Movement member in his home and that she offered her body to the Spaniard as a form of payment for lodging and breakfast. He accepted. She never said that she had asked permission from that Spaniard's Orientor to have sex with him. She did ask Adam if he was disgusted by her values and behaviour. He was indeed disgusted but did not have the courage to tell her. Over time, Adam learned that M-C was the Council Slut, and her vagina was a sort of public utility for men in the council. Indeed, her long-suffering gynecologist said that her vagina's chronic infections were caused by the frequent introduction of foreign bacteria, namely a great variety and multiplicity of exotic penis bacteria acquired from her world travels and frequent changes of sexual partner. M-C became emotionally distraught during each vaginal plague, cried and expected

Adam to comfort her and remind her to insert her medicinal ovule into her infected vagina at night.

By the third Saturday in August, they had agreed his moving date would be around September 1st and that he would have to inform Enrico of his plans to leave Frère-André and join M-C, who had already told Rania. Soon, M-C's cycle of repeated domestic mistakes would be completed to her near satisfaction. That evening, she made an emotional scene on her back stairs. "I believe what my mother said. When I meet the right man, it'll just flow." She hysterically insinuated Adam was somehow to blame for her forcing him towards her ends. Adam thought she had some nerve, considering everything she had told him about Vittorio.

Rania asked her mother for a bottle of warm milk; M-C told her to get it herself. Later that evening, they were in bed and M-C said she would not be available to attend the upcoming modern dance show they had discussed because she had Movement business. Adam said she was neglecting her own hobbies and putting too much time into her Admi duties. She leaned right into his face and with eyes flaming red, yelled, "*NOW YOU'RE GOING TO HATE THE MOVEMENT?*" In so doing, she achieved a perfect replica of her same problem regarding Vittorio's alienation. Adam was terrified that he had become the living embodiment of Vittorio, that he had become Vittorio in M-C's eye and that when she looked at Adam she saw Vittorio.

On Sunday afternoon two weeks before Adam was to move in with her, M-C asked him a series of four questions and told him to take some time to think about it then write down his answers. She asked him for the first time ever about his "needs and limits" — some three months late. In explaining her own "scenarios," she objected to his input: "No! It doesn't have to work! You have your scenario; I have mine. If it doesn't work, I keep my scenario, but I change the actor," she said, snapping her fingers at "actor."

On Sunday evening, M-C and Adam were in bed talking about what it would be like to live together. Like a bad cover of a good Jim Croce song she said, "With Vittorio, it took me years to figure out that I loved him more as a friend than a lover, or a partner. I just don't want to make that mistake with you." She had already repeated the exact same mistake, on schedule. She asked Adam what would happen if it failed to work out. Adam answered, "Whatever you do, just don't kick me out on the street in the middle of winter." She began crying and exclaimed, "*That's what I did to Vittorio!*"

M-C had spoken in the previous days about a recurring dream she had about falling through the Earth and how it led to a discussion with her Team Delegate Support, Ned, about an advanced function in her internal process called the "biographical knot." In the dream, she called out to the Support Sector to catch her, but nobody did. The new support, Yorgo, continued the work in the same job as Ned and explained to M-C the "biographical knot" involved identifying the central elements of repetitious suffering from the cumulative story of her biography. The knot at the centre of her biography was the part of her life that M-C was always unable to resolve, despite resolving other problems: her relations with men.

Over and over, M-C spoke to Adam about biographical knots, plots, scenarios and actors. Insight into the meaning of these keywords is given in a Siloist book titled *Self Liberation*, a central document in Siloist thinking and a book with which both M-C and Enrico were familiar in their positions as Team Delegates. Adam looked through the book further and was alarmed by the chapter titles "Converting Tense Biographical Images ... Cathartic Probe ... Deeper Cathartic Probe and Exercise ... Transferential Probe ... Self-Transference." Adam read further. The book described M-C's persistent life problems and also the means she had used to resolve them. M-C had been exposed to the Siloist doctrine for ten years and had developed her own homemade technique for resolving her biographical knot. Her cathartic plot involved her past sexual traumas, ordeals, pains and frustrations. Having identified her goal as "reconciliation," she then identified the characters she would use as players in her psychodrama and defined her situation by "fixing her interest."

Like Queen Midas in reverse, everything M-C touched turned into corruption. Over time, Adam came to understand that she had used him all along as a cat's-paw, an innocent male vessel and character actor sub-contracted and pimped by Enrico to act out and relive with her all the terrible scenes from her life with men. In each scenario, Adam had played the part of a different man without his knowledge or consent. Only she knew the script she re-enacted, except this time she resolved the conflict in a different way, doing to Adam what she had wanted to do with those previous men from her past, for her own satisfaction. She had used Adam as a surrogate or catalyst man, and she used sex as a kind of "fire of purification" to melt away all the violent problems from her past and untangle her biographical knot. That was why she had selected Adam to sexually assault: she knew he was so soft and absorbent, he would be the perfect receptacle for her toxic emotional waste. In siphoning all the goodness from Adam, she tore a strip off his soul and put all her "marbles" in him.

On the third Monday in August, Adam started to tell her his answers to her questions: What would he like to see happen in a relationship? What did he want? What was his scenario? What did he want to change in their relationship? What couldn't he accept in a relationship? What were his limits?

Although he had worked hard on his responses in writing, she did not let him answer. Before he could say a word more, she cancelled the moving plans and did not want to hear his answers. This was effectively the end of their "relationship" before he ever got a chance to define what he wanted from it. It took her less than twelve hours to reject the principle of her asking him what he wanted, just as it took her only five days to betray her offer of friendship the previous Friday in May. Adam was already emotionally, psychologically, sexually and physically exhausted. He lost concern for his own interests and did not even care any more about what would happen with M-C. He knew intuitively that they had only two weeks before oblivion, before the ball of energy dissolved in his mind.

On the fourth Friday in August, Adam had one of the worst days of his life. He was overwhelmed by all the violence M-C had inflicted on him, and everything seemed completely without hope. The ball of energy was starting to leak. Sinking further into the abyss of deep meaninglessness and without any feeling but pain, he wandered the streets of Montreal aimlessly all day. Not even a meal at his favourite Chinese restaurant could lift his spirits. During the entire summer, every moment that he had spent with M-C was always uncomfortable for him and always felt wrong. During and after each of her assaults, he always had that same dark feeling in his stomach and in his soul. He was weak, immobilized, submissive and terrified, and he did not know how to defend himself. They talked at Waverly in the evening. Somewhere deep inside him, he hoped she would let him off the hook, that she would stop raping him. Adam did not have the courage to accuse her bluntly any more on that evening than he had during her previous assaults.

On Saturday, M-C raised the topic of his needs and was in tears on her back balcony, almost hysterical. « Je ne veux pas être responsable de tes besoins » [I don't want to be responsible for your needs], she said.

As in the week leading up to the Saturday in May, she withdrew her question only six days after asking it, revealing its insincerity. The same day, Adam attended a lawn party given by Lima in Montreal North. When M-C showed up, she ignored him. Adam went to say hello to her and she refused even to say hello. Adam tried to confront her about why she would not acknowledge him in public. M-C treated him like scum, marching away angrily. Adam approached her again to discuss their lengthy list of unfinished business and told her he wanted to ask her questions about the events of that Friday in May and the conditions that led up to her actions on that day — the involvement of Enrico and other details. Adam had done his best to get information from her, but once again, she showed that verbal communication was impossible.

M-C did agree to give him a lift, however, to the Henri-Bourassa Metro, which was on the northern shore of Montreal Island, across from Laval. In the car, Adam started to feel a small modicum of self-respect returning, long enough to make a decision for his own self-interest. He formulated certain thoughts about her but kept most of them to himself until later in the evening. He spoke to her about his burgeoning feeling of freedom from her emotions. She listened from the driver's seat, tense and breathing hard through her nose, her lips

Marie-Claude Avenges Herself on the Male Species

sealed tighter than a shell-mouth. When he tried to leave her car, he again acted completely casual and disinterested in her as he did before her "construction worker" assault. She grabbed him by the arm, turned him around and pulled him back in. Feeling her control on her slave loosening, she kissed him roughly on the mouth then let him go. She showed him again that he was not allowed to leave until she had first shown her sexual jurisdiction over him.

Later in the evening, M-C phoned. He told her, "I noticed that you have a lot of moods … I will continue to be your friend and you can continue to have your moods, for I will not react to them anymore, and I don't care what happens to them or myself as a consequence." As a consequence of his new assertiveness and self-respect, M-C lost nearly all interest in knowing him while conserving her fear of losing him.

On Sunday, Adam went to Waverly at noon to collect a hand-written letter she had prepared for him. They talked briefly then he told her he had to leave early. She did not accept this, grabbed him by the arm and started dragging him to her bedroom. "I want to have sex with you," she said.

He pulled away and resisted her physically for the first time. She could not get him to stay down on the bed. She said she did not want to see him go. He said she could drive him to the Metro to spend a few more minutes together. She drove him to the de Castelnau Metro. Leaving the car, he kissed her goodbye. She leaned over, pulled him back in and told him to close the door. She drove them back to Waverly where, upon entering she wasted no time immediately dragging him by the arm to her bedroom, where she sexually assaulted him. She handled his penis roughly, performed oral sex on him and mounted him. Her average-sized breasts flip-flopped with the motion of her sexual assault until his ejaculation. This was Marie-Claude's "power-grab" assault.

M-C returned Adam to the Metro by car around three in the afternoon in the same manner as she would return a vacuum cleaner to the original upright position after each use. There, Adam had his first chance to read her letter, in which she confessed to many of the things of which he accused her:

J'ai tendance à être attirée plus par quelqu'un qui est centré. C'est vrai. Mais quand la personne s'éloigne de moi pour quelque raison que ce soit, je panique aussi. Je cherche à ce qu'il revienne à mes côtés, ou au moins qu'il me montre qu'il est encore amoureux de moi. Quand il me le montre ... j'étouffe ... j'ai besoin d'air ... je recherche ma liberté.
[I tend to be attracted by someone who is more focused. It's true. But when that person walks away from me for some reason, I panic too. I want him to return to my sides, or at least to show me that he is still in love with me. When he shows me ... I can't breathe ... I need air ... I seek my freedom.]

M-C admitted in writing that this was part of her motivation for refusing to answer his line of questioning during her first assault. She had written this letter to justify her aggressive and violent behaviour during her "Dust-in-the-Wind" assault; her twinned "sick-not-an-excuse" assaults when she assaulted him to drain him of his strength; her "Bastille Day" assault when she assaulted him for his emotional support ; her "pet-shop" assault; and her "construction-worker" assault. Even the day before she wrote this very letter, she was unrepentant and, in a crowning feat of egomaniacal misandric hatred, sexually assaulted him the same day as she handed him the letter! Even at that, she was still not finished spewing her venom:

Je n'aime pas dire ce que je veux comme relation car mes tchums essayaient de faire ce que je voulais pour que je continue à les aimer, mais leur attitude n'était pas VRAIE. Leurs motivations [...] ne partaient pas de ce qu'ils voulaient pour leurs vie mais du désir compulsif d'être aimés par moi. Tôt ou tard, leurs vrais désirs ressortaient et revenaient hanter la relation.
[I hate to say what I want from a relationship because my boyfriends tried to do what I wanted so that

I would still love them but their attitude was not REAL. Their motives did not come from what they wanted for their lives but from their compulsive desires to be loved by me. Sooner or later, their real desires emerged and came back to haunt the relationship.]

M-C admitted that she had hurt and manipulated him; all of her previous "boyfriends" had been put through the same meat grinder of her sexual violence. None of the men she knew had acted in their own best interests, and none had authentic motivations for their actions. Rather, just like Adam, all had been manipulated by M-C. Even after their real motivations came out, she saw it as merely an inconvenience for — and distraction from — her selfish control. As for his case, M-C admitted that she had never given him a chance to make his own decisions regarding his sexual activities with her. Indeed, throughout the summer, an image emerged of her as a woman obsessed with suffering. Every letter she had written to him, every action she took and every threatening comment she made had gone in the direction of deepening her suffering.

M-C admitted in writing that she had offered him friendship and used it as a ploy to keep him coming back to her. She used the demise of their friendship as a constant threat hanging over his head:

> J'ai très peur de ça, Adam. Quand je t'ai parlé au téléphone hier soir, j'ai senti que tu as décidé ces choses pour toi. J'ai quand meme un doute qui reste quelque part, alors je veux m'en assurer avant de changer quoi que ce soit à notre entente (l'idée de l'amitié).
>
> [I am very afraid of that, Adam. When I spoke to you on the phone last night, I felt that you decided these things for yourself. I still have a certain remaining doubt somewhere, so I want to make sure before changing anything to our agreement (the idea of friendship).]

This letter clearly showed there had been no friendship to speak of as of this advanced date. Friendship was only her "idea" at this late stage. On Monday, she sent him yet another hand-written letter, this time in English:

> I think we should each follow our hearts and not follow somebody else's heart. If our scenarios coincide, if our hearts reach that's fantastic, that's the adventure … but we don't want to make our scenario out of the image of someone else, [...] no matter how much we love that person.
>
> Adam, I want you to take your time. Find out [...] who you really are, who you really want to be, and try it out. There's no rush (and I'm telling myself as much as I'm telling you).

M-C wouldn't know anything about his scenarios, because she refused to hear them after having asked for them in writing. Only two days after Adam rejected her emotional violence and only one day after he stood up to her physically, she admitted that she could not accept the idea of being his friend without sex, or knowing him when he was assertive and self-respecting. She effectively gave him his walking papers. At Frère-André, Adam informed Enrico that moving plans were cancelled. Enrico was delighted Adam had failed and used this to expand his orientation and remind Adam about "the problem of sex and death." He went on at length about Adam's road accident and how his problems with M-C reminded Enrico about his own suffering with Lola. In Enrico's mind, everybody's problems were all mixed together in a simmering broth of suffering. Adam sat on the living room carpet while Enrico lectured him about "possessiveness" and told Adam for the nth time how to catch a monkey — with a banana placed inside a cage. No need to lock the cage once the monkey has grabbed the banana within, for the monkey will never ever release his possession. The summer air was heavy with pipe smoke and the sound of Enrico's nasal voice when Adam started to see through Enrico and perceive the malignant workings within this supremely irritating devil.

XI — MARTYR TO THE CAUSE

*[The totalitarian nature of this philosophical movement
that uses the concept of humanism
with a greater taste for power than for charity, is disquieting.]*
— Judge Jean-François Tritschler

ON THE FIRST Saturday in September, M-C phoned Adam to say she had something important to discuss with him, just as she did on that Thursday in May. In the same manner, she refused to say in advance the subject of their discussion, but she took care to arrange for the meeting at a neutral site, just as he had requested and been refused on that first Friday. On the lawn of St. Joseph's Oratory she told him "I don't want to be your girlfriend anymore," and added in French, « Ce n'est pas le bonheur qui grandit en moi, c'est la souffrance! » [It's not happiness that grows in me, it's suffering!] Abandoning her earlier metaphor about the spider, she reversed her previous position on suffering and blamed Adam for the suffering she herself had predicted and created. Less than two weeks after her "friendship" letter, she broke it off unilaterally without respecting their agreement, or her promise. She also made a conscious yet selective echo of Silo's question about suffering:

"Here is my question: As life passes by, is it happiness or is it suffering that grows within you?"

Instead of changing her own life for the better, she inverted Silo's stated doctrine and made Adam responsible for her suffering, just as she had been doing throughout the entire summer — it had all been one big long emotional, spiritual, psychological and sexual rape. As a Team Delegate in the Movement, she had a position of trust over Adam. By blaming him for her own suffering while invoking her garbled and selfish version of the Siloist doctrine, she made Adam into her martyr – a convenient group delegate who would absorb the Central Admi's suffering while providing for her sexual and emotional needs. She neglected to consider, however, the very next passage in Silo's works:

Though you may be wise and powerful, if happiness and liberty do not grow in you and in *those around you*, I will reject your example. (Emphasis added.)

M-C's inversion of the written record was an aberration of the Movement doctrine of non-violence and therein lay the essence of her abuse of power. Thus spoke Silo:

We have lied from dawn until dusk, and we have falsified our thoughts, our affections, and our actions. We have assaulted life at every turn for we have created suffering.

These passages were central to Adam's understanding of the Movement since his earliest days in the HP.

She was a soldier in Silo's Army. Freshly refuelled and sexually recharged, she returned to the front lines ready for combat in the woman-eat-man business of Humanizing the Earth. With her summer recreation over, she returned Adam to Enrico's team the same way she would discard a spent cartridge; she cast Adam off like a used penis delegate and hoped he would return to a student lifestyle and forget about her.

He had more quiet time on his own in private reflection. The doubts, suspicions and feelings of uneasiness that had been submerged under the surface since May began to surface. He resumed asking himself the same questions she had refused to answer. He reviewed the chain of events, dialogue, and persons involved in an attempt to understand what had happened that whole summer. She called him in late September and he put his questions to her more directly; she became enraged and refused to discuss it.

"What do you want from me?" she asked and continued, "We can still see each other on Friday nights, at parties and things. I'll still see you there, like all the others." M-C made another false promise. Immediately, he saw her hypocrisy. She had offered him a friendship outside of the Movement, but all the events she mentioned were part of the *social* life of the Movement and were the same activities that he already attended on his own without her friendship offer. He was interested in having her friendship without sex, just as he always had been. She refused, treating him like a group delegate, like "all the others."

All September, Adam asked her a number of pointed questions about what she had done to him, starting with the events of May and the events that led up to it. She accused him of "always coming back to the same thing." She partly admitted she had put him in a difficult situation but claimed he had "said yes." Stunned, he reminded her he had accepted her offer of friendship only, the Sunday before that first Friday. She falsely claimed he had said "yes." Also, Adam began complaining in public about M-C to other members of the Movement like Tara and Mina. This violated her condition of silence and she became angry with him. She complained to Enrico, who abused his position of power to protect M-C.

M-C called Adam the following week and reprised her lesson from her "dust-in-the-wind" assault; « Je ne pense pas que tu devrais garder l'idée qu'on va s'en parler au mois d'octobre. C'est un faux espoir... [I do not think you should keep the idea we're going to talk about it in October. It is a false hope...] I want to get on with my life. Let go of me!"

Leaving the abusive relationship with M-C did not bring Adam instant relief. Day and night, images of her burned in his mind. Sleep brought no rest. He dreamed horribly depressing and miserable dreams; dark, Kafkaesque images polluted his nightly slumbers. His lucid dreams were filled with Enrico's themes and Enrico's words. Indeed, Enrico appeared as an unwelcome character in his dreams and an ever-present irritant in his daily life. Upon waking, Enrico was always eager to tell Adam how his situation with M-C resembled his own situation with Lola. Enrico took sadistic pleasure in reopening these wounds to rub in salt. Once, Adam awoke from a long sleep with the feeling he had not rested at all; instead, he had a great tension in his body. He looked down and discovered he had been sleeping with a tightly clenched fist the whole night!

Adam's introspection and self-questioning also allowed a greater understanding of how Enrico had manipulated people and events for years, resulting in great harm. Enrico also developed a new, vindictive attitude. As Adam's anguish over M-C increased, Enrico supported her consistently and made a point of telling him that Adam *knew in advance* she was going to sexually assault him. Adam asked Enrico how did *Enrico* know in advance? Enrico became evasive and told Adam he should "take it like a man," misquoting the popular song lyrics: "Sweet dreams are made of these, some of them want to hurt you, man. Some of them want to abuse you, fuck. Some of them want to be abused. Welcome to life."

Enrico's explanation meant nothing to Adam, who had the lyrics to Jefferson Airplane's "Somebody To Love" racing through his mind: "When the truth is found to be lies and all the joy within you dies, don't you want somebody to love?"

Enrico continued, "You know, it's like I said at the time, man. You take a confused person, you take another confused person. Put them together and you get a confused situation." Enrico never actually said that to Adam; nor did Enrico say who did the taking or the putting.

On the first Sunday in October, Enrico told Adam about a conversation he had with his peer Ned about the imperfect nature of memories. Enrico warned Adam that the Council of Team Delegates would turn against him and file a SLAPP (strategic lawsuit against public participation) against him if he tried to complain about M-C in public, to say anything about her or the Movement to the media or to write a book. Enrico added that no information about the Movement existed in the outside world and nobody would believe him anyway. For each stage of his pain and grief with her, Enrico told Adam he had gone through the same with Lola and gave a mirror description of his problems. Enrico said Adam's persistent desire to resolve his problems through investigation was a "mental trap" from which he would never escape until he adopted Enrico's attitude toward women and resolved "the problem of sex and death." To make Adam feel worse, he referred to Silo's doctrine of the "Great Mistake" and asserted the incident on that Friday in May was a big mistake for Adam and that he would forever be haunted by how his life could have been different if only he had acted differently.

Enrico had a new trip of speaking of the human body as "the envelope" and said its existence was transient compared to the immortal soul. Enrico thought it would be a good idea to update Adam about bad news that had befallen Yorgo in recent weeks. Years after being kidnapped, tortured and murdered in Chile, the remains of Yorgo's brother were identified there. Shortly thereafter, Yorgo's father died in Toronto just days after Yorgo and his wife Victoria had discovered her elderly parents dead on the floor of their home. They had been lying there for several days undiscovered. Enrico made a point of describing their decomposition when Adam asked him to shut up. "The body is only the envelope," Enrico added one last time.

Enrico again raised the subject of Adam's accident and compared its status as a painful memory from his past to his experience with M-C. Enrico recounted the story in a twisted and sick way, inventing details or incidents that never happened. He defended the responsible parties from civil litigation, saying the accident was Adam's fault and it would be as ridiculous to accuse M-C of anything bad as it would be to hold the driver of the car that hit Adam responsible. With this last statement, Enrico's motives became clearer. Since the accident, Enrico had inflicted upon Adam the Movement's doctrine of overcoming pain and suffering, using the accident as a paradigm example for his own dark purposes. If Adam allowed Enrico to complete the loop, to create endless new situations of suffering to be overcome with the Movement's doctrine of healing, as Enrico wished, Adam would have become his willing victim, forever enchained without any hope of freedom. When Enrico heard that M-C wanted to sexually assault Adam, he recognized this as an excellent way to reinforce the Movement's doctrine and to test what Adam had already learned about it. In so doing, he tested Adam's resolve by "allowing the cream to rise to the surface."

Just like M-C, Enrico also distorted the Siloist doctrine to allow her assaults against Adam and included it in his orientation regarding "the problem of sex and death." For every statement Enrico made to him after that, Adam asked if M-C had told him to say that. Visibly irritated and off-balance, Enrico refused to answer and claimed to be uninvolved in the situation. Just as Enrico had controlled Adam's dreams, exploited his handicap to weaken his resistance and interfered in and controlled his relations with women, so did he use the same abuses to defend M-C.

Enrico told him, "It was all a dream. Everything you had with M-C was a dream. Forget about it." He said these instructions came to him from Josh. Adam asked Enrico which part was a dream, the part where she sexually assaulted him or the part where they had planned it together? Enrico refused to discuss it but gave Adam further Siloist propaganda: "If you have a bad dream and I'm a character in your dream, you don't try to take it out on me when you wake up or address your grievances with me. Everything you had with M-C was a bad dream. It never happened in reality." He pushed Adam closer to insanity.

On the last Friday in October, Adam had already figured out during the previous six weeks much of what M-C and Enrico had done. The ball of energy was dissipating quickly and all that was submerged before rushed into his conscious mind. He was in the worst emotional pain of his life. Nonetheless, he attended the Friday night gathering where Renato and M-C were sitting around a table. Renato said to M-C "Adam, eh? Adamo, eh, Adamo. Look at Adam, Hmmm? He's a gigolo, eh? He's a gigolo. Adam is a gigolo."

"Yes, yes I do feel that way sometimes," Adam responded to both of them. M-C gave both her sexual victims very dirty looks and gave Adam hell for it the next day. She said that she would also have words with Renato.

Aside, Adam confronted M-C and complained about the suffering and sexual exploitation she had put him through. With libertine insouciance, she twisted the ideology of the Movement pathologically out of shape « Chacun est responsable de sa propre souffrance » [Everybody is responsible for their own suffering.] The statement cut right through him and the image of the spider spinning a web of suffering resurfaced. There could be no more doubt that M-C was the spider and had sexually assaulted Adam on purpose, knowing that it would hurt him greatly, but not caring a jot for his health and safety. She had abused her position in the Movement to get cheap sex. She repeated this and other similar statements throughout the autumn. Each one contradicted the many similar statements she had made in the summer.

Just as Enrico had suddenly shifted his attitude to the situation, so M-C also used three different attitudes to address her assaults against Adam. First, her attitude to her own conscience before the first assault was ostensibly "I'm worried that I might hurt Adam if he has sex with me; I feel responsible for Adam's suffering; therefore, I'm going to call Enrico."

Second, her mutual understanding with Enrico was "Stand aside and let me have sexual access to Adam; be responsible for Adam's suffering and follow up on him; support me fully in case of his complaints." M-C was willing to consider taking responsibility for the suffering she created in Adam only before she had created any suffering at all and as long as there were no real consequences for her! Once she had sexually assaulted Adam, she passed off her responsibility to Enrico, as they had planned.

Third, when Adam confronted M-C about the suffering she had created in him but had wanted so strongly to avoid, she replied indolently, "Everybody is responsible for their own suffering."

Also at this time, Suzette surprised everyone in Enrico's team by revealing her pregnancy by Santito. Most members of the team knew Suzette had been dating the myopic Guatemalan Enrico referred to as *La Cometa* [the Comet] owing to his extremely haphazard attendance of weekly meetings and cameo appearances at Movement events. It appeared Suzette made a very thorough study of the member *fiches*, as supplied by M-C. Santito had lived in Canada for years but had never been known to work at a job, preferring to spend his days on welfare discussing philosophy in cafés or hanging out at a public library. Aside from that and appalling bad breath, most people agreed Santito was a fairly decent man but also lumpen — a bit of a loser not at all prepared for the responsibility of marriage or fatherhood. Suzette expected their baby the following May.

On the first Thursday in November, Adam restated his desire to M-C to be her personal friend. "No. As for talking with you about my personal things, or sharing things with you, no," she said while adjusting her glasses. "That's something I do with Team Delegates because I am one myself," she said, revealing again but at a deeper level that her offer of friendship was never valid and she never stopped seeing him as a group delegate. She continued, "I didn't want to hurt you ... I didn't ... but it hurt you more than I thought it would."

He was surprised by this confession and asked her, "So you *did* know you would hurt me? How much did you intend to hurt me? And since when do you wear glasses?" But she refused to answer other than saying she had worn glasses for years. It was like he didn't know her, and he grew frustrated with her curt answers. Finally, he cut directly to the question she had always refused to discuss: "Did you ask Enrico for his permission to have sex with me?" She became extremely enraged and resentful but promised that they would talk about it the next night.

She visited him at Frère-André the following evening and asked him to return the key for Waverly. The instant the key was in her hand, she said « C'est aller trop loin. Toi-là, ne m'appelle plus!! Je ne veux plus entendre parler de toi, pas de messages laissés sur mon répondeur, rien! Je ne veux plus jamais te parler! Et si tu m'appelles quand même, ça se peut que je ne réponde pas à tes appels » [It's gone too far. You, you don't call me anymore! I do not want to hear from your calls, from messages left on my answering machine, nothing! I don't ever want to talk to you! And if you call me anyway, it's possible that I may not return your calls.] She stormed out of the house and imposed a communication ban on him that lasted until she, Fan and Enrico had forced Adam out of the Movement.

Starting on the first Friday in November and repeated nearly every Friday night until the end of January, Fan worked on instructions from the silent M-C to force Adam from the Movement while Enrico claimed to be uninvolved. He denied all knowledge. With unbridled enthusiasm and scintillating nastiness, Fan harassed Adam with repeated anti-Semitic insults about money-grubbing Jews, reinforcing

M-C's "pot calls the kettle cheap" and her "genocidal maniac assault." He was so infuriated, he could not sleep the whole night until Saturday morning and worked off his rage by walking from Frère-André down Côte-des-Neiges all the way downtown. For her part, M-C shunned Adam, refusing even to acknowledge his existence. Later the same month, Enrico approached Adam from behind when he was in profound emotional pain. Enrico leaned in very close to him, touched his back and said in a honey-sweet, mellifluous voice, "Do you miss her warm, soft vagina?"

Adam fired back, "What about your mother Consuela or Esmeralda or whatever the fuck her name is? Do you miss *her* warm, soft vagina?"

Adam was filled with a consuming rage and hatred for M-C, Fan and Enrico. He wanted to know if M-C was solely responsible for her actions or if Enrico was also to blame. He ruminated endlessly and reviewed every detail of every conversation and event involving M-C for signs of her guilt. Once established, he shifted his attention back to examine Enrico's role. Weeks turned to months and blame alternated between M-C and Enrico, twenty-four hours a day. At times, his grief was so great he strained to remember who he was or who he had been before the Movement and before the accident. He walked the streets of Montreal at night chanting Hebrew prayers, though he could not speak Hebrew. He sang Hebrew children's songs or parts of the Bar Mitzvah *maftir* though he did not know all the lyrics. He recalled inspiring lines and scenes from *Star Trek* and repeated them to motivate himself, particularly lines attributed to Khan Noonien Singh and Captain Pike's defiant resolve: "There's a way out of any cage and I'll find it!" He did anything he could to remind himself of who he was or who he had been. His parents invited him to supper in a nice Italian restaurant on Jean-Talon Street, but Adam could not even concentrate enough to get through reading the menu. "Look at him!" said Adam's father to his mother. "He's physically, emotionally and mentally exhausted. Look at him."

The stress and headaches caused by M-C and Enrico merged with the stress and headaches from his unhealed road accident and united into a single unending headache. Adam could no longer tell the difference between his many problems, since Enrico and the Movement had already linked them all together. Adam was losing his grip on reality and feared insanity was not far behind. He could no longer sleep and failed miserably at his attempted return to university. Everything, every time, place and person became contaminated with thoughts images, memories and sounds of M-C.

In time, Adam's review and reflection permitted him to have profoundly personal internal revelations. These revelations could happen at any time and in any place and often had the effect of loosening a great tension in his mind, followed by his body. Such revelations arose about once a week and were short-lasting in their comfort and relief. All was in play at this time as he was regurgitating his whole life and dealing with every source of tension. Demons appeared at his bedside from every difficult or painful situation or person he had ever lived or known to torment him. They were palpable and he feared them. There were so many demons, he did not know which to fear first and ordered them to line up in single file at the foot of his bed. When the demons agreed to do so, he knew they were artefacts of his own mind. From his childhood and family to his posture and health since the road accident to career and school to his breathing and the Force to finance and work to the position of his head to Enrico and M-C to his mood and attitude, the direction of his actions, his level of communication his future in the Movement, great progress was needed in all areas.

He summoned memories of his childhood, which he could see clearly for only a few moments before they morphed into the odours associated with the memories. These odours were fleeting and lacked a sense of smell. He was left incapable of re-experiencing their scent and was thus deprived of his own childhood memories. His senses, thoughts and memories each lost their distinctiveness and blended one into each other. Colours, sounds and sights were co-experienced with similar memories and the events of the present day, words, shapes and feelings without distinction until he no longer understood his own thoughts. He was tormented by other such synesthetic hallucinations throughout the autumn and into the New Year. The doctor had never diagnosed

"Involuntary Induced Dissociative Synesthesia", but then, Enrico was not a doctor. At times, Adam forgot the names of many ordinary things and could only see the relation between objects without recalling their original or intended usefulness. His mind raced and burned on overload until he declared out loud, "These are not my thoughts. The thoughts I am thinking are not my own. They are Enrico's thoughts and I am thinking Enrico's thoughts. Forget about them and Enrico. Clear your mind." This was a major turning point for Adam.

The phrase from one Saturday in May returned to his mind and its origins became clearer. Adam recognized it as something he had learned in school:

Under the spreading chestnut tree
I sold you and you sold me —

Adam repeated the line every day and contemplated its meaning. It was a story of profound betrayal from Orwell's *Nineteen Eighty-Four*, where Winston and Julia betray each other under torture in the name of Big Brother. M-C had betrayed Adam, and he wanted desperately to betray her and the Movement! He strained to recall the lesson from school and knew it had great significance for what he had lived in the Movement, especially M-C's sexual assaults. The society in *Nineteen Eighty-Four* is a totalitarian world and a police state obsessed with controlling the individual. Now, the Movement must be something very similar. There was a word for it; he thought he almost had it after her "genocidal maniac" assault, when he identified the Movement as an extremist group, but there was another word…

Two days before Christmas, Adam could no longer take the silence and the pain of being shunned by M-C; her embargo restricted his self-expression and his questions went unanswered. He wanted to speak with her very much but was terrified of actually calling her on the phone. Instead of risking her rage, he contacted the BBS and left her a message telling of his suicide attempt three days earlier. To this day, he has never heard back from her about it. Indeed, Adam had fallen into self-destructive behaviour when he received the only good news in the form of a cheque from the student loans people for over $5,000 and a letter of apology for having miscalculated. But it wasn't a loan, it was a grant. Adam deposited the gift money in the bank and went out to drown his sorrows on Park Avenue, a street much like Côte-des-Neiges to the west, which zippered Montreal together on Mount Royal's eastern flank. After two beers and a large supper which he could no more taste than enjoy, as for the past two years, he failed in his attempt to get drunk and broke down crying. He couldn't forget her and he couldn't give a damn about the money.

On Boxing Day, Enrico returned to Frère-André after a trip to Toronto. Enrico told him to sit down at the table because they had to talk about something. Enrico told Adam that he had spent Christmas with his family in Toronto and had also visited Josh. He was having a good time until Josh got a phone call from M-C in Montreal. She was freaking out, hysterical because Adam had left her a message saying he had attempted suicide. M-C desperately pleaded with Josh to handle the situation. By calling Josh, M-C identified Adam's suffering as a structural problem in the Movement, after having said emphatically and repeatedly that it was not.

Josh — not Adam's father, nor his employer nor his teacher — gave Enrico specific Movement orientation on how to handle Adam, refusing also to contact Adam directly or the authorities. Josh was reported to have told several Movement anecdotes and "Silo stories" and to have said that everybody has "bad climates" (a Siloist expression meaning "bad times") but that the Movement was not there to accommodate Adam's. Josh did send one special message for Adam personally, through Enrico. It was the word *kartofln* [potatoes] in Yiddish. Adam did not get the point of Josh's one-word message, but if Josh were appealing to his Judaism, Adam felt he no longer had any respect for or anything to learn from Josh, given the high level of anti-Semitism prevalent in council.

Josh had answered a question that Adam never asked him but was forwarded to him by M-C. Josh identified Adam's suffering as a structural problem after having just said that it was not. Enrico reprised the messages from Josh and told Adam he was lucky Josh was not there in person. Enrico laughed at his suicide attempt and told him he'd had a good laugh with Josh at Adam's expense. Josh asked Enrico to report if there was much blood on the floor upon Enrico's arrival at Frère-André.

Enrico became grim and gave Adam his own orientation, saying the real question to ask was "Am I serious about the Movement?" After a long monologue, he told Adam that if he wanted to stay in the Movement, he would have to prove he was serious about the project. He said that the best way for Adam to prove he was serious about the Movement was to get "a new girlfriend."

Enrico told him the way to do that was to build structure in the team. Adam should talk about the Movement at school, especially, and invite women to come to his apartment with him, to meet Enrico. From that meeting, Enrico would decide which women he wanted to have sex with. The rest he would expect Adam to integrate into the team, then himself sleep with. From the women Adam had slept with, he could pick one steady girlfriend, if he wanted. After Adam broke up with her, he would have to repeat the process. Enrico also said he might sometimes pass Adam down his used women, after he was finished having sex with them.

Enrico said that until Adam did as he was told, Enrico would not consider him to be really serious about the Movement. He also said that if Adam failed to do this indefinitely, there would no longer be place for him in the organic structure of the Movement. The next day he told Adam, "You know, you're really lucky I was so soft on you yesterday… If Josh had been here, he would have told you 'Either you cut the bullshit, or you get out.'" Enrico and Josh had effectively ratified M-C's assaults and made Adam's submission to them a new condition of his continued membership in the Movement, thereby adding yet another level of sexual harassment.

"First we resolve the suffering of the Human Being, then we worry about your suffering," Enrico added, and Adam understood the Movement more clearly than any time in his life.

To hell with that noise, Adam decided for himself.

During the second week in January, Adam seriously considered leaving the Movement and spent that time considering his future. He wrote down all the questions that concerned him and composed a letter

Lies My Guru Told Me

to Enrico, hoping they could discuss his future "within and without the Movement." He mailed the final version of his letter on the third Thursday in January, and Enrico received it the following Monday. Enrico refused to arrange a structural meeting with Adam or answer any of his questions. Adam recapitulated all his questions and accused Enrico of having lied to him and engaging in a cover-up to protect M-C.

Enrico told Adam to "meditate on lies." It was the last orientation Enrico ever gave him, but Adam refused Enrico's version of his own sex life, refused his oriention and refused to meditate on what Adam called "lies my guru told me." Later in the evening, Adam called M-C. During that conversation, he confronted her again with the suffering she had created in him. In a sharp change of attitude, M-C responded with « Ça se guérit, ça!» [That heals on its own.] He felt it was a stark change of attitude from her previous "I didn't want to hurt you."

During this difficult time for Adam, nobody in the so-called Support Sector made any effort to help him. Neither Yorgo nor Josh's peers Isaias and Salvatore, both of whom had been Support in Silo's triangle, offered any help. Even local Supports Mina, Tara, Dwight, Curly or Adam's own peer Support Lisette never called or contacted him in any way to offer their help for what he was going through. Gus, himself a former Support in Enrico's triangle, did arrange to go out for coffee with Adam and Popo. Adam told them the entire salacious story with M-C and Enrico. Gus shrugged and said he didn't know, like he didn't care. Eyeing the desserts on the countertop, Gus added that if he learned Enrico was a child molester or murderer, maybe he would work with Renato instead or directly with Josh, but it wouldn't affect his faith in the Movement. Popo said he was « abasourdi », speechless and stupefied to the point of near deafness and incredulity. With good timing, a letter arrived from Raymond in Japan who encouraged Adam to

> Watch out for your feelings if people start treating you like a fallen angel. You know: the unconscious, subtle hints that you've fallen from the flock of the elect and joined the masses of heretics. I recognize this tendency

... when I think of those who've come and gone. It's a ... tendency which goes totally counter (to) the spirit of human solidarity. A human being is incredibly precious and unique, and valuable, despite the fact that he or she doesn't dedicate every fibre of his or her being to the project of the Movement.

The following Saturday, Enrico's team held a potluck supper at Lisette's apartment on Foucher Street, east of Jarry Park and not far from Waverly. Adam waited patiently to use the bathroom. Standing across the hall was Marie-Josée (M-J) herself, a group delegate until that time. Enrico asked M-J questions about her personal life. He inquired whether she still wanted to learn English, and when she said she did, Enrico told her, "You know, the best way to learn English is with an English boyfriend ... You know, Adam here is an English teacher."

Enrico offered Adam's sexual services to her in plain view and full earshot. He expected Adam at that moment to start talking to her for the purpose of starting a sexual relationship. Adam also noticed she had expectations of him; she looked curiously for his reaction to Enrico's innuendoes and sexual interference. Adam had no particular interest in talking to her and said nothing. Enrico continued to press him about M-J during the car ride by Rocinante to Frère-André. He looked at Adam in the back seat in the rear view mirror with a great grin and taunted him. "So, Marie-Josée is looking for a boyfriend, eh?"

Adam responded, "I didn't hear her say that. I heard *you* say that..." The incident was Enrico's way of saying that if Adam did not like his interference with M-C, he would respond by doing it again with M-J!

Adam set aside a night to confront Enrico at Frère-André about the events of the previous year. By that time, he had already figured out most of what Enrico had done, but he had amassed enough courage to confront him more directly. He dispensed with the formalities and told Enrico he was interested in knowing Enrico's true role in what had happened with M-C. He accused Enrico of having pushed her toward himself. Sitting up straight and confident, he pointed at Enrico and said, "You deliberately set me up with M-C and her with me. You forced us together to see how I would react, so you could watch and laugh at us. You set her loose on me! You sicced her on me!"

"Shh! The lady upstairs! She will hear you!" Enrico shushed Adam while motioning to his mouth with one hand and the ceiling with the other.

"I don't give a damn about the lady upstairs!" Adam shouted and stormed off to the bathroom, where he shouted imprecations up the ventilation shaft, intended for Brianna, then returned to the living room.

Enrico, who was cleaning his pipe, said he would tell Adam something very personal.

"You see, Adam, M-C and I ... and Renato and Josh, and Fan and Pigpen and Yorgo and Ned ... and Colleen; you know, the old gang. You know, we've been through a lot of things together; we've helped each other through some very difficult personal things over the years; and we've had our little battles between us and our little victories, but we've been working together for a long time, man ... we're friends. You get to know people after a while ... you know what I mean? You know, Adam, when you first came here, all those years ago, you were the laughingstock of the council, man. Everybody was laughing at you behind your back, man. You used to tell weird stories, and when you left everybody said "Wow! Who the hell is that guy? What a weirdo! What's he doing in the Movement?" You know, with all your *Star Trek* stories and weird stuff; they even thought you were gay! But I stuck up for you, man. I put my neck on the line for you, man. I told them, "You wait and see, this guy is gonna be really something, man.""

Adam knew what game Enrico was trying to play, but it no longer worked on him. He resumed his line of questioning from a few short minutes earlier, this time more agitated.

"You set her loose on me! You set her free on me! You sicced her on me! The Council Slut! The Whore of the Council! Marie-Claude-the-Council-Slut! You sicced the Council Slut on me and you pretend to be my friend who 'stuck up for me?,' HEY, FUCK YOU, MAN! IN FACT, WHY DON'T YOU TAKE A FLYING FUCK AT A ROLLING DONUT? WHY DON'T YOU TAKE A FLYING FUCK AT THE

Martyr to the Cause

"MOOOOOOOOOOOOOOOOOOOON! You knew what kind of a sick person she is when you sicced her on me, but you did it anyway! You knew in advance she was going to maneuver me into her apartment and assault me, but you didn't even warn me. You knew what kind of a sick, twisted, demented individual she is and you let her have access to my body without a warning! You could have warned me, Enrico."

"Now, how would I know that she's such a sick person as you say she is?" Enrico asked, puffing away.

"Because you already had sex with her yourself. You had an affair with Marie-Claude when you first came to Montreal. You made her pregnant and she had an abortion. You never supported her emotionally and she felt like shit. She lived out the horror of her abortion with me; I was the first man who ever supported her for the abortion. So you already knew how she uses sex to hurt men," said Adam.

When Enrico heard this, his jaw fell to the floor, and Adam saw him like he had never seen him before, vulnerable like a Siloist Wizard of Oz, hiding behind a veneer and projecting a grand image of false bravado. Enrico's true being was revealed to be one far less endearing than that from the classic children's film. Just as Adam had peered through M-C's soul while in her kitchen to perceive all her previous victims lamenting, Enrico's bad qualities became transparent and undeniably stark. He was a sophist and master-manipulator, a liar who misrepresented himself and his Movement, a haughty, arrogant, pompous and egocentric upper-class twit. Possessed of a rabid anti-Jewish hatred, Enrico was also a first class pervert who masqueraded as a closeted homosexual and a voyeur, alternately hiding and exhibiting his acute and utterly unresolvable Oedipus complex. Fully expecting people to believe he was raised in the Andes by Spanish-speaking jackals, Enrico was a phoney alchemist and failed magician who feigned omniscience. Suffering from the delusion of being a medical doctor, he was disrespectful of personal boundaries, nosy and prying and a sexual harasser of both women and men. Clinging to prestigious symbols, status and knowledge, supercilious and derisive, he was an intellectual fraud, a confidence trickster and esoteric pseudo-scientist who engaged in incoherent, overly complicated mental masturbation.

He was also a violent antinomian who laughed alone at his own jokes, an absent father and a philanderer. Enrico truly believed he was part of Silo's ten percent. Compounded by his narcissistic personality disorder, despicable and immoral behaviour, Adam saw Enrico for who he really was, in all respects, a thoroughly ugly excuse for a human being.

Enrico looked like he would cry and truly seemed not to have expected that Adam would know all this about himself and the Council Slut. M-C had spilled the beans on Enrico, and Adam spilled the beans on M-C. Enrico regained his composure and told Adam at least part of what he wanted to know but did not expect to hear. He said that M-C had called him on the phone the previous year, just weeks before that Friday in May, and inquired about Adam's sexual availability. "There's nothing about it in the *Norms*," Enrico told M-C. It sounded familiar to Adam, who felt he had heard that before and searched his memory. The memory of a sunny afternoon in April, of M-C's partial confession in her car the Tuesday following the Friday in May and Enrico's warning about Christine the plump Frenchwoman came to him, and suddenly it all made sense. Enrico had kept the identity of the mystery woman to himself until revealing nearly a year too late that she was M-C! Adam's mind reeled once again and he went into shock.

Enrico had confessed part of his own involvement and had spilled the beans on M-C, implicating her as well. For her part, M-C's story did not jibe with Enrico's. After all his speculations and failed attempts at asking her, Adam did not get confirmation until now that she had planned her assault weeks in advance, with Enrico's knowledge! This was crucial information of which she had deliberately deprived him! The position Enrico took with her was not consistent either. Enrico claimed to have answered her query with, "There's nothing about it in the *Norms*," as if her behaviour and intentions were unacceptable in an organization like the Movement. Why then did Enrico not make a more thorough effort to warn Adam about her, or report the incident to Josh, the Orientor of both M-C and Enrico, who could then take appropriate action? Otherwise, why did Enrico bother referring to an official document like the *Norms*?

It was only then that Adam began to understood more the full impact of M-C's sexual assault and her conspiracy with Enrico to keep it secret. She had an obligation to tell Adam every detail of that telephone conversation, but she instead concealed its existence. During each of her innumerable assaults, she knew that she had already conferred with Enrico behind Adam's back about assaulting him and obtained Enrico's consent to do so. She had never fully revealed to Adam what Enrico did that night, and she intended to keep it secret from him forever. In her mind, the image of Enrico was standing over her bed, watching her sexually assault Adam, nodding his approval, puffing his pipe and making prescriptive remarks.

M-C claimed to have sought an indication from Enrico that sex with her would *not* "fuck him up in his process." In fact, she got no indication from Enrico or from anyone that sex with her would *not* screw up Adam.

Adam was never asked this question. However, if she were so concerned with not messing him up and if she did not get any such indication from Adam, then how could she go ahead with her plan of having sex with him? It was never her intention to get such an indication of safety from anybody. She made that phone call to unburden her conscience, more specifically, to get Enrico's *consent* to have sex with Adam. Otherwise, what indication of safety did she get? The answer to these questions left no doubt in Adam's mind that Enrico and Marie-Claude had grossly abused their power.

Adam confided his earnest troubles to Raymond during lengthy transpacific telephone calls at sleepless hours. One of the few remaining people Adam could trust anywhere in the world, Raymond told him, "I will always be your friend, no matter where you are on this pebble" and sent him an insightful letter, observing:

> You were used, and what's more, there's the shadowy presence of members of M-C's clique, who were supposed to be your comrades. It's all a very weird, filthy affair...
>
> I think that the *viejos* are venting their structural

frustrations with these games. They've been through thick and thin together, fought many battles, and have forged what might seem to them to be links of solidarity with one another. However, there came a point where these links mutated into a kind of factionalism, an "old-boy" network, an elite mentality. It's sad really: they had almost understood the Movement, even to the point where they could claim they had ... that's when their self-deception fucks up the functioning. They alienate people, treat them like objects, which causes people to leave. Then, in frustration and their elitist sense of superiority, they blame the losses on changes in the norms, or getting rid of "the flan", "the chaff", and all the other dehumanizing ways they refer to people who leave the structure. It's a delusion to believe that only those who leave are to blame. The orientors are supposed to create conditions for qualification, not only put resistances.

The element of the abuse of the Movement by M-C is especially disturbing. You put things succinctly when you notice that Enrico was questioning M-C's understanding of structural work by saying that sexual relationships between members of the Movement, or the sexual life of group delegates, or any such thing is NOT to be found in the norms. The norms define the scope of Movement activity. I also believe that Enrico had a responsibility towards his peer, especially one such as M-C who holds a very important position, to clarify her.

Adam considered himself incredibly lucky to have a friend like Raymond, without whose assistance he might not have survived the winter of his discontent. By the end of January, M-C, Fan and Enrico had succeeded in forcing Adam out of the Movement, and there remained nothing to hope for. He left the Movement for good. The very next day, M-C called him just to tell him she didn't want to be his friend and also to insult him one last time.

« Je ne veux pas être ton amie. T'est une personne laide. Je voulais juste te dire ça ». [I don't want to be your friend. You're an ugly person. I just wanted to tell you that.]

She hung up without saying goodbye. It was merely one month after his suicide attempt, which she still refused to discuss with him. He was the only other person in the world who had known the details and felt the pain of her wretched stories and personal traumas. Unwilling to look upon the reality of what she had done, Marie-Claude's scabbed and ulcerous personality — her entire being — was the blank canvas upon which Pablo Picasso had painted his *Guernica*. With all her negative history transferred into Adam, it would have been the best possible outcome for her if he had indeed killed himself, so the world might never hear another word from the last remaining person to know her personal story, so she might be forever protected from herself.

EPILOGUE

When remedies are past, the griefs are ended
By seeing the worst, which late on hopes depended.
To mourn a mischief that is past and gone
Is the next way to draw new mischief on.
What cannot be preserved when fortune takes
Patience her injury a mockery makes.
The robb'd that smiles steals something from the thief;
He robs himself that spends a bootless grief.
— The Duke of Venice

IF ADAM HAD NOT left the Movement, he would have died of grief. He left by formal verbal notice to Suzette, after which all overt harassment stopped abruptly. Nothing improved, however, in Adam's mental health and would not for many years. He was invited to return to the council's Friday evening gatherings by friends who were still in the Movement and those who were no longer but who, like Adam, maintained social connections there. After all they had done and all their insults, Enrico and M-C each took turns trying to re-enlist Adam in the Movement; there was no chance. As a former member, Adam was offered no help whatsoever by the Movement in readjusting to life in society: no financial compensation, no psychological counselling, no medical or dental insurance, no explanations, no apologies, nothing. In time, he found it too painful even to attend the Friday nights and drifted away.

The first winter was bleak, depressing. Adam was just barely surviving and he was extremely fragile. He saw an advertisement for

Epilogue

a made-for-television movie featuring a fourteen-year-old girl who had cancer and was supported by her family. He broke down in tears. The morning radio brought news of a college girl named Chantal who was raped and murdered overnight on the lawn outside of a church on Vincent-d'Indy Street. Although Adam had never heard of her before or who she might have been, his hands trembled. He shed a tear in part for Chantal, but in part too because he knew he would always be inadmissible to grieve for her. The feminist establishment wouldn't allow it because he was guilty of being a man.

M-C had mastered the lessons and exercises in *Self Liberation*; springtime brought a new outlet for her to publish the transformative results from her exploitation of and self-transference onto Adam, in a Siloist rag:

> Pour la première fois depuis des mois, je sens plein de possibilités... Mes problèmes, qui étaient comme des boulets que je traînais, deviennent beaucoup moins lourds. Ils ne sont plus mon point de mire, ils prennent une place beaucoup moins grande et bizarrement, ne semblent plus être aussi problématiques.
>
> [For the first time in months, I feel full of possibilities... My problems, which were like a ball and chain that I was dragging, have become much lighter. They are no longer my focus, they occupy a much smaller space and oddly, no longer seem as problematic.]

Refreshed, renewed and revitalized, M-C returned to school and took her first degree. With her experience in crushing, destroying and exploiting men, she was rewarded with a new and lucrative career in what else? Human Resources Management. Indulging in white flight, she bought her own home and lives a suburban, unwed lifestyle in Laval, working for the city. She has no problems.

For years after, Adam's attempts to get legal or psychological help did not bear fruit. The psychologists told him to get legal help while the lawyers told him to get psychological help. With very few exceptions, nobody helps cult survivors and the stigma attached to cult *survivorship* (and not cult leadership) is extremely negative, impeding the progress of cult survivors. In Quebec, rape and sexual assault centres are reserved for women and French speakers. Survivors turn in circles with few resources in a perfidious, cruel and utterly stupid society that rewards racism, hypocrisy and cult recruitment. Case in point: Fan was awarded the Peace medal from the YMCA of Montreal. Enrico was awarded a Ph.D. in biomedical engineering; he now makes a handsome living working in a hospital on the South Shore of Montreal and resides in the chic Lachine Canal district, where he has gone undetected by society.

Raymond settled in Western Canada and has a stable family life, unlike Popo, who has become an anarchist, an anti-police activist and a fixture on Montreal's street scene of "revolted and revolting" agitators. Renato returned to Chile, where Adam hopes he has found happiness and genuine friends.

As for Adam, his exit from the Movement and subsequent reinsertion into society has been very slow and for the most part, difficult and disappointing. Adam has suffered a wide gamut of problems that typically plague cult survivors: financial problems and near bankruptcy to depression, low self-confidence and other health problems. He cried himself to sleep every night for twelve years while reliving all of M-C's traumas. Her miscarriage was the most difficult for him, since every thought of M-C always came back to it. One long night, he understood that he felt bad for her because she had been in a cult for over thirty years. At supper in his favourite Chinese restaurant, he hummed unconsciously to himself until the diner at the next table said out loud, "I suppose I could go to bed early tonight."

Adam thought about it for a moment and asked the man if he had been humming the lullaby, « Fais dodo bébé à Maman. » The man confirmed it was the same song Adam had sung to M-C for her unmourned miscarriage. *This has got to stop,* Adam thought, but it did not.

If there was a bright side, Adam did feel gradually unburdened

Epilogue

and relieved of the Movement. In his brighter moments, he identified with songs that became his anthems, such as Johnny Nash's "I Can See Clearly Now" in addition to John Mellencamp's "Jack and Diane." New musical discoveries such as Daniel Lanois, Kashtin and Axelle Red were soothing landscapes. Though it was a pleasure to walk down the street on a sunny day humming one of those tunes, he remained melancholic. There were many other pleasures which Adam did not enjoy for years after. A renewed exploration of literature led to readings of Robert Bly, Alexander Pope, Jonathan Swift, Harold Pinter, Eugene O'Neill, John Ralston Saul and David Sedaris, among others whose writings sometimes comforted Adam. The birth of his first nephew or niece brought renewal and became the happiest event of his life.

He did research in a special cult-documentation library in Montreal and was astounded to learn the amount of information available about the Movement! Adam's cosmology was transformed and he began collecting information about the subject and reading widely on cults in general. A few years later, he founded a newsletter for survivors of various cults in Canada. The newsletter had a run of five years, while Adam contributed essays, editorials and book lists until it ceased publication.

Several years after that Friday in May, Adam was surprised to read a newspaper article in which Suzette was photographed strolling through a park arm-in-arm with Vittorio, M-C's ex-husband. Suzette and Vittorio looked like a couple of very happy people, smiling and gazing into each other's eyes. It didn't make any sense to Adam, since Suzette had her son to raise with Santito. They were last known to have become parents together. For his part, Vittorio was divorced from M-C and had shared custody of his daughter Rania. *How did that happen?* Adam wondered.

Twelve years after that Friday in May, Adam bumped into Santito on Park Avenue in Montreal. He told Adam that Suzette had kicked him out of her home soon after the baby's birth. She had also expelled Santito from her life and kept the baby for herself. Santito left the Movement as a result. He had lost all custody rights to his son long ago and had not even seen the boy in five years. He was extremely distressed about this. By concealing her intentions, Suzette had sexually assaulted and exploited Santito and used him as a sperm donor without his knowledge or consent, after M-C had supplied her the confidential member data from the *fiches*. M-C supplied not only the male victim but was instrumental in supplying the surrogate father by recycling Vittorio onto Suzette, just as Enrico had taught her. Rania spent half her time at her father's house, where Suzette's baby became her stepbrother, and the two families were blended. *Was there no end to the violence this evil woman could do?* Adam asked himself about M-C.

Fifteen years after he left the Movement, Adam was quite surprised to receive a lawyer's letter informing him he was being sued by M-C, who wanted to prevent the publication of this book. It was the disguised SLAPP Enrico had threatened. Matured and emboldened, Adam hired a lawyer of his own, and they agreed her lawsuit was weak, rapacious, vexatious, borderline frivolous and ill-considered. Having developed something of a Captain Ahab complex, Adam welcomed the lawsuit as a chance to rattle her cage while telling his story before the courts and perhaps be vindicated. Through many procedures, expenses and more than two years of litigious wrangling, Adam made his defense and in a final judgment delivered under advisement won his lawsuit against M-C. She had thirty days to decide if she would appeal. Her father Moritz died barely halfway through that period of reflection. Perhaps taking a lesson for a change from the man she had ridiculed and whose old school French Canadian values she had rejected, she chose not to launch an appeal of the court judgment against her. Where the Quebec Human Rights Commission, Quebec IVAC, Transport Quebec, Quebec Administrative Tribunal, Quebec Legal Aid, Quebec Police Ethics Commission, Quebec Social Services and Quebec society had all failed Adam, the Quebec Courts system ultimately championed the triumph of his reasonableness and Canadian Charter rights over cults and abusive cult leaders.

On a bright, sunny, clear Tuesday morning in September, Adam stood sipping his morning coffee while looking out the window of his New York City apartment. He was reminded of the Silo story where the Argentine guru had been a passenger on an international flight

Epilogue

encountering heavy turbulence. The passengers were directed to return to their seats and buckle up. Everybody was concerned, worried and upset, except Silo. As the plane passed through the roughest parts of the turbulence, Silo sat there impassively, breathing freely, serene and completely relaxed while all others around him were deeply concerned and fearful for the worst fate that might await them. Once the danger had passed and the passengers were allowed to leave their seats, a woman approached Silo. She asked him why he sat there calmly reading his book the whole time when everybody else was so out of their minds with fear? Silo shrugged and replied dryly, "No es mi avión." [It's not my plane.] Silo is just so cool in the eyes of his flock; it would never occur to him to be concerned for his own life when he has immortality to offer the masses.

Adam took another sip of java just as a hijacked jumbo jet carrying nearly 10,000 gallons of jet fuel crashed into the World Trade Center's North Tower, killing all on board. If Pierre Trudeau had not died the previous year, he would have said about the event, "Well, welcome to the twenty-first century!" for a completely new reality had exploded upon the world. Adam wondered if Silo had been on board that commercial flight, and what would his saving action in the Armageddon have been? Seated at his kitchen table and with an eye on the now closed window, Adam ate his breakfast and recalled Enrico's quote from Silo: "What is time other than the biological processes of our own bodies?" Pensive, Adam wondered if Western society had learned any lessons at all about cults in the previous century that could help better understand terrorism.

While he mulled it over, a second hijacked jet crashed into the World Trade Center's South Tower. "Too late," concluded Adam and thought about Rantes at his sink, slicing a cadaver's brains and crumbling bits of it into a sink with running water. "There goes Einstein, there goes Bach," Rantes said as brain matter washed down the drain. He continued, "Mr. Nobody, an assassin, a madman. What do you think, Doctor? Will this drain lead to heaven or hell?"

Experienced in navigating his internal landscape, Adam knew what matters is not the fire in the sky or the crazy society that makes celebrities of people like Silo, Roch Thériault, Jim Jones, Shoko Asahara, David Koresh, or Osama bin Laden. Their violent plans all originated in the mind and in the heart, and it's what we feel, think, and do in life that counts. If he had still been a Siloist, Adam might have thought it was the end of the world foretold in "The Saving Action." In the disaster that followed, Adam kept his wits and did not panic or lose his nerve when all around was chaos. Between heaven and hell, he knew the road all too well.

DEDICATION AND ACKNOWLEDGEMENTS

Lies My Guru Told Me is dedicated to cult survivors everywhere who struggle to overcome their many burdens, to heal, to understand, to learn, to survive, to strive, to thrive, and to speak out.

It is dedicated also to my dear old dad who, in his own quirky way, gave me my gift for observing people and describing their foibles.

Lies My Guru Told Me was made easier to write thanks to some special people to whom I owe a debt of gratitude. Thanks to all my friends and (some of) my family who have helped me over the many years. Thanks to Solange Cantin of the Université de Montréal, Mike Kropveld and the good people at Info-Cult and also to Sébastien Nadeau of CAVAC. These special people in Montreal had rare patience and understanding.

Special thanks to all the friends who helped, supported or encouraged me along the way, including Barbara R., Richard and Marie, Patti and Tim, Paul B., Glen and Doris, Brenda P., Jason and Chris, Nicole D., Julie B., Pierre and Jane, Eric D., Jimmy Z., Robert T., Alexis D., Benoit M., Vlad R., Zahra B., Colin and Josée. Thanks to the good people of Chayi and the former staff of Café Perk Avenue. Thanks to the late Alain Létourneau.

Very special thanks to Louis and Rima for everything they have done, their specific insights and material support in perpetual friendship and unfailing solidarity over the many years.

Thank you to Constable Claude Jutras badge 5079 for being the only known competent member of the Montreal Police Force and for her insightful interview and concise written report to the Sexual Crimes Unit.

I recognize the existence of the Laval Police Force, ever valiant in

Dedication and Acknowledgements

their efforts to brush donut crumbs from their unionized moustaches.

Thanks to Louis-Philippe Paquin for teaching me the difference between complicated and complex.

Thanks to Neil O. and Caroline E. — I owe you a bundt cake.

Thanks to Robert Y. for keeping my focus on my goal and my eyes on the prize.

I respectfully thank the Honourable Madam Justice Pierrette Sévigny for her sound and clever judgment, which I fully support.

I wish to thank, acknowledge and pay tribute to the wonderfully talented writers of the original *Star Trek* series, among them D.C. Fontana, the late Robert Bloch, the late Shimon Wincelberg and the late Jerome Bixby, all of whose words inspired a few of my own.

Thanks to Peter F. McNally, Howard Roiter and the late Hugh Hood for being sensitive and responsive to the needs of their student.

As corny as it may sound to some, I still believe in what I learned in my first year of college writing at U de M: "I COUNT MYSELF AMONG THOSE WHO WRITE AS THEY PROGRESS AND WHO PROGRESS AS THEY WRITE."

—Rex Voluntas, 2012

BIBLIOGRAPHY

Ammann, Luis. *Self Liberation*. York Beach, Maine: S. Weiser, 1981.
Blake, William. *Collected Poems*. New York: Routledge, 2002.
Burns, Patricia. *The Shamrock and the Shield: An Oral History Of the Irish in Montreal*. Montréal: Véhicule Press, 1998.
Deutscher, Isaac. *Stalin: A Political Biography*. New York: Oxford University Press, 1967.
Freud, Sigmund and Peter Gay. *The Freud Reader*. New York: W.W. Norton, 1989.
Hatch, Alden. *The Miracle of the Mountain: The Story Of Brother André and the Shrine on Mount Royal*. New York: Hawthorn Books, 1959.
Hesse, Hermann. *The Glass Bead Game (Magister Ludi)*. New York: Holt, Rinehart and Winston,1969.
Hirigoyen, Marie-France. *Stalking the Soul: Emotional Abuse And The Erosion Of Identity*. New York: Helen Marx Books, 2000.
Hofstadter, Douglas R. *Gödel, Escher, Bach: An Eternal Golden Braid*. New York: Basic Books, 1979.
Karma-glin-pa and Padma Sambhava. The Tibetan Book Of The Dead. London: Arcturus, 2009.
Klein, Shelley. *The Most Evil Women In History*. New York: Barnes & Noble Books, 2003.
Nazare-Aga, Isabelle. *Les Manipulateurs Et l'Amour*. Montréal: Éditions de l'Homme, 2004.
Norms and Ceremonial of the Movement. Paris: The Community for the Equilibrium and Development of the Human Being, 1989.
Orwell, George. *Nineteen Eighty-Four: A Novel*. Harmondsworth (U.K.): Penguin Books, 1954.
Pearson, Patricia. *When She Was Bad: Violent Women & The Myth Of Innocence*. Toronto: Random House of Canada, 1997.
Shakespeare, William. *King Lear*. Harmondsworth: Penguin, 1972.
Shakespeare, William and Kenneth Muir. *Othello*. Harmondsworth: Penguin, 1968.

Bibliography

Shakespeare, William. *A Midsummer Night's Dream*. New York: Oxford University Press, 1994.
Swift, Jonathan. *Gulliver's Travels in The Writings of Jonathan Swift*. Robert A. Greenberg and William Bowman Piper, eds. New York: W.W. Norton, 1973.
Silo. *Collected Works*. San Diego: Latitude Press, 2003.
Silo. *Tales For Heart And Mind: The Guided Experiences, A Storybook For Grownups*. San Diego: Latitude Press, 1993.
Stapledon, Olaf, 1886-1950. *Star Maker/Olaf Stapledon*. 50th anniversary ed., 1st ed. New York: Distributed by St. Martin's Press, 1987.
Wende, Markus. *Siloismus Tarn- und Unterorganisationen einer Psychogruppe z.B. Humanistische Bewegung, Humanistische Partei, Grüne Zukunft, Grüne Internationale, Zentrum für Direkte Kommunikation, Die Gemeinschaft*. Dortmund (Germany): Humanitas-Verl., 1995.

DISCOGRAPHY AND VIDEOGRAPHY

"An American Prayer." Jim Morrison and The Doors. Prod. John Densmore, Robby Krieger, Ray Manzarek, Frank Lisciandro, John Haeny, Elektra/Asylum, 1978.

"By Any Other Name." Dir. Marc Daniels. In *Star Trek*, Jerome Bixby and D.C. Fontana, Paramount, 1967.

"Dust In The Wind" by Kansas. Prod. Jeff Glixman and Kansas, Kirshner, 1978.

Man Facing Southeast (original title *Hombre mirando al sudeste*). Dir. Elisio Subiela. Cinequanon and Transeuropa S.A. Cinematografica, 1986.

Misery. Dir. Rob Reiner. Columbia Pictures, 1990.

"This Side of Paradise." Dir. Ralph Senensky. In Star Trek, D.C. Fontana and Nathan Butler, Paramount, 1967.

"Raining In My Heart" by Buddy Holly. Prod. Norman Petty, Dick Jacobs, Bob Thiele, Coral, 1959.

"Sweet Dreams (Are Made Of This)" by Eurythmics. Prod. David A. Stewart, RCA, 1983.

"Somebody To Love" by Jefferson Airplane. Prod. Rick Jarrard, RCA Victor, 1967.

The Wizard of Oz. Dir. Victor Fleming. Metro-Goldwyn-Mayer, 1939.

"Wolf in the Fold." Dir. Joseph Pevney. In *Star Trek*, Robert Bloch, Paramount, 1967.

www.ingramcontent.com/pod-product-compliance
Lightning Source LLC
Chambersburg PA
CBHW031346040426
42444CB00005B/202